THE LAST HURRAH

FROM BEIJING TO ARNHEM

SECOND EDITION

DES MOLLOY

Kahuku
Publishing Collective

Publishing Collective

The Last Hurrah

© **Des Molloy 2020**

Text design by The Design Dept.
Cover design by The Design Dept.
www.thedesigndept.com.au

Editing by Kahuku Publishing

Second Edition published in 2020 and 2023 by
Kahuku Publishing
PO Box 149 Takaka
Tasman 7142, New Zealand
www.kahukupublishing.com

First Edition published in 2006 by
Panther Publishing Ltd
10 Lime Avenue
High Wycombe
Buckinghamshire HP11 1DP
United Kingdom

All rights reserved.
This book or any portion thereof may not be reproduced or used in any manner whatsoever without the express written permission of the author except for the use of brief quotations in a book review. All inquiries should be made to the author.

ISBN: 978-1-7386002-2-9

In the memory of mum and dad who encouraged my early wanderings and Dick Huurdeman, without whom this adventure would have been a shallow travelogue

THE LAST HURRAH

CONTENTS

Gestation 1

Beijing & beyond 29

Across the Gobi 55

Stars in Mother Russia 103

The `stans` 135

Bummed out in Bishkek, cruelly cured in Kashgar 169

KKH triumph 187

Pakistan & Persian disappointments 221

Racing for home 245

Aftermath 275

PostScript 284

CHAPTER 1

GESTATION

Breath shoots noisily out of my mouth the way it does when I'm extremely scared or about to tell the boss to take his job and shove it.

It sounds deafening. The more I try to stop it, the louder it gets. This is so unfair. How dare my body let us down now? We've already dealt with our versions of tempests, famines and locusts. Wasn't that enough?

We should be blissfully hitting the road through the Tian Shan mountains towards the Chinese border, but here I am in a tawdry hospital corridor watching my son Steve with a charming and vivacious young woman. Dick, the other member of the team, is back at our accommodation dutifully loading our bikes for take-off, unaware we won't be going anywhere in a hurry.

I sense Steve is concerned for me, but he's still enjoying flirting with this exquisite dark-haired, petite Kyrg. They parry and banter with smiles and light trilling laughter. There are shrugs and arm twirling gestures. She has the medical instructions and she is the key; she has the English and is telling Steve the prognosis. I must be operated on immediately and stay with them for seven days. Impossible, Steve explains. We have to travel on. She counters with an offer of four days. No! We just can't spare the time.

This all seems so unreal. We've come so far, struggled so hard and now we are bartering with my health against a silly time scale, a paper itinerary. I'm almost twitching with nervousness. This is Kyrgyzstan and I'm in trouble. I feel the thousands of kilometres separating me from home.

Just as acutely, I feel the thousands of kilometres separating me from the successful conclusion of this already eventful odyssey.

I try to be composed, will myself not to tremble. I want to believe in the competence of these medics, but I can't help my first-world prejudices. Perhaps this is just a bad dream, but hell, the pain seems real enough. How did we get into this mess? The start of the Last Hurrah all seems so long ago.

This project had a long gestation, a bit like an Indian wedding; all the stars had to be in the right place and the right players ready to play. But let's go back further, to before the adventure was even a twinkle in anyone's eye.

I might be looking back through rose-tinted glasses, but my twenties had been a delightful period of enjoyable adventure. Back in the 1970s I'd travelled to more than 35 countries on various motorbikes and quite a few more in the ubiquitous Combi van. I'd even found the woman of my dreams, Steph, and in 1976 shared with her a year-long idyll riding from New Orleans to Buenos Aries on simple British single-cylinder motorcycles.

At the time I owned three of them, Penelope, Samantha and Bessie. Penelope and Samantha were 1960s Yorkshire-made 650 cc Panthers. They were the last of a long line of simple, robust machines manufactured by Phelan and Moore in the small town of Cleckheaton. Obscure and unloved by mainstream motorcyclists, they were chiefly used by that bunch of eccentric enthusiasts who insist on ruining the enjoyable characteristics of their motorcycle by adding a sidecar, then ruining the purity of motorcycling by carting their family along. These sloped-engine bangers are throwbacks to a gentler time. They are long in wheelbase and ungainly in appearance whilst only gentle in performance. There aren't many folk around who would enthuse about something as ungainly and, quite frankly, ugly, but they do exist. There is a Panther Owners' Club whose members love and cherish these big pussy cats, loyally defending the indefensible with a blind love. For us the love was requited. We loved Penelope and Samantha and they returned that love with untiring reliability and loyal service.

In comparison, Bessie was svelte, perky and loved by all, quite the show pony, even though already a 40-year-old. She was, and is, a delightful, semi- sporty 1937 BSA 500 cc Empire Star. Light, nimble and attractive, she had been produced by Britain's (and the world's) largest motorcycle manufacturer whilst at its peak. A stunning performer, with reliability to match, she was to have only US$10 spent on her during the 30,000 kilometre adventure. Since those halcyon days of our youth, Bessie continued to be a good friend and shared many long journeys and good times. She is now quite elderly, wearing the patina of age like a badge of honour. This doesn't stop her embarking on ambitious trips of 600 kilometres or more.

My brother Roly and an Aussie friend Lawrie, shared Bessie and Samantha, whilst Steph and I were as one on Penelope. It was a remarkable saga of guileless youth and naivety. We wandered without aim or constraint. There were numerous dramas and mishaps, many brought on by our lack of money and matching lack of caring about such a fundamental. The bonds we formed with Penelope, Samantha and Bessie became extremely strong, as these iron steeds were so central to our lives. There was a fusion, as each couldn't do their day's work without the other. We were nothing without those wonderful bikes.

Unlike Peter Pan, our lives moved on. Our youth passed, we returned to New Zealand. Steph and I embarked on another huge adventure. It involved poverty and deprivation but included marriage, mortgages, old falling-down houses and four children. We each had long periods of being wage slaves. It was a good adventure and, whilst we included Bessie from time to time, Penelope lay abandoned, languishing in neglect.

Then, sometime during my children's pre-school years, probably 1981, I happened upon a Readers' Digest magazine. I was fascinated by an account of the newly constructed Karakoram Highway from China to Pakistan. This amazing engineering feat had taken 10 years to complete, had cost over 400 lives and at 4,730 metres (16,200 feet) was being claimed as the highest public road in the world. I fantasised. It transported me back to the Andes, where I was sure that we'd crossed higher roads. Such was the inspiration from the article that I vowed to one day ride the Karakoram Highway. It didn't quite become an obsession, but I did read everything that came my way related to that magical road. I remember being extremely envious of a Dutchman riding overland to New Zealand for an International BSA Rally on a 350 cc B31, who on the way detoured to ride up the Karakoram Highway.

Another fascination during this time was Mongolia. My sons remember me telling them that one day I'd take them there. I knew that Ulaanbaatar was a dull Soviet-style city with little or nothing to recommend it, including a terrible climate. I also knew that given the choice between two weeks in the sun at Club Med Tahiti or a visit to Ulaanbaatar, my leaning would not be towards the palm trees of the Pacific. I yearned for the exotic. Possibly it was a 'Look at me! Look at me!' phase I hadn't outgrown. The humdrum and ordinary holiday held no appeal. All that took was money and a giving in to the enticements of the travel industry. It required no imagination, no passion. There was no 'wow!' factor. Nobody would say "Bloody hell, Des … why?"

These fascinations remained as fantasies for years as the family grew, and then grew up. I did have many adventures within New Zealand, including a lot of years when a week-long midwinter adventure with friends would be planned and executed, taking in the old gold mining roads of the South Island. Then in about 1990, after a fit of the guilts (away with my mates having a great time while the family back at home ate gruel), I stopped doing these trips because of the imbalance of enjoyment. There was always the thought at the end of the week away, "God this is good. I wish it could go on for another couple of weeks". You don't know how guilty I felt having those thoughts. To overcome this, I instigated an annual weekend which had to include our loved ones. "You can only come if you bring your wife or girlfriend – not both, unless you have a sidecar", read the invitation to the first Consenting Adults weekend. These events became the main motorcycling rides we now do with our wives. Over the years we've explored many of New Zealand's back roads and country pubs. You can only come if you bring your consenting adult (and we sexist males add that she has to be consenting). These were great rides and great times with great friends, but lurking in the back alleys of my imagination, there was always the call of the Karakoram Highway.

Sometime in late 2003 I was sitting at the computer when I looked at the cheap inflatable globe which hung at my shoulder. I love maps. One day I'd love to own an expensive, stylish, tasteful globe but in the meanwhile this gifted balloon-thing which hung on a string, hitting my head as I sat at the computer would have to suffice. On this night I focused on China and Mongolia, then twisted the globe around to look at Pakistan. I felt that maybe, just maybe, you could travel from Beijing up to Ulaanbaatar, hook a lefty, go across the Gobi Desert and … it all started to look like a ride.

So, another daydream to go with the others. I'd also been going to ride around Australia with Steph in two sidecar outfits, two kids in each. Another time I'd planned a ride to Uluru (Ayers Rock) from the south, exiting the interior of Australia in far north Queensland. I'd loved planning these trips in my head, dreaming the rides, knowing that they were unlikely to come off. That didn't lessen the enjoyment. During an earlier period of eight or nine years, when I commuted nearly 200 kilometres a day by motorbike, all sorts of things were planned as I relentlessly droned to and from work. Novels were written. Trips were planned on wonderful fantasy motorbikes. Riding a motorcycle takes you away from reality and gives you time to think and dream and scheme. Sometimes you sing; sometimes you play rugby for the All Blacks; sometimes you win the Isle of Man TT races, and sometimes you win outrageous fortunes or meet mysterious strangers. There's no limit to your imagination while you are experiencing the solitude of a long trip on two wheels.

But as with the Indian weddings, all the stars need to line up. After moving from the useless globe to some not-quite-as-useless maps, I scoped out a route.

There couldn't be any harm in that, surely? After Mongolia, it crossed into Russia then headed south down into Kazakhstan then Kyrgyzstan, Uzbekistan and Tajikistan before going back into China and onto my beloved Karakoram Highway, onwards to Islamabad. I had a rough route but how far was it? And how long would it take? Even for a dream trip I needed better maps. At the time that I was filled with this rampant enthusiasm, Steph went away for a weekend to Nelson to visit our daughter Kitty. Taking advantage of this quiet time and not having to account for my whereabouts, I went to the appropriately named Map Shop and bought the most detailed maps of Mongolia and Central Asia available. It was a start. Nights were spent poring over them and data was entered into spreadsheets. Soon I had a two-month-long, approximately 10,000 kilometre adventure to drool over. A fantasy, maybe not yet with teeth, but at least with gums.

This new fantasy exhilarated me hugely, but I really didn't know what to do with it. I couldn't share it with friends or family because it was all too ludicrous. You can't just go and ride motorbikes through all those countries can you? For a while I dreamed, living this exotic trip in solitary wonder. I had included Samarkand and Bukhara from the mythical Silk Road. What a star-studded adventure this would be: Mongolia, the Silk Rd and the Karakoram Highway. For several months I shared with no one, not even Roly who is usually included in my motorcycling fantasies.

Finally I could contain myself no longer; I had to share with someone benign. John, a favourite workmate of mine, encouraged me to walk at lunchtimes. During those walks we would bare our souls. We'd been at school together years ago, we'd travelled together for work for weeks on end and had a good rapport. We would talk about our families, gripe about work, and share wishes for the future. I felt able to share my fantasy. John didn't express particular amazement; he was non-judgmental about this frivolous, irresponsible fantasy, this ludicrous out-of-reach adventure. When I enthused endlessly, John appeared to be swept along with my helter-skelter ramblings. In time I think I even convinced him he could come along, although he wasn't a motorcyclist. I wanted a loony companion who would share the joys and challenges. Years earlier, Lawrie also hadn't been a motorcyclist, yet was the best travelling mate you could wish for. For a trip like this you needed an optimistic dreamer with only the faintest touch of realism or responsibility.

I still hadn't shared this possible interruption to the family dynamics with the family, and it would be a while yet. I couldn't quite see how to broach the subject. It wasn't practical to just say one night, "Oh, by the way, I'm thinking of going to Mongolia for a motorbike ride soon". I did, however, share with an English friend, Terry, who is an affable, quietly spoken, competent and confident Yorkshireman. A lifelong motorcyclist, he had also travelled to many countries including China and Tibet, so had a good idea of what my adventure would entail. Terry likes to travel quietly and slowly, meeting the locals, listening to their music, socialising with them. Sometimes he shares his trips with his wife Di, sometimes not. You can tell a lot from a person's choice of life partner. I like Di a lot, so Terry must be OK. I emailed Terry a copy of my potential trip and waited for his response. It was positive. He thought the trip looked great and wanted to be in on any planning to make it happen. It was still a dream trip, but the plans continued to evolve.

There were all sorts of minor details missing such as "Where do you get the bikes from?" and "What happens when you get to Islamabad? What do you do with the bikes then?" I'd felt it would be a good idea to buy Chinese motorbikes in Beijing. I love it that China still makes copies of the Russian copies of the pre-World War Two German BMW machines. Using a local machine would result in travelling with the minimum of impact. We wouldn't be coming into villages like invading spacemen on gaudy modern bikes in lurid colours, things the locals had never seen before. We would use the Chang Jiang, which would also be very suited to the low-octane fuel that would be served up. Being a copy of the Russian copy, there would also be a good chance that if parts were needed in Russia or any of the 'stans' then maybe parts for Urals would fit. To this end, in early 2004 I established contact with two different suppliers in Beijing who could prepare these bikes for the intended journey.

When travelling through Third World countries I like to be seen as a traveller, not a tourist. I don't want to be served so I don't need service. Whilst I don't mind being the centre of attention to a degree, I want the locals to empathise with me, not look upon my presence as an intrusion or feel threatened by me or my companions. For this reason, I don't like big groups when travelling. Our 1976 trip through South America on three bikes had a good balance to it. There were enough of us to have group fun, yet not so many that it was a pain to organise things or get consensus. I wanted no more than three bikes and I was quite keen on one being a sidecar outfit to maybe film from and carry extra fuel, etc. By now I was fantasising about making a documentary of this adventure.

For many years I have also secretly harboured thoughts of taking paying clients on my adventures, but always I have stepped back when I admit to myself that I probably wouldn't like the fee-payers. I kept coming back to my preference for friends rather than clients. This, however, could be an answer to "What are you going to do with the bikes in Pakistan?" I could do the anticlockwise loop in spring, ending in Islamabad and, in autumn, armed with all the knowledge and experience of the first trip,

I could take clients back the opposite way. After all, there are successful escorted motorcycle tours in India, Nepal and Tibet. Of course this threw up other problems, like needing more than three bikes to make it viable financially. Fortunately, dreams are cheap and easy to change, modify or delete altogether. I would wake, and the old employment treadmill would call me, dragging me from my contentment and the warm nuptial bed.

But John and I kept walking at lunchtimes and I continued to rhapsodise. How nice it was to be able to do so without fear of ridicule. I wanted a team and the team I wanted needed to comprise people who were resilient, durable, supreme optimists, slightly irresponsible, able to give up their lives for a couple of months and, be compatible with me. I would have loved to put together the old team from our South American times but I felt that Roly wasn't quite up to it physically, having an ailing knee and also neck problems. When asked, Lawrie demurred, citing a recent hip replacement, a new relationship and an intended van trip around Australia. That was quite some length to go to, to avoid having to follow me to Mongolia, I thought. Sadly, the Blues Brothers wouldn't ride again.

At some time during this early planning stage, maybe March 2004, Terry emailed me his intended travel plans for the following year. There in black and white was an option for London to Beijing and from Islamabad to New Zealand. This was listed as an alternative to some more mundane plan. Hell, this was like it was being taken seriously and it could even happen. Maybe the dream should come true. The hardest thing about anything bold is the first step. I now started to pretend it was a real journey I was planning. The stars were beginning to line up. With bated breasts and girded loins I even let the immediate family know that something was on. The thought of this moment had been scary, the reality not so. Steph was amazingly accepting, possibly a little too eager. Would our place become Party Central as soon as the wheels of the big silver bird left the tarmac, I wondered?

I had absolutely no idea of how much it would cost or how I would pay for it. I just knew I had to do this one magnificent adventure; money would be one of the last things to organise.

For my dream crew, initially, I had overlooked the obvious. Living in Wellington, only a couple of kilometres away, is a legendary motorcycling hard- man, someone who should have been at the top of the list for any adventure. I'd known Dick Huurdeman for over 25 years, loved him as a friend and admired him immensely. Sure, he was now old, an insulin-dependent diabetic septuagenarian who'd had a couple of strokes, but hell, he was still a match to any man on a bike and more than a match off it. An ace mechanic who still raced his Manx Norton on the track, there was also the bonus of knowing that Dick had been planning a trip to Russia a few years ago, a trip that was ultimately stillborn. He'd taken a bike around Europe though in the late 1990s and was still a keen adventurer. Dick and his partner Sharon had also been enthusiastic participants in our Consenting Adults weekends.

Dick is also a hunter, with a hut in the hills. Casually one night, with an eye to the future, I enquired about his fitness. Yep, he still hunted, still tramped the hills for days on end, his only concession to age being a bivvy camp he has set up a couple of hours from his hut, just in case he can't make it all the way back before dark. I enquired about his diabetes, but that didn't seem to be a problem. He just had to manage it. It didn't take much to get him interested in my idea. I took my maps around and showed him what I'd like to do. The next day Sharon told Steph how Dick would love to come on my adventure. Wow. Saying Dick is an ace mechanic sells him a little short. If it's mechanical, Dick can make it talk. Forty years earlier he'd made his Manx Norton lighter and quicker than the factory ever did and in more recent times he was the engineer who made the late Robert Holden's race Ducati one of the fastest in the world. This was the sort of man that people would pay to have along.

Dick, Terry and me, and maybe John. Although I wasn't so keen on four bikes, I was keen on the personnel so would make compromises. But I didn't want a whole troop. It may seem a small thing, but I know how hard it is just to get six bikes fuelled up, started and all pointing in the same direction. Keeping them all in contact with each other and going the same way in big cities would be a nightmare. Also, I know from experience that if one rider stops for a call of nature or to take off a jersey, someone notices him missing and also stops. Slowly, one by one, they all notice the emptiness of the rear vision mirrors and stop. Then someone turns around and goes back. It is so hard to get cohesiveness from such a number. You can't really be tight-knit, and too many compromises spoil the fun.

Now that we had an embryonic team, I could start the real planning. By now I knew that the paperwork would be hard. These are countries that you can't just go and visit as you feel fit. It's only in recent times that they've started to let westerners in and they still make it difficult for you to bring your own vehicle. Russia and all of the 'stans' require 'letters of invitation' before you can even apply for a visa. New Zealand doesn't have resident representatives of all the countries we intended visiting so when the time came our passports would be going all over the place.

Around the middle of 2004 I became aware of two other motorcycle groups doing the Silk Road. The first involved movie actors Ewan McGregor and Charlie Boorman. When I heard they were riding from London to New York via the Silk Road I was envious and a little disappointed. Envious because their adventure was real and happening whilst mine was still in the planning stage and disappointed because I felt they had stolen a rumble or two of my thunder. Of course, I was also envious of the money they would have to do their trip. I had absolutely no idea how I would fund mine without leaving my loved ones totally bereft of support. I had a job and a sizeable mortgage. I knew I'd have to take leave without pay from work and leave without love from home, but I had this little flame burning inside which meant that lack of money wasn't going to stop me. I know many people with the money to do any trip or adventure in the world, but they don't because they lack the imagination. I've never lacked the imagination, just the opportunity … and this time I was determined it was all going to happen. But because of a fear of failure and possible ridicule, I still kept the planning under wraps. Very few knew of our intentions.

A sad postscript to this was Mum dying in September 2004. She left a modest inheritance that would enable me to pay for the trip without increasing the mortgage. I would now have the money but would miss being able to share the thrills and spills with her. It wasn't a good trade. Mum had been a great influence in our lives. Afflicted with a debilitating degenerative pelvis problem from early middle age, she always encouraged others to chase their dreams even though she could no longer do so. Dad was quiet and reticent, Mum was forthright and opinionated. They made a good pairing and never seemed to interfere with our paths to adulthood or beyond. They had actively helped in earlier pedal-powered adventures and I know that they would have been happy for me to be spending, in three months, what had taken them a lifetime to accumulate.

The second group who were intending to ride the Silk Road were also from New Zealand and some were local to us in Wellington. A group of prominent businessmen and one of their wives were going to ride from Germany to China at the same time we would be going the other way. They would be on six new BMWs and they would try and follow Marco Polo's route. Their planning was further advanced than ours and they appeared to be well sponsored and well prepared. They had a good web site (www.silkriders.co.nz) and were already getting publicity, even though their trip was many months away. Their paperwork was being handled by a small South Island tour company, aptly called Silk Road Adventures. I decided it would make sense for them to also look after ours, as the research for the trip was proving to be time consuming. Bloody work was getting in the way of my life! I needed to be full time on the planning but couldn't be.

Lots of things were happening at quite a speed, as they needed to. I'm a writer by inclination and also by employment. I knew that this time I should write a book, not just serialise the exploits in the club magazine. With this in mind, I contacted Rollo Turner of the Panther Owners' Club. Rollo is another Panther rider, but also a publishing consultant and shareholder in Panther Publishing. Panther Publishing had been set up to re-publish the definitive book on the marque when no publisher could be found. They have gone on to publish other motorcycling books and actually advertise for motorcycle-related topics. I explained my project and asked if he would be interested in the chronicles. Quick as a flash, Rollo responded that not only was he interested in publishing but he wanted to come along. He was serious about this. I found we shared a lot of philosophies when it came to taking groups away on trips. Rollo had toured Europe extensively and was planning a sortie around the perimeter of Europe. He was reckoning on six weeks or so for this ride and was struggling to find mates who could or would put their lives on hold for that length of time. I knew quite a bit about Rollo through his exploits in the club and liked what I had read, but it wasn't ideal to just add another because he wanted to come. I had my team, so declined his offer to join us.

Within a few weeks things had changed. First, Terry came back to me and said he wanted to keep helping with planning and support, but his research had led him to the decision that Mongolia would be too tough for him. He would rather be outside the group cheering us on than be in the group being carried along. Fortunately, he never did show me the research that led him to this decision. If he had, possibly we all would have given it away. Thanks Terry, your silence contributed to the realisation of my dream. There was another minor setback when John also came to the conclusion that my dream had to stay as my dream. He had his own vision that led him to a new job opportunity that he felt he couldn't turn down.

This of course led me back to Rollo.

"Do you really want in? We're not normal people. We sleep under bridges, we get lost regularly, sometimes only eat occasionally, it isn't a five-star junket, our hygiene is suspect, but if you're serious, there's a spot." Rollo was absolutely earnest and keen. He loves camping and wanted in. One of the amazing things about putting together this road trip was that no one mentioned money. The two mates who declined did so without knowing the worst and those who accepted the challenge did so knowing it would cost what it would cost.

The next significant turning point came at a social gathering. We were having our Consenting Adults debriefing (this may sound salacious, but it's merely a shared meal after the latest adventure). Dick and I happened to end up together at some stage during the evening and started discussing our secret mission. This was quite a thrill as here we were in the midst of our closest friends, talking about something we couldn't share, yet. Perhaps it was the amber fluid that encouraged Dick to slur, "If it was my adventure, I'd prepare my old Norton single instead of relying on the Chinese". Phew, now that was an insight. I admitted that if I were to give in to the romantic side of my persona, I'd love to ride the ride with Penelope, my long abandoned and neglected old friend. Dick's response was "We can do that".

We quite quickly justified the use of the old bikes. They were used to crap petrol – they were born to it, and the bad roads as well. We also rationalised that we would know their condition intimately and wouldn't be relying on the work and word of a stranger. Hell, that was a good idea. A classic adventure on classic bikes! My next email to Rollo had advice something along the lines of, "How crazy is this, we're now thinking of taking our old bikes. What are your thoughts?" His response was quite unexpected. Not only did he not think it crazy, all his adventures had been on his Panthers. He'd been all over Europe on his tame pussy cats.

Whoohoo! What a trio, a 1948 Panther 600, a 1954 Norton 600 and a 1965 Panther 650, fine machines all. This made the whole thing even more exciting. Penelope was going to live again, soon.

I need deadlines, I am crap and lazy without them. Some people DO, whereas I dream and only occasionally DO, but now there was a frisson in my life. My secret life was so exciting. It was like riding a roller coaster. There were ups and downs at an amazing pace. I even set a date for the off. THE FIRST OF MAY 2005. There were only about eight months left.

Soon yet another direction change came about after a night at Dicks. He told me he would be going to Europe for his 'kid sister' Willy's 70th birthday party. Initially this was going to be in Arnhem on April Fool's Day 2005 (the date of the actual birthday) but she decided that she really wanted to wait until summer when she could have a big party in the outdoors. This now meant sometime in July, after our adventure should finish. Dick hinted that it would really be nice to be there and he'd like to have me there too. I went home, sat in front of the computer with more maps and soon I had added another 9,000 kilometres or so to the proposed route. This would solve the question of what to do with the bikes in Islamabad. It might give rise to another question – "What'll we do with the bikes in Holland?" – but somehow this seemed easier to handle and at least Rollo would get his bike home. I knew I couldn't really extend my 'missing in action' time for another two months. I resolved that after the big anticlockwise adventure from Beijing to Islamabad, we'd race for Europe as fast as our ancient wheels could spin. I reckoned this would take a month. Accordingly, I went in to work and asked for three months off work "next May, June and July". I wouldn't be drawn as to what I was going to be doing for three months. I just wouldn't be at work. This was exhilarating. We were going to do it. The Last Hurrah was born – well not actually born, but at least the sperm had started swimming.

Of course the pregnancy wasn't without its dramas. Rollo had the first. One of his daughters was chronically unwell. She needed tests. If the prognosis was that it was life-threatening then he was out. If it was debilitating, he was still in. This kept us on tenterhooks (whatever they are) for a month before they knew the answer and, phew, he was still in. His progress went very well. The bike was unbuilt, then rebuilt.

We'd all talked about getting fit for the challenge. It was spring, coming into summer for us in New Zealand whereas it was still winter for poor Rollo. Bullied by a sporty daughter, he was pounding the roads in very cold conditions. I kept putting it off; I would start on September 1, October 1, November 1. I started with walking and never really got to do more than run a bit, walk a lot, run a bit. I tried to change my diet. I weighed in at 104 kilograms and targeted 90 as an ideal starting weight. Out went the chips with meals, rabbit food was nibbled at, I walked at lunchtime and each week my weight would be sent around the traps. Others joined in and a spreadsheet of weight loss was produced. I wish I could report that I withered away but not so. I did make it down to 95 kilograms though. Dick was the oldest, but probably the fittest of us all. He is naturally lean, always walks a lot and living near the top of a substantial hill means that he gets a regular cardio workout. He also had the advantage that he didn't have paid employment to get in the way.

Thank God for emails. Messages flew around the world, sometimes on an hourly basis. Murray and Pat Reedy at Silk Road Adventures were amazing with their cool, efficient planning on our behalf. They'd email me and say, "No, you can't travel through that area as fast as that; the border is closed over the weekend; you need to get a visa in xxxx and they only issue them on a Wednesday", etc. We did sometimes clash over the itinerary because I had a clear need to get us to the end for a given date. We now had the 24th of July as a set-in-concrete date for the party. I'm an optimist and one of my failings is not always being realistic in my goals. I had to eat humble pie many times on the trip as I had to concede that Silk Road Adventures were right.

But all that was many months in the future. An early test of our patience was the requirement of the Chinese government to have photographs of the bikes, taken from the front, rear, and both sides, by the end of October 2004. For me this was not possible because Penelope was miles off being ready. There was nothing for it but to mock-up a slightly earlier model Panther of Roly's with Penelope's petrol tank on it. Fortunately, they didn't need a real number plate as we were going to have to get the bikes registered in China and travel with Chinese plates, after we'd got Chinese driving licences. The process of obtaining the 'letters of invitation' and what visas were available in Australia or New Zealand was set down to take about five months. Although Silk Road Adventures were looking after the planning and getting the letters, Rollo would chase his visas in the UK and we'd do the Wellington ones.

We also had to get a 'carnet de passage' for each bike. This is like a vehicle passport. It appeared that only Iran and Pakistan actually wanted these documents but we knew they would be useful as ownership-type papers. They are issued by the Automobile Association of the country in which the vehicle is registered. A substantial bond is lodged. After your travels are finished, you surrender your carnet and get your money back. The intention is to stop you from selling your bike along the way. At the border on the way in the carnet is stamped and on the way out it is stamped and a section removed. The bond required varies from country to country so the most onerous one on your journey is chosen. In our case this was Iran and their requirement was for 470 percent of the new value of the vehicle. Thank God they don't make Panthers or Nortons any more. We were able to value the bikes ourselves and accordingly lodge the money required. I won't say what value we gave the bikes. It was realistic, but not too realistic. After all, you have to win occasionally. We laughed later in the trip when a border official was suspicious because he felt that the value on the carnet was too high. He didn't know that bikes could be worth so much money, especially old ones like ours. Of course he was used to seeing Russian 250 cc bikes which may be worth only US$100 second hand or less.

Even though it was only six months before the off, our plans were still relatively secret. We'd been told the Chinese documentation was tricky. In theory they didn't allow private travel. Quite a few government agencies had to agree to let us do this trip. We also knew it would take three to four months to get this resolved and if China wasn't on then we'd have to have a whole rethink. For this reason we kept the lid on things. I was dying to tell the Panther Owners' Club and my local classic club but kept quiet until Christmas time, when we admitted to the intended folly.

Hell, in four months we'd be twisting the throttles in China. How exciting was that? The reactions of our acquaintances were many and varied. Some were excited for us, some a little fearful, some were bewildered and some strangely seemed embarrassed by the news and started babbling about themselves. But the news was out. Now people knew why there was feverish work being done on Penelope and many folk helped with this refurbishment. Looking at the Silkriders' web site, I could see that there was only one place where our paths could cross, Tashkent in Uzbekistan. Our dates almost looked like it could work. I'd thought it would be quite cool to be nonchalantly resting somewhere when the Silkriders rolled into town. We knew a couple of them slightly, and I could imagine the fun we'd have when we would agree that "yeah, it had been tough". We'd then point out the old bikes and tell them of the 3,000 kilometres or so of off-road riding we'd done across Mongolia to get there. What a surprise that would be. I wondered if we could keep it all a secret and really blow their minds. Just when they would be thinking how intrepid they'd been, even though they hadn't left the tarseal, there we would be, unheralded, unwashed, etc. Despite my enthusiasm, Silk Road Adventures didn't think it would be fair not to let them know that they were working on a similar project for another client. Reluctantly I agreed, but I made no attempt to share the forthcoming adventure with the other group. We were both planning quite different trips and there was so much to do that there didn't seem to be the time for social chit-chat and mutual backslapping. Besides, we hadn't got anywhere yet and what if our bikes failed to cut the mustard?

Dick's 19S Norton is a legendary old warhorse, having dipped its wheels at each of New Zealand's extremities over the years. It usually pulls a box sidecar filled with camping gear, tools and all sorts of luggage. It had been specially built with a long adventure in mind. After Dick and Sharon had toured Europe on his Norton Dominator special in the late 1990s, Dick didn't feel he had finished with the Northern Hemisphere. He really wanted to launch a full-on exploration of Russia. To this end he made the special sidecar which he could attach to either side of the bike so it could be used

GESTATION

at home in New Zealand or the UK and be changed for riding on the other side of the road in Europe. He designed and made special 'trailing link' front forks. Dick is a great fan of this design and his best description of why they work better is his wheelbarrow example. If you push a wheelbarrow at some steps, the wheel bounces up, but if you pull the wheelbarrow up the steps the wheel follows much more smoothly. It has long been recognised that this is a good design for sidecar use. Fortunately, the bike also works well without this ungainly appendage on the flank because we had decided not to take any sidecars. The 600 cc long-stroke design engine has been put in a slightly more modern Norton 'featherbed' frame. The bike has always drawn huge raves from Dick. Sadly for Dick, his trip into the European East never came off. It was probably conceived a little too early and it is unlikely that the right permits would have been able to be procured. The old Soviet Union wouldn't allow tourists or travellers on two wheels and things took a long time to change after the break-up. Still, we were intending to take in a corner of Russia, so he'd get there finally. The Norton didn't need a lot doing to it to get it in suitable condition for the trip, just a freshen-up and new rings.

Penelope, however, was a different kettle of fish. She had come back to New Zealand with only half of the frame, no mudguards or toolboxes, and the engine worn out. Over the years I'd slowly had bits refurbished, or purchased new bits. Virtually every nut and bolt was replaced. My own skills are quite limited when it comes to the clever stuff. The engine had been with John Saywell, a very talented engineer, for over 10 years. Whenever spare money came my way, I slipped John a bit and when spare time came his way, he did a bit. This was a fine arrangement except I got a bit ahead and, now that the pressure was on, poor old John was working for free. He didn't seem to mind, but I felt bad about it. The main clever bit involved re-engineering the big end, crank assembly to use a modern roller bearing from a Japanese bike. Also lots of frame bolt holes had to be sleeved to make a snug fit for the through-bolts, etc. Many small things were missing when it came time for the final assembly, so these had to be made. Roly was also great with his help and, being family, was probably taken advantage of. However he was very supporting of the adventure, and seemed to get quite a kick out of the bike preparation having 'been there and done that' with me before.

Whilst John did most of the engineering and machining work, Dick prepared the cylinder head and incorporated a few oil-saving mods that the Panther Owners' Club folk have come up with. My model of Panther is a very reliable machine, but they do have a thirst. Not a thirst for fuel, but for oil. It's too complex a subject to fully explain here, but they can be insatiable. When new, their oil usage seemed OK at 1,000 miles per gallon. That was the industry norm – hang on a minute, all the other bikes were 1,000 miles per pint. The engine design incorporates an oiling system that is not wet-sump but is not dry-sump either. The engine is oiled quickly from cold, which is good, but it seems they are massively over oiled to the cylinder which results in the eight times as much as normal consumption. Restrictions were put in place, which appear to help by redirecting the oil elsewhere. Another weakness is the single row primary drivechain and Burman clutch. These purchased-in proprietary items are OK in normal use but especially when used on a big, thumping single, hauling a double-adult sidecar, they can be overwhelmed. Our solution was to fit a robust more modern Norton Commando clutch and match it to a rubber- toothed belt drive. This was to prove perfect for the trip and hasn't been adjusted since installation. Dick has a similar set-up on Dutch Courage (as his bike had now been named).

One of the areas of motorcycling preparation where Dick and I differ in opinion, and quite strongly so, is in the area of sparks. My long trips have always been achieved on bikes powered by magnetos. A magneto makes a spark by having its armature rotated. It doesn't need a battery or coils.

Turn the engine, it turns the mag armature, a magnetic field is broken and, wham, a spark is made. I have travelled tens of thousands of miles without ever being let down. The great thing is that you don't need to have your generator, which charges the battery and enables you to have lights, working. I reckon, start with a good magneto and you can't go wrong. Dick, however, has an almost pathological hatred of them which dates back 40 years or so – he was about to win a New Zealand beach racing title when his magneto failed within sight of the finish line. He did push home for second but he never won a national title. The item that caused this ignominy was a new Lucas Racing Magneto that had cost an enormous amount of money (incidentally, they are worth an enormous amount of money today). The reviled magneto was ceremonially whirled around Dick's head by its spark plug lead and thrown far out into Wellington Harbour. From that day on, none of Dick's bikes, for either the road or racing, have been powered by a magneto. He always cobbles together a set-up involving a battery, a coil and points. Charging the battery is a separate issue and he treats it as such. This approach has worked well for him over the years. So he went his way and I went mine, having my magneto rewound. As it happened, we both were to experience only the smallest of problems with our chosen systems. Thank God for that as it would have been so humbling to see my magneto being sworn at. "I told you so" probably wouldn't have been articulated but it would have been thought by both of us.

Finally, on New Year's Day 2005, Penelope spoke to us. She fired into action with the first kick. She had lain dormant since 1977 and now she was back. Lions are not the only felines to roar. Her throaty bark was barely muted. It was great. There's something about the deep booming thump of a big long-stroke single that is stirring and so evocative. It's from an era of long ago. It sounds so lusty even when only coming from the tail pipes of a 27 horsepower weakling. Roly and I both went for rides around neighbouring blocks before heading up to Dick and Sharon's. It was pouring with rain but that didn't diminish the joy. We were duly admired and complimented. We thought we made a handsome pair. Steph brought us back to earth a little when she saw Penelope and, instead of exclaiming how beautiful she was, expressed disappointment in all the shininess. She didn't feel that this freshly chromed and painted beauty was her beloved old Penelope. Well, I bet Penelope appreciated the makeover complete with cosmetic surgery. She looked like she should be in a showroom somewhere, not about to head off roughing it in the desert.

This was good progress. We now had both New Zealand bikes on the road and were able to put a few thousand kilometres under their wheels before the off. Meanwhile, back in Britain Rollo had initially made good progress in giving his trusty old late 40s Panther a birthday, with a similar conversion to his bottom end as Penelope had had. He'd fitted folding footrests and he'd booked an off- road training day. Back on the road, he did have a small problem of the bike not running true when he took his hands off the handlebars. I can almost hear you shouting the answer to that one. Quite simple really – don't take your hands off the bars, Rollo. His carnet had been obtained and his fitness was coming along well. Things were gelling nicely.

Well, they were and they weren't. Rollo's wife Elaine's mum Joan had recently shown signs of disorientation and confusion. This was quite out of character and concerned them considerably. In a short time she had gone from being a dynamic, independent elderly person to being needy. Every couple of days a new prognosis was hinted at. Dementia and Alzheimer's were both mentioned. Tests were needed. Suddenly their world was unravelling. There was now no way that Joan could go back home. Worse was to come. Rollo had to make the hard decisions before time. The end of February was set as the cut- off date. They hoped to have the test results back before then. If it was a stroke, how would she bounce back? I tried to offer encouraging words as my mum had seemed down and out for the count after a stroke yet came back to have another year or more in reasonable comfort. Sadly, Joan's condition worsened and a biopsy confirmed she had a couple of brain tumours. She would not have a long twilight to her life. This was hard for Rollo and Elaine and at the end of February, Rollo made his decision. He would not be going on the big adventure. His Last Hurrah would have to be postponed. He would be staying to support Elaine and help care for Joan. Modifications would be needed to their house to make homecare possible. Running off to the other side of the world on a frivolous adventure was not an option. We respected and admired him for making that choice.

Meanwhile, not only was my dream world possibly coming to life but another of my still deeper down fantasies might be coming to fruition. Even before I heard of the 'Long Way Round', as the two actors Ewan McGregor and Charlie Boorman had called their adventure, I had been thinking of making a documentary of us riding the Silk Road. A camera crew would be out of the question. We would have to film it ourselves. It didn't take me long to think of the right cameraman.

Action Man, second son Steve, was currently cycling through Vietnam and Laos with Hannah, our youngest. Dependable, sturdy Steve was having some time out from his studies because the Olympic Games had clashed with the final year of his Masters in Environmental Planning. He'd gone off to France and worked in a backpackers hostel/café before following some of the Tour de France, getting down to Pamplona for the running of the bulls, catching up with some of my old London rugby club friends (also in Spain) and then doing his time as a volunteer in Athens at the Games. Some more time was spent in Grenoble and Alsace before he went cycling for a month in Nepal. After that as an entrée, he'd met Hannah in Hanoi after the end of her school year. Two months of cycling the old French Indo-China followed. When they finished in Bangkok, the plan was for them to come home and Steve would return to Dunedin to finish his studies and Hannah would return to school for year 13. Would Steve be interested in postponing his studies even longer and coming with us for the ride of a lifetime? He'd emailed me in the affirmative. Great, an energetic youth along would make it all the more exciting. I knew he'd get along with Dick. The team dynamics were different but still strong. I liked the idea of a young man filming two silly old fools on silly old motorcycles trying to ride across half the world, not even the easy half. How many lads would get to ride across the Gobi Desert with their fathers?

There's a wonderful stimulus that comes from planning the implementation of a fantasy. It's like a constructive daydream. You're visualising the future but you only have the past to inspire you. Racing into the planning of The Last Hurrah were all sorts of crazy ideas about where to go and what to do. Planning a grand gesture with a fresh sheet of paper in front of you is often harder than being led by circumstances beyond your control. The things that I noted down as being important to do, became like 'activities on nodes' on an old fashioned critical-path plan for a construction project. Some plans have the activities on the arrows leading from chore to chore, but others have the activity as being a node with the arrow between not really meaning much. My nodes were the important bits, the arrows between portraying the journey to them.

It seemed also to remind me of a landmark black-and-white movie I had seen as a boy whilst holidaying with some of our many cousins in the sleepy little South Island hamlet of Murchison. The whole experience was quite feral for sophisticated city lads like Roly and me. To see kids racing through the the dank, musty old picture theatre banging on the piano as they passed, with little adult admonition, was new to us. The images of that afternoon linger, as does the romance of the movie's topic. It was the tale from classic Greek mythology, Jason and the Argonauts. Jason was the rightful heir to the Greek throne but somehow when he reached adulthood he had to prove himself worthy, to win his rightful place. So he was sent off with his Argonauts to get a golden fleece and consequently win the kingdom. Along the way were a number of almost impossible tasks. Of course Hollywood made these so scary and nail-bitingly suspenseful. The film was famous at the time for the high quality special effects. My tasks were much simpler and we hoped there wouldn't be the nerve-wracking experiences that those valiant celluloid souls endured. Accordingly, lined up on our promotional flyer were our aims:

- Navigate to the degree confluence point 49N:90E in western Mongolia and construct a small ovoo (stone cairn) and leave some small treasures for future generations, etc.
- Meet with and surprise the Silkriders (expedition of six BMW motorcyclists riding the Silk Road from Venice) in Tashkent.
- Visit the Silk Road towns of Bukhara, Samarkand and Khiva.
- Cross the Karakoram Highway (one of the highest public roads in the world) from China to Pakistan.
- In Esfahan, Iran try to locate Ernie, the ES2 Norton that Des sold to 'Shaking Minarets' in 1974.
- Ride to Willy's 70th birthday party in Holland, arriving on the bikes (a 9,000 kilometre detour).
- Collect enough memories and tales to last through our dotage.
- Write a book of the journey and produce an accompanying DVD.

So The Last Hurrah was finally born. Hurrah is listed in my Collins Dictionary as a cheer of joy, victory, etc. I picture the troops in the First

World War giving a last hurrah as they leapt from the trenches and charged towards the enemy. I also picture the Light Brigade charging down the Valley of Death with a rousing last hurrah. I see both of those images as magnificent follies. Similarly, I could see us thundering across Mongolia, in this last huge, magnificent and outrageous adventure, but deep down I also believed there would be sequels. The Last Hurrah Returns, Son of The Last Hurrah, Daughter of The Last Hurrah, Revenge of The Last Hurrah, etc. These would be more dreams to savour, but we all know that sequels are never as good as the original.

Let the odyssey begin.

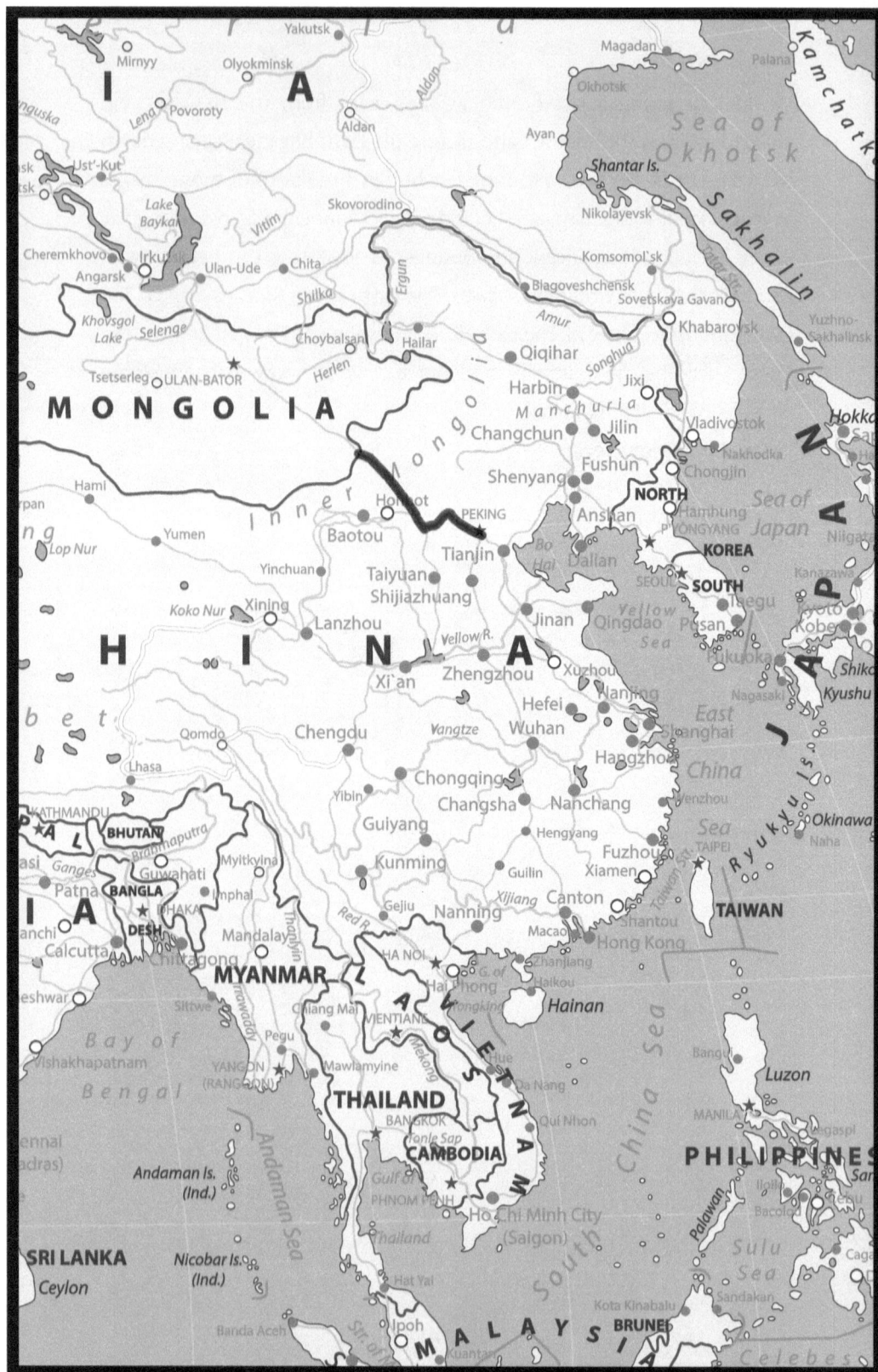

CHAPTER 2

BEIJING & BEYOND

Some of what follows overlaps chapter one, but the postings and emails were written as the trip was unfolding, not afterwards from the comfort of my resumed life. We had wanted to tell the world of our adventure as it happened via the aether and whilst we couldn't bask in the real-time amazed wonderment of friends and family, we could imagine it. This allowed us the obvious advantage of being able to indulge in self-praise at will, even when neither due or true. Among the gadgets brought along for the ride was a Palm One computer – only as big as a cigarette packet with a folding keyboard that wasn't a lot bigger. This enabled me to write postings for the web page as we went. I could email them when we found suitable computers with USB ports. The first posting resets the scene for the beginning of what we were hoping would be a memorable and entertaining three months.

First web posting: reflections

Sitting in an Airbus at 36,500 ft reflecting on the beginning of our adventure, seems a good place to start. Dick is asleep, head slumped forward in a post-brunch slumber. The posturing is over, now we must stand up and be counted ... ride the ride. There have been hurdles, personnel changes and an enforced last minute dropout. We've had serious financial challenges as first China then Mongolia required us to pay for guides to look after us while we transit. Our guide for China comes from something like 3,000 kilometres away in Beijing, where he meets with us. He will meet us again for our second entry into China from Krygyzstan in seven weeks time. The Mongolian follows us 2,000 kilometres across the Gobi Desert then drives home again. Reluctantly, we've had to dig deeper into our wallets. The euphoria of our going-away party and the triumphant, successful crating up of the bikes was tempered by learning that they were being delayed a day and would only just reach Beijing before us. This meant that our advance party in Beijing (Steve) would have more time sightseeing. But wait ... there's more. Not a Ginzu steak knife but another challenge ... the airlines rejected our bikes and on Saturday night upon arrival in Auckland we were soon uncrating them and removing the tanks and carbs. On a generally not amusing night, it amused us to see the crate addressed simply to Des Molloy, Beijing. There had been at least six emails trying to sort out an address, and somewhere along the way they must have given up. Late in the evening we left the removed bits on top of the crate (fingers crossed that our freight man came back for them) and brother-in-law Warren took us off home for a late-night snack and a few ... very few, hours sleep. 4.30 saw us having our first coffee of the day and Warren soon had us back at the airport and on the big silver bird. Two years of planning are behind ... the die cast, the warmth of our closest's hugs and kisses fading. Will we get our bikes back? Will we find Steve ... or our guide ... or Geoff (a loyal supporter) ... will my threatening cold lay me low?

And just to give you a laugh ... I left my Visa card at home ... hell I remembered the arnica, the homeopathic rescue remedy, the lip balm, the maintenance tools for the Primus, Dick, spare plugs, points, the Rover piston, the tent, the balaclava, the Aids Certificate (don't ask), bandages for Africa, the first aid book ... I even remembered the maps. So I left one small piece of plastic behind.

Beijing is only 10 hours away ... time for 8,000 games of solitaire on the *palm computer.*

Email of Monday, 2 May 2005
Subject: Molloy and Huurdeman reach Beijing

Well actually it's two Molloys, but we're not sticklers for accuracy. Beijing has been reached but we haven't knocked the bastard off as they say. NO, the Last Hurrah is a bit of a fizzer so far because although we've found Steve, Dick... mate Geoff, our guide Wang and his Beijing 'fix-it' man Lee, and their driver, the bikes are missing and we think they're still in Auckland.

Beijing has been found to be already occupied ... seems like several million got here before we did ... we'll shortly press on to the north ... we may be gone for some time.

~ Des

PS, we've just had a huge meal and a 680 ml beer for under US$20 for the three of us.

Fancy being so disappointed, so soon. Things were to get worse ... and better. For the worse ... read on, and the better? We got meals down to $1.00 per head including beer once we knew what we were about. To keep it simple, all dollars mentioned are Uncle Sam's ones, as that was the Western currency we mostly used.

Excerpts from second web posting: another few thoughts from Beijing

The city is big – very, very big. It bustles with life, laughter and a million oriental sounds. For me the highlights are too numerous to chronicle so I'll just try and portray a little of our time here. We've been staying in a hotel for Chinese nationals, which has been ideal – always someone exotic to observe. Until last night the temperature had only fluctuated between 23.9 and 26.9 degrees Celsius. Last night it rained and the temperature dropped.

Steve has been a treasure, slipping into a clear leadership role. The three months he spent travelling in Nepal and Indo-China show in the confidence and competence he displays. He was also particularly caring when I wasn't well with coughing asthma/chest infection/ cold. Our experiences here have been very sensory, with meals in raucous market cafes that stimulate every olfactory tissue. We've endured numerous crazy taxi rides, we've walked the streets and we've tasted the diesel fumes close up with a day out on bicycles. Scary? Well ... Steve has worked as a cycle courier so is a known road warrior. Dick hadn't ridden a self-powered two-wheeler for 40 years but "hey ... how hard can it be?" With Beijing's 15 million people, 2 million cars, 65,000 taxis and God knows how many buses, all wanting to go to Tiananmen Square at the same time as us, it made for a memorable comeback. Should we be surprised with the man who still races his Manx Norton shoulder to shoulder at 200 kilometres an hour just like any other youthful 72-year-old? There were many duels with the various four-wheelers who challenged for the same road space. A totally stimulating day was made even more challenging by the bikes having no discernable brakes. Some respite from the craziness was found in the tiny lanes off the main roads. These Hutong are a labyrinth of dirt lanes between walled, courtyarded traditional dwellings. They're too small for a car and we struggled to pass a rickshaw at one stage. The narrowest is reputedly only 400 mm wide. Seeing the real Beijing close up has been great and we often catch each other sitting, usually in a bar, just grinning. It's so dream-like. The local beer is amazingly cheap and damn nice. It's refreshing to drink from big 680 ml glass bottles. Our cheapest meal was at an Islamic (kebabs, etc) place not far from the hotel: three beers and three very replete lads = $3.00.

Frustrating as it's been to be waiting for our trusty steeds to arrive, there have been some very funny moments, not the least being our driver's licence medical inspection. Wang, our guide (once we're on the road) took us to a suburban hospital and in the grounds was a small bunker-like building with two nurses and a more senior looking gentleman. Dick was up first for an eye test. Initially, he thought all the characters were Chinese so couldn't say where he could read to. The symbols were rotated versions of a capital E so all you had to do was show whether the tongs of the E were up, down, to the left, etc.

This had the old fella absolutely confused and us rolling about with laughter. Wang would say "up?," so Dick would try to describe the symbol above. At one stage he got up and said he could read five lines down, which showed letters about 75 mm high. I'm thinking "this can't be true, he'll need a white stick." This was all done with a spoon held over one eye. Finally, after a lot of hilarity, he was led over to the boss-man who did the paper stamping and Dick was asked to look at two pictures and describe what was there. These were a bit like the hidden object kids' books. I can't believe it when he says he can see the number 52 and a horse. For me the number was a clear 89, but also a horse. This might have been a colour-blindness test. Our permits were both stamped, although I suspect that Dick's might have been notated 'Imbecile'.

We've seen an acrobatic troupe, we've walked dozens of kilometres, Dick and I have been temporarily 'geographically displaced' once, and I misplaced the other two at The Forbidden City. All in all, things are going OK but the bikes are not going to be with us until Friday 6th May, having left Wellington on the 26th April. Don't tell the hygiene police, but our clothes are in the box with the bikes. Dick and I have what we wore on the plane to come to China. It seems all the incompetence is in New Zealand.

~ Des

Our days in Beijing were in no way unpleasant – quite the contrary. We were enjoying it far more than we'd anticipated. The people were friendly and most of the women stunningly attractive. There isn't yet much obesity in China and usually the women are slim and willowy, with nice complexions. And no, they don't all look the same. Dick and I would often start the day with a walk which might take in a market or a park where we would watch the locals of all ages doing tai chi. There were a few occasions when the morning walk self-extended, as our sense of direction wasn't always unerring. Breakfast with Steve would follow. Wang would arrive and we'd usually go off trying to get some of the visas needed later in the trip. The one first needed would be Kazakhstan. Unfortunately, the May Day holidays were now in full swing and the embassy didn't seem too concerned about reopening. Typically, Wang would go to there early and, in the local custom, write our names on a piece of paper and stick it to the fence which established the order in which we would be seen later (when they deigned to open). After breakfast we would go en masse to take our place in the now-forming queue. One morning Wang got there early enough to place us fourth. The pity was that yet again at 9.30 the consular underling indicated that the ambassador wouldn't be seeing anyone that day. We would often then wander around the other embassies trying to find one that was open and would let us have a visa. Wang suited us well. A man who was a little sturdier than many Chinese, in his mid-twenties, he spoke good English and had a friendly, engaging personality. He and Steve struck up a strong rapport and comfortably wandered along together like long-term mates.

The days flowed into each other in a bit of a blur. We'd do a bit of sightseeing, once we'd established again that the bikes and the visas weren't forthcoming. Occasionally, we'd see a tourist or two but we weren't in those sorts of places very often. We did go out to the main night market once, which was entertaining because of the outrageous variety of food available and the forceful way the stallholders do the hard sell on you. The market has been relocated, regulated and sanitised for tourism, which diminished its appeal in our eyes but it was still a great night out. I started by buying a small 300 millimetre long snake about as thick as your thumb. Unfortunately, it tasted hideous. It was complete with all its insides but had been skinned. You buy the skin separately. It seemed to have been marinated in something that made me gag. Or maybe that was when it popped as I bit into it. This rates high on the list of the most repulsive things I've eaten. Steve and Dick each had a small portion before moving on to the more wholesome common sparrow. Fortunately, we were able to strike quite a good deal with a shifty pirate hawker of beer, so we weren't thirsty. These entrepreneurs moved through the crowd carrying a few bottles of the local brew and put the hard sell to any westerners they found. I'm sure many would pay the asking price first up. If you resisted, prices would tumble. Occasionally the stallholders would shoo them away.

The climate wasn't totally pleasant because although the temperature was no higher than 30 degrees, the humidity was usually below 20 percent. (How did I know all this? Because I was carrying a maximum/minimum digital thermometer which also records humidity.) The skies were never blue because of the air pollution. The visibility was usually about 1,000 metres and on a bad day it would be down to 500 metres. If you looked down a big road, you could clearly see the first couple of buildings, then the third would be blurry, the fourth hard to see and the fifth almost invisible. The pollution, combined with the low humidity, meant that you often had a dry throat. The city's traffic is initially overwhelming in its volume and intensity but when you're in the midst of it you realise the system is working. Merge like a zip takes on a whole new meaning as cars never hesitate to change lanes or leave intersections. If they did, the main roads would clog quickly, as they do in many other big cities. If you just go with the flow, and go quite aggressively, all is well. There are still many tens of thousands of ordinary bicycles on the roads of Beijing, along with many small motorbikes. The big growth in recent times, however, has been in electric battery-powered bicycles which possibly will enable the population to become fat and lazy, just like the rest of us. Many of the middle class have also become affluent enough to own cars, and the numbers are staggering.

Just how huge Beijing is, was clearly shown on the day of our sidecar outing. Amongst the millions of vehicles doing battle on the streets, we occasionally saw Chang Jiang sidecar outfits (CJs). I enjoy the flat, deep, menacing purr that their exhausts emit. They sound like a V8 car, powerful but smooth. Of course they aren't at all powerful, they just sound that way. I also love the look of the old-style open steel sidecars which haven't changed since they started making them after the Second World War. Some CJs we saw were adorned with large speakers, large woofer things, so antisocial rock'n'roll music could be played at a loud volume while cruising the streets, real outlaw stuff. Remembering that China is still a communist regime makes this all the more unusual. They seem caught halfway between the old and the new philosophies. There are still unbelievable numbers of people in uniforms just monitoring the state, yet there are also a surprising number of wealthy flaunting their status.

I had ascertained that there was a dealer in CJs only a few kilometres away from our hotel. With nothing special to do on this particular day we walked the 5 kilometres or so to a back street just off a main arterial route where we found some lock-up sheds and a line-up of CJs in the road outside. Some appeared new, whilst many were tatty and forlorn looking. Some had overhead valve engines, but most seemed to have the less powerful side valve configuration last favoured by the West in the 1930s. We found a young man who seemed to be interested in dealing with us. The plan was to hire an outfit for the day. We thought we would ride into the country and have a picnic by a river or under some trees. He seemed to grasp what we wanted.

Travellers are always told never part with their passports. Good advice, but sometimes worth ignoring. I swapped my passport for the sidecar that day. No deposit was required. He had my passport, I had his new CJ. He even gave us new rego plates to take with us. I did a trial run up the road to demonstrate that I could indeed pilot a three-wheeler. No sweat. I've had a couple of sidecars over the years and I'd even had the real deal, the Russian copy of the BMW, a Ural. Dick is also a sidecarist from way back but this day he had a sore arm which restricted him and meant he was confined to

the chair. So, with no helmet, no gloves, no jacket, no insurance, no papers and lots of false bravado, we were off. In our minds, we were off to a quaint rural repast. In reality we rode forever through suburban developments. I judge the activity in a city by how many tower cranes I see. I reckon we passed a thousand or more. Large housing blocks and whole suburbs were being built. I suppose in some way this compensates for the huge swathes being cleared through the older parts of the city, all in the name of progress. Sad though. We found a great market where Steve had his new boots repaired and I bought a hat which looked like a military cap from the Chairman Mao times. Later, I was told that the writing on the front showed it to be a fruit inspector's cap.

Finally we had to give up on the country dream. Like Hansel and Gretel, I was running out of bread crumbs and we might never find our way back. Without Steve's unerring navigation skills, we could still be going. A severe dust storm attacked us on the way back and the ride became even more challenging. Our CJ was a side valve and made 22 brake horsepower, but they are very small ponies, we reckon – it struggled with the three of us aboard into the strong head winds. The build-quality of the bike was so bad it made us laugh. Not everything worked and the front wheel was egg-shaped. The engine even stopped on us. Steve and I pushed the outfit off an expressway to the side of the road. We did wonder how we'd get it back and what we would say to the owner. It was probably fuel starvation in the hot going, as it fired up later with no apparent ill effects. We found our way back (no mean feat), paid the guy $35 and got the passport back. We'd had a great day out and I don't believe I frightened the others at all, although Dick does slightly dispute this. Nobody hit us and we hit nobody. That's a huge success, surely. I bonded with the machine despite its failings. They're a great throwback to more gentle times. They're like a lamb in wolf's clothing (a modern 750 makes over 100 horsepower).

Each succeeding day we would try to locate our bikes and get visas. After a while we were becoming used to failure. We were comfortable. Our hotel may have only been two-star, but it suited us by being clean, cheap, quite good fun and bright yellow, which often helped us find it. We had a variety of eating places we used, we knew where the email place was, we were on nodding terms with our doormen. We felt for Wang who was several timezones away from home with a job to do, namely guide us to the Mongolian border. He'd been waiting for us since about the 28th of April. We had thought that we'd have the bikes around the 3rd or 4th of May, do a bit of sightseeing and definitely be on the way by the 6th. This seemed to give us quite a bit of flexibility. We hadn't reckoned on the bikes ending up stuck because of the May holidays. We had met with the local agent, Jack, who tried hard on our behalf, but it seemed that apart from choosing the wrong airline to carry the goods, quite a bit of the problem was back in New Zealand. The bikes didn't come with us or follow close behind. Emails went back and forward to our New Zealand freighting agent Ralph, who didn't seem to grasp the gravity of the situation. Dick and I were out of undies and T-shirts. The plan of us taking the heavy tools and spares on the plane with us in our allowance and sending the light clothing, etc, in the bike crate, which we paid by the kilo, had backfired on us when we arrived first.

There is a limit to how many times you can turn your clothes inside out, upside down, or back-to-front to use them fully. Although we did do a bit of overnight hand-washing, we kept clinging to the hope that today our bikes and clothes would arrive. How hard could it be? You just put the box in the plane. We finally capitulated and bought underwear in the hope that it might bring the goods quicker. I bought the extra large size only to find myself so constricted I was out of breath. Dick bought a pack of medium size and the result was that he even walked funny. Maybe their sizing is done in a way to compliment you by making you feel bigger. Which is a bit like the Japanese who sell their condoms in three sizes ... large, extra large and super-extra large. Or so I'm told. Imagine going into the chemist and asking for a gross of super- extra large caramel flavoured featherlight ticklers. It would be almost worth a trip to Japan just to have the fun of going from shop to shop buying condoms. Dick's mate Geoff had been keen to wave us off from Beijing and he had even thought he might get up to Ulaanbaatar to see us ride in there. Now that we seemed destined to have to wait out the holidays, it would be touch and go whether we'd even be on the road before he headed back to New Zealand. Geoff is a big fellow who oozes bonhomie and largesse and who reciprocates friendship in the way that is easiest for him. He refuses to let Dick pay for anything when they're out together. This probably evens out the score quite well as Dick provides a skill and knowledge level that often can't be bought and he has long since given up working for reward. Being adjuncts to his mate meant that we also were swept along by Geoff and we had some good nights out together. He was able to go half way across China and see the buried army, muck about at other attractions and come back to find us still there, doing the same things as before he left.

Dick and I entertained ourselves looking for the tricycle with the slackest drivechain. We marvelled at these pedal-driven three-wheel delivery trucks that cart all sorts of loads all over the city. The loads they carried were very impressive, as was the apparent lack of maintenance on these work vehicles. Sometimes we'd spot a driver, standing up, pedalling hard with the top row of the drivechain tight, but with the bottom row almost dragging on the road. A small thing to be enthused about but it kept us amused, especially each time we found one more droopy than the last.

Of course this couldn't go on for ever and finally on the night of the 10th of May the bikes were delivered to the hotel on a truck with no way of being unloaded. A ploy to get some more money from us perhaps? We'd already paid a bundle to the customs agents and others. More money changed hands. Suddenly, there were swarms of eager helpers. Many hands not only make the lights work but get heavy loads off trucks. Later, Jack had some friends come around on their latest model, big, round-the-world type BMWs, to look at these relics that were going to attempt to ride to Europe. They were blown away by what they saw and insisted on taking us all out for a meal that night, including Wang and Geoff. And what a night it was. There was Jack, the two BMW guys who we called the older TV guy and the grinning photographer, and two 4 x 4 adventurers who had been in some sort of off-road rally in China. One of them also had his wonderfully attractive, much younger wife along for the night. A delightful lady, she had quite good English comprehension. Not so the rest of them, apart from Wang and Jack, but that didn't matter at all.

A posh restaurant had been selected and we were treated to course after course of delicious food. This was accompanied by bottle after bottle of Chinese beer. China is now the second largest consumer of beer in the world and it's now the drink of choice of the masses. The local beers trace their origins back through Germans who established the hops and breweries decades ago. Outside brewers had come and gone in the

90s, mostly with unhappy results. Wrong place at the wrong time. Now Chinese beer is more than acceptable, it's bloody delicious, especially with good company. We had the bikes so were naturally happy. There were numerous toasts and presents were given and received. Steve got the best of it, receiving a stylish shirt from the desert rally the two 4 x 4 guys had been in. Dick and I got hats and a CD of the event with a plaque. We gave flags, I think. Geoff conspired to get Wang drunk, and succeeded. Dick, the cunning old fox, managed to get some of the Chinese into 'skolling' races. He told us next day that the secret is to always make sure that your glass is only half full and the toasting partner's is much fuller. We finished the night late but happy in more than one way. I was a bit concerned that Wang was legless, away from home and we needed him on the ball at 7.30 next morning, as it was a big day for us. We now could assemble the bikes and go for our Chinese licences. Wang would lead Dick and I to do that whilst Steve would go and get the Kazakhstan visa now that the embassy was open for business. If we managed everything, we would leave town in two days.

Wang turned up on time looking a little yellow (I had to say that didn't I?).

The day started with a lot of grumbles as we unpacked the dangerous goods parcel which turned out to be nothing more than a cardboard box with the tanks and carbs wrapped in cellophane. No bubble wrap or anything. My super- expensive chromed and enamelled petrol tank now had big scrapes and gouges in it. I don't mind adding the patina of adventure to my bikes but this was pure incompetence, almost wilful damage. Only an imbecile would put two motorcycle petrol tanks and two carburettors in the same box without good wrapping and padding. We photographed the damage and went out into the courtyard of the hotel to assemble the bikes. Generally this went well. In went the new batteries, in went the new oil, but when Dick put petrol in Dutch Courage, one of the petrol taps leaked significantly. Because the tanks had been drained and left for such a length of time, the cork seals in the taps had dried out. Normally, the cure for this is to boil the cork in water so it swells, then smear it with oil and replace it. One seal stubbornly resisted this dodge and was not going to stop dripping. If we had time, we could have found one of the 4 x 4 drivers and got him to locate a couple of gas pipe taps of that size. This may not have been as easy as I make it sound. It's in situations like this that Dick excels, however. He quickly whittled a wooden stopper with his trusty Mercator knife to replace the tap and reduced the flow of leaking petrol to a few drops an hour. Penelope had a broken tail light but we didn't see that as being of much consequence and there wasn't time left in the morning to deal with it. With Wang as a pillion, we went out into the Beijing traffic, in eager anticipation of doing the Chinese driving test. It took us a while to find the Police facility but after a bit of taxi-hiking (similar to hitch-hiking) we were at a new and impressive operation that looked like a suburban shopping mall. The test involved a ride around the carpark and a display that the brakes worked. Wang seemed to have smoothed the waters. There was no comment about my lack of a brake light. So now we had Chinese driving licences and new number plates, which unfortunately we would have to later give up. Our time in Beijing was nearly done.

Steve had been successful with getting the Kazakhstan visas so now we could relax and prepare for the big day. Wang advised us that due to our lateness we would have to put in a couple of really hard, long days to get to the Mongolian border non-stop, with little time for sightseeing, as the border didn't stay open over the weekend. We would visit the Great Wall out at Badalang and then do some big distances. We were OK with this as we were aware that already we were a week late. Our plan had been to gain a week if possible to meet the Silkriders (the other New Zealand group already en route). We were a little disturbed to learn from Wang that our re-entry point to China was down in all his documentation as being through the Torugat Pass from northern Kyrgyzstan. Our documentation and our accommodation bookings were for a much more southerly route taking us through the Erkistam Pass. Despite our protestations that his documentation must be for the Silkriders, he was adamant that the plans could not be changed. This was the route that had been agreed to by the government and it would take months for any alteration to be accepted. This was a blow. It would add to our journey if we continued with our plans to get down to Samarkand and Bukhara, because we would have to backtrack a substantial distance. There was nothing we could do about it except moan to Murray at Silk Road Adventures. We were nearly away, but the butterflies had returned. It's hard to describe the slightly scary feelings of anticipation. The thought of actually riding off into the hinterland of China and then on to the even more exotic Mongolia was almost too much.

Geoff wanted to take us all out for a Peking duck meal but I really didn't want a big night out. Steve and I opted out, settling for a quiet meal at a pretty scungy cafe within walking distance from the hotel. It was a reflective night with just the two of us sharing thoughts about the future and what it might hold. I knew Dick wanted to join us and I admired his loyalty to Geoff by going out for the Peking duck ceremony. We all had a reasonably early night as Geoff was heading off to the airport at some outrageous hour and we were heading off at a similar hour on an outrageous adventure. Yeeehaaaa!!!

As the big day dawned we packed, some stuff on the bike and some stuff in the van that Wang had hired for the next few days. Jack turned up in his Mercedes Benz 4 x 4 (the only one in Beijing) and soon we were off, following him out through the suburbs to a rendezvous with the others from the party night. This was a surreal moment. Finally it was happening. I couldn't help but sing, which is something you do sometimes on a motorbike. I had a helmet camera running and tried to express myself as we rode. A couple of times Dick and I rode side by side and grinned at each other. We're not grinning sort of people, but there was no stopping us today. Shit, it was a good feeling. We were in bloody Beijing on our old champions, riding through this huge bustling city, going to the Great Wall and beyond, way beyond, all the way to Mongolia. If only the folks at home could see us now! The network of expressways seemed pretty good and soon we were greeting our new-found friends and yet another matching big Beemer. This third rider I christened Meat Pies after the kid's rhyme. Who stole the meat pie? Who me … couldn't be! Unlike almost all the other Chinese we had met, this one was rotund. He also spoke good English and was yet another friendly chapter in our book. With Jack in the lead we headed for the wall. Steve was filming from Wang's van while we hummed along. We were also being constantly photographed by the grinning photographer who kept zooming ahead to click away at us as we passed. The two rally 4 x 4s followed in the rear. They were impressive, complete with every adventure extra you could imagine. They had spades and axes strapped aboard with jerrycans and rows of spotlights along the front and up on the roof rack. There were also sponsor's stickers all over. What a convoy!

This was immense fun and highly satisfying as we savoured the anticipatory delights of riding into sights seemingly from the pages of the National Geographic. Soon we would reach the foothills where we would see the Great Wall running away over the hills. I'd read enough to know that there wasn't one wall but several, and also that it wasn't really able to be seen from space by the naked eye. But who cares. Back on Earth, I was the centre of some excitement. While happily holding my course on the expressway I was carved up by a small yellow car coming at speed in from my right, presumably coming from an on-ramp. The incident was a near miss, close enough to shake me and invoke an involuntary expletive. We

are always vulnerable on motorbikes. We don't ride because it's safe, we ride because we love it and because they haven't found a cure for it yet (and isn't that great?). I reassured myself that a miss was a miss, a bit like being nearly pregnant; you aren't pregnant and you'll live to ride another day. No real harm had been done. Then one of the big Beemers came by at an outrageous speed, scything through the traffic, presumably in pursuit of the perceived felon. The road was three lanes wide. We were making steady progress in the middle one but I jumped a little as that first avenger whistled by. Within a few seconds the other two followed, giving full vent to the power of their 1200 cc machines, curving across all three lanes and back as they cut through the traffic like a knife through soft butter. It looked like they were doing a slalom race with the cars as markers. What a chase! Soon they were out of sight and my first thoughts were that these guys might be more than just successes of China's new economic policies. They were sure on a mission. It was quite some time before we finally caught up with them . They had the culprit boxed in, with a bike in front and one on each side and they had him down to 50 kph or so in the middle lane. He was weaving from side to side trying to get away but they doggedly kept him pinned, all the time shouting abuse (and probably threats). They kept him there while we passed by and it was another long time before they rejoined the convoy. The little yellow car never appeared in my mirrors at all. Well, that had been exciting. Later Meat Pies told me that they would normally have beaten up the offending driver, but there wasn't time.

The first sight of the wall is memorable because it's just like in the pictures.

I've found this to be case with all major sights of international significance. You stand there like an idiot saying that it's just like it is in the movies or some such drivel. Of course it looks like that because that is what it is. This doesn't lessen the thrill though. You are prepared for it but seem so unprepared when you finally see it. You can't help but laugh or smile because now it is you in the frame. It's all the better when you have kindred souls with you, so you can share the "Will you look at that!" moments.

Badalang is, for many, one of the lesser spots to view the wall. It's deemed to be a bit touristy and over-exposed because of the high level of worldwide recognition. We didn't care. For us it was all we needed. The wall snakes away over the misty hills just like in the colour glossies. It is an amazing feat of human endeavour, especially as the scale is so evident and we can so easily imagine the difficulties of planning and execution. However we didn't spend much time with the wall. We spent the time down in the car park taking photos and laughing with our new friends. We'd had a good time with them and we savoured this last gathering. There were tour buses arriving and some of the tourists were from Holland.

They were most impressed that we were going there, albeit slowly and in a roundabout fashion, on motorcycles that should be in museums. We quite liked being the centre of attention even though we knew we hadn't really earned it. We hadn't gone anywhere yet. All we'd done was turn up, but there are always a few leaps of faith needed to even get to the start line. We knew dozens back at home who were quick to say they wished they were coming with us. We knew, but never said so, that most lacked the commitment and audacity for the step off the high board, but hey, we were planning to leave the roads there more or less undamaged, so they could do it any time they liked.

We had a big distance to cover on this, our first day on the road, so Wang had us climbing through the hills away from the plains before lunchtime. We didn't really know how far the ride would be as there weren't road signs that we could comprehend, but we knew it was more than 400 kilometres and that it would be a challenge. Once past Badalang, the tour bus numbers lessened, the truck numbers increased and we began to feel we were really in the hinterland. The roads were good, the weather warm, the bikes great and our spirits were as high as the sky. We had hills and corners to entertain us, we had views to dwell on. Everything was alien to us and interesting. Small towns were passed through. We lunched in one. This was the real China.

No longer were there any road signs in our script (Latin alphabet) as an alternative. I liked this as I'm always disappointed when travel becomes too easy. I lament the loss of individuality now apparent in most of the world's big cities. China started to introduce Pinyin, which is their language written in our characters, in the late 1950s. It's now starting to take hold in the major towns, with big signs and advertising hoardings often being presented this way. Already all their vehicle number plates are in our numbers. They've got more than 6,000 characters of their own so you wonder why they want to learn a few more of ours. This is OK, but there's the danger that in time they will lose their own written language, as so many other nations have before them. Well-meaning politicians will make this decision for them and part of their heritage will be lost forever. Some of the Central Asian republics we would shortly visit had lost their own scripts in recent history. Mongolia is another example, as are Vietnam and Turkey.

The towns and villages were all quite different from Beijing. There weren't the gaudily dressed young folk, aping the Tokyo Shock Girls. This was a bit more of the Chairman Mao utilitarian world with more socialism and less market economy. There may have been less colour in the clothing but we were loving it all the same.

The afternoon saw the team make a small navigational error. This wasn't Wang's part of China and his driver was a city boy from Beijing. We knew there were two routes up to the border point. One looked shorter but Wang had explained that we wouldn't be taking it as it was the coal truck route which went through the hills and was nowhere near as good as the longer, more developed road. So you can guess which road we ended up on. It's hard to imagine there are more trucks on the planet and for a while the constant stream was just an annoyance. We had the ability to pass easily, Dick and I by way of having skinny motorcycles and our van by being driven in the typically dangerous fashion of ignoring oncoming traffic. But in the mid-afternoon we started to run into a full-scale truck jam. We were able to crawl up either side of the line and, on cresting a long hill, we could see right down a valley and up the other side into what appeared like infinity. It was a gobsmacking sight – trucks nose-to-tail in both directions. The tailback must have been at least 50 kilometres long.

The road was now narrow and unsealed, with trucks trying to go the opposite way as well. It was no longer a matter of just going onto the other side of the road and blasting along. Dick and I snuck our way ahead sometimes in the small gap between the trucks in the middle of the road or between the trucks and the bank. The casual behaviour of the drivers was a revelation to us. Some were definitely broken down, but others seemed to be carrying out quite major maintenance while they waited. We saw driveshafts being replaced, gearboxes being taken out, and several wheels were off. If the line was able to move, it would move around them. For a couple of hours Dick and I forged ahead. After finally getting out of this chaos we took refuge in a roadside cafe, of a sort, to wait for the others. We idled away the hours with cups of tea, a couple of beers, a few photos, visits to the loo. We watched a young woman knitting sleeves for a jersey with four needles (this was fascinating and we were quite disappointed to be told later that it's quite normal to do it that way).

It was a windswept desolate place and it was sad to see what our culture has introduced. Plastic bags were everywhere in northern China. Every bush has the remnants of shredded plastic clinging to it. Sometimes from a distance it looks like cotton fields, but close-up the reality is depressing. The lack of care about the disposal of rubbish throughout this whole region depressed me. There were occasions when you almost had to wade through rubbish to get to an outdoor privy.

Finally, the van slewed to a halt outside, Wang having spotted our bikes. They had tales of cross-country driving – paying money to farmers in return for taking short cuts across their land – and the like. It had been frustrating but all part of the adventure. We tried to think of how many trucks we might have seen but the maths got a little too hard and we settled for thousands. It was now getting towards dusk and we still had a long way to go. We'd come through the brown grassless hills and valley and now seemed to be out on the featureless tundra. The driver had ascertained that with a bit of effort we should be able to get onto the sealed highway being constructed parallel to the dusty road we'd been enduring. And so another type of fun was engaged in – zooming down nicely made smooth highway. Oops, it ends here. Back onto the crap road, back up onto the new road, up to full cruising speed, wave to the road workers (hell they work late, it's already dark). Oops a barrier, better move that, and so on. We went on and off the new highway many times. It might not have been quicker but it was cleaner and a lot of fun, although there was a bit of frustrating backtracking a couple of times.

On one occasion, I saw a local vehicle pulling off to the right when the road appeared to carry on for a while, so I made the decision to follow. Dick must have been in his own twilight zone because only at the last minute did he become aware of me having slowed for the turn. I heard the squeal of skidding rubber and flinched as I looked back to see Dick with the Norton all locked up and smoke coming off the tyres. Lucky he has such good brakes on the old girl. Having built the bike for use towing a sidecar, Dick has mated a pair of brakes back-to-back in the front wheel and the resulting braking is better than the British motorcycle industry managed until they introduced disc brakes. "What the hell were you doing?" Dick wanted to know. "Um, just following the van in front," I replied. If I had continued straight ahead I would have plunged off the end of that section of made road.

It was now 8 o'clock and we were getting tired and really needed to finish for the day. We knew the town we wanted to stop in was near but it was resisting discovery. A period wandering through little lanes and fields followed before finally we were in Jinin. A miserable hotel without hot water was found and after something to eat we were soon asleep. Wang wanted us up at 5 a.m. and away so as to get to the Mongolian border before lunch if possible. This was about 500 kilometres and would be touch and go with bikes lacking in speed. We'd geared the bikes for crossing sandy deserts and climbing mountains, not for blasting along, eating up the miles as quickly as possible.

I can't say we were very frisky first thing in the morning. The hotel only had intermittent lighting, no heating and, as mentioned, no hot water.

The beds hadn't been great either with their hard, wheat pillows. We did take a big thermos to our room though and had hot drinks and 3-minute noodles for breakfast. It wasn't long after dawn when we were fetching our bikes out of the secure compound next to the hotel. All sorts of trucks and commercial vehicles, including mobile cranes, were also being unlocked and fired up for the day. It seemed funny to be in a work-day situation with working men so different in culture and appearance from us. They had their jobs to do and so did we. I felt a bond with them even though in reality it was probably only that we'd all shared the same sleep-deprived night and lack of amenities with staunch resolution. I hoped they could sense an ally.

Now we were finally away from the pollution influence of Beijing, the skies were beginning to clear for the ride across the rest of northern China and Inner Mongolia. The villages were fascinating for their lack of colour. They were the colour of the surrounding countryside. Some had earth roofs and the houses were all similar in mud brick or unpainted timber. There were plots of intense horticulture with long growing houses of semicircular tunnel construction, their coverings were being rolled back as we passed in the morning sun. The road was now good and the traffic light. The sun was out. We were happy and it was at one of our stops that Dick shared with us the song he'd been singing. Dick isn't known for his singing or overt passion, but here was something straight from the heart. The words and message were not difficult to grasp. "We're going to Mongolia, we're going to Mongolia, we're going to Mongolia," repeated 4,000 times before the added refrain, "to Mongolia we're going". He had sung this succinct song for a couple of hours. I knew just how he felt. All morning we rode hard, but we needed to rest a couple of times so weren't going to make the border in the morning session. We did reach the Chinese border town of Erenhot at lunchtime and met with another local agent as deemed necessary by someone, somewhere. Wang had established contact with our Mongolian guide and we would be met at the border after 2 p.m. when the border reopened. We ate, we chatted with Wang and reminisced. We wouldn't be seeing him at the other side of China as he would be guiding the Silkriders by then. We'd enjoyed his company and help. He'd shared our frustrations with good grace.

China had one last event for us. We'd heard that Mongolian petrol was quite a bit more expensive so decided it was sensible to fill up at the classy looking petrol station just back from the border. Dick and I rode into this modern service area and stopped in front of the pumps, only to be shooed away by the quite fierce female attendant. We couldn't grasp this as we wanted petrol and this was a petrol station. She seemed to understand what we wanted but she didn't seem to want us to be there. This confused the hell out of us and lots of silly miming followed. It transpired that they wouldn't fill our bikes because the engines were hot. We had to go 20

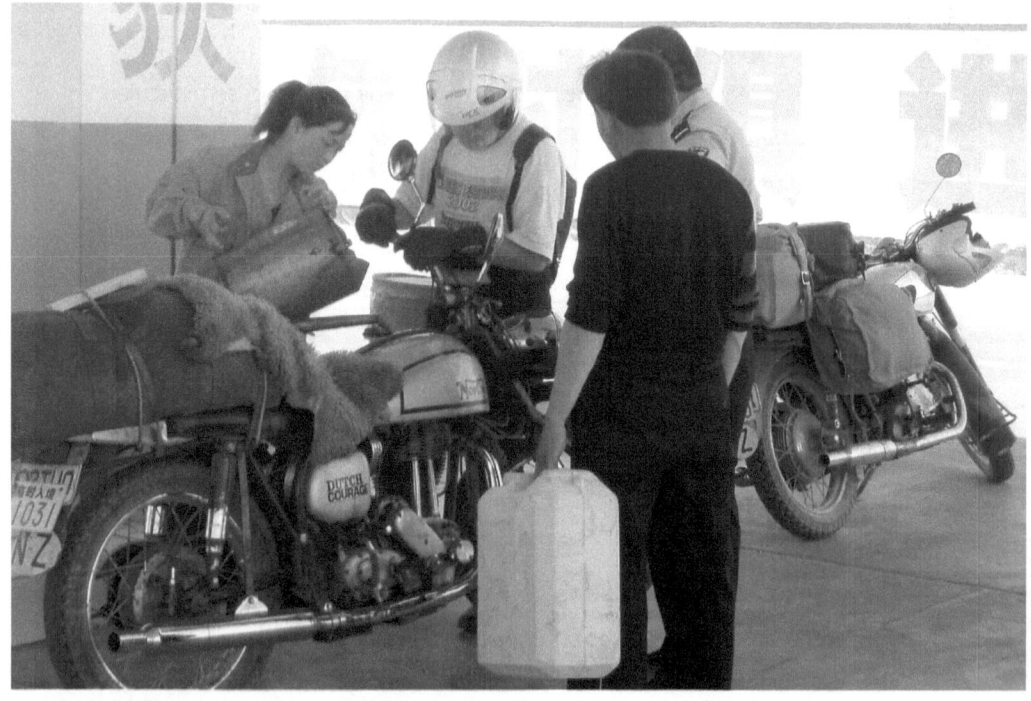

metres away and the pump attendant assessed how much fuel would go in the tank. She then went back to the jealously guarded pumps, put that amount of petrol in a watering can and brought it over and tipped it in. To us this seemed much more dangerous than just plonking the nozzle in the bike's tank as done at every bowser in the world for the last 100 years. She was accurate in her guesses though, and we were quite impressed, but walking around with open watering cans full of petrol defied all logic.

The final step of our adventure in eastern China was to remove our number plates and give them back. We had hoped to be able to keep them but supposedly Wang had to surrender them to officialdom. We did get to keep our licences though. Wang would be driven back to Beijing and then he would fly back to his home province of Xinjiang to await the arrival of the Silkriders. He would also go back to our yellow hotel and see if my Visa card had finally arrived and if it had, he would get it to the other side of China for me to collect upon re-entry in six weeks or so.

Whilst still at the Chinese side of the border we were surprised to have a startlingly beautiful young woman bound up to us and introduce herself as Maggie. Well that's what we thought she said her name was. Actually she said, "Hi, I'm Eggie and I'm your guide for Mongolia". Dick called her Maggie for quite a few days, but that's Dick.

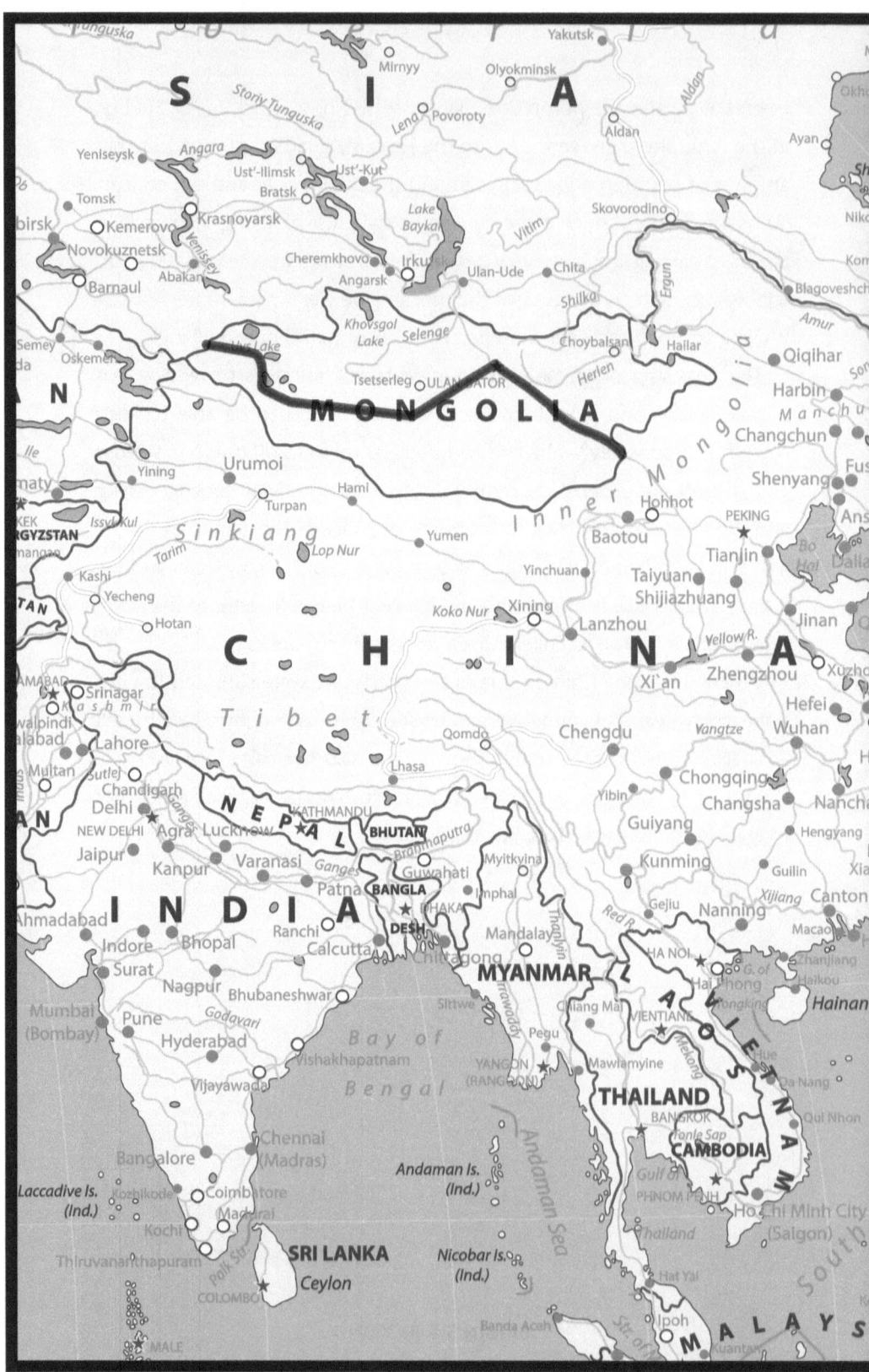

CHAPTER 3

ACROSS THE GOBI

Having a 19-year-old English student as our guide to take us across Mongolia seemed a little bizarre. Would she know where to take us?

Had she been across the Gobi to the Russian border? The answer to both of those questions was no. She was with us to provide the English. Her driver, Ganbaatar, was a 21-year-veteran of the Mongolian tourist industry. There weren't many places in Mongolia that he hadn't been, or many things that he hadn't seen. Their vehicle was a newish Mitsubishi Pajero with air conditioning and a good sound system. It seemed like Steve was in for a cruisy ride.

The China to Mongolia border crossing was our first and possibly the quickest, but we didn't know that at the time. It was some time after 2 p.m. when we farewelled Wang and faced officialdom. Even though we were reasonably confident that we had all the right paperwork, this would be the proof. A lot of confusing forms were filled in and scrutinised by several different officials. It was a little bewildering to learn that this was just to get us out of China. Our next step was to get into Mongolia. Our first introduction to Mongolia's border personnel was to a very smart, quite beautiful but tough looking miniskirted female border guard wearing a tight green uniform with gold buttons all over the jacket. The uniform

was bottomed-off with shiny knee-high leather boots (well, you can't say topped-off for boots, can you?). She was scary with her stony silence and piercing but impassive glare. I felt guilty and didn't know what of. She wasn't the least bit impressed by us but ultimately brought my passport back to me. I took my opportunity to leave and rode off through a couple more checkpoints until I was in Mongolia. What a feeling. I stopped a couple of hundred metres up the road to wait for Dick and the Norton. I waited and waited in quite hot conditions, watching all sorts of overladen trucks grind their way by at walking pace. There were some broken down at the border and another one dead-in-the-water between me and the last checkpoint. The trucks were old Russian ones and didn't seem to be maintained at all. One had clearly visible collapsed wheel bearings. The loads were colossal but the speeds very low. It is possible that they were just carting to a local railhead or depot although that didn't make sense. I really couldn't see these loads being carted 800 kilometres to Ulaanbaatar.

After a long wait, Dick threaded his way through the dead and dying trucks and came with the news that I had to go back. The scary Gestapo lady had made a mistake in letting me go and it seemed there were other procedures to be gone through. We debated this a bit and wondered if we shouldn't just keep on going as we were now both in Mongolia. Ultimately,

we reasoned that there was probably another checkpoint and they would be bound to get us. Besides they still had the Cabin Boy, as we had taken to calling Steve. We joked at his expense about the right to eat cabin boys should the need arise (it was only the case against the crew of Maignonette in 1884 that judicially made it illegal). Just as we'd reached this conclusion, we saw Eggi running up the road to fetch us. She looked just as appealing with a sweat-induced glow. She wouldn't ride back with me though and chose to again run all the way. At the customs building the bikes were searched and our paperwork taken away. We sat sweltering in the shade outside, the temperature probably in the mid 30s. Dick removed his jacket to reveal a completely sodden T-shirt. Not an inch of dry fabric was to be seen. He took it off and wrung it out like an item of hand washing. He was finding it very trying in the heat.

A few of the local labourers wandered over from time to time. These were pretty hard looking characters. We weren't completely at ease with them. One took the opportunity to flip open one of our tank caps and have a good sniff of the petrol. Others sat on the bikes and generally poked and pulled at things. In time they wandered away to where a few others were wrestling; Mongolia's national sport. This wait was quite frustrating and we were beginning to worry about being let into the country at all before they closed for the weekend. We saw lots of uniformed men and women (including Gestapo lady) packing into Russian 4 x 4s and driving off. Earlier, Eggi had said she would like us to ride 280 kilometres before getting a place to stay. This was before we'd even started the border processes and our immediate refusal was based on being knackered from already having done 500 kilometres getting there. This distance would have been out of the question anyway as it wasn't until the late afternoon that we were given permission to leave the control point. So we followed the Mitsi into the rundown dusty brown Mongolian border town. This was quite a challenge as the bikes slewed and weaved alarmingly in the loose softness of the sandy streets. Our Mongolians had located an old rooming house with a reasonably secure compound for the bikes. They would stay elsewhere. They had the director of the company with them and I think he may have had a place there. He would be staying on for a few more days and not travelling back to Ulaanbaatar with Eggi and Ganbaatar. We had just enough time left in the day to change some money before the facility closed at 6 p.m. – $600 got us an amazing 709,000 togrog. We could have been millionaires. We were all quite excited, although buggered from our long day. We managed to arrange some food and a thermos and more noodles for the morning. There was a building sense of anticipation. Each day seemed to have greater possibilities than the last.

We assembled next day and were given our instructions by Eggi. They (with Cabin Boy) would go and get some supplies from a store. Dick and I should head off out of town and they would catch us up. Dick and I nodded our assent and rode off along the paved road to the town's end. But it wasn't just the town's end, it was also the road's end. Snaking away ahead of us, going in all sorts of directions, were numerous tracks with varying degrees of definition. None of them looked main enough for us to be bold and strike off into the Gobi alone. No way! As it happened, Dick's bike also had a bit of a misfire so he was happy to look for and find a loose

wire while we waited for our support crew. It was nice just to look around at a town that was so far removed from anything that we'd seen to date. There were streets of gers, each surrounded by a wooden fence. Town folk do indeed live in these traditional tent-like felt houses. We found it funny calling them gers when we were more familiar with the term yurt, but yurt is a little offensive to Mongolians (being the Russian name). We were to get even closer to these fascinating dwellings within only a few hours.

It was astonishing that we could stand at the end of this one paved road and just look out into the Gobi Desert. The nothingness was fascinating. Everything was a tawny brown and there were no hills to be seen, just a few minor undulations in the foreground. There were no trees, not really any scrub at all.

Ganbaatar laughed at our indecision and hesitation. It didn't matter which track we took. It was 800 kilometres to Ulaanbaatar and as long as you kept the railway on one side, you weren't lost. There was also a line of power poles that went all the way so it would be hard to get lost. We were to find his observations only partially true.

We headed off in the general direction the tracks went and soon were each taking the one which we individually preferred, so sometimes I would see Dick well off to one side of me, making steady progress. It was nice knowing I was riding with someone who was matched to my ability in dirt road riding. Neither of us would profess to be an expert but both of us are proficient and confident on what we would call gravel roads. However, on the first day in Mongolia both of us struggled badly. The tracks were just too sandy. We were often veering from side to side, out of control. There were ruts and bumps, potholes made for hiding in – it was very hard going. Our skill levels probably weren't yet up to the level needed to travel fast enough to make it smooth and enjoyable. I remember thinking that I might never get out of second gear and, when would I ever get to look up long enough to admire the crazy, wild view? There was a niggling feeling of despair, as I knew it would be a hell of a long trip to Ulaanbaatar at this speed. It was also hot and we were sweating like pigs.

We hadn't really ridden for too long before we came to a small rise and our first ovoo. An ovoo is a Shamanist religious monument, being a stone cairn topped with blue ribbons and rags onto which seem to be thrown all sorts of objects from crutches to beer bottles. We stopped and were told to walk around the ovoo in a clockwise direction three times, each time throwing a stone onto its construction. We did this and were rewarded by being made to drink a toast of vodka by Ganbaatar. It was awful Chinese stuff. Eggi just smiled, saying it was tradition and had to be done by travellers. We had Steve film us riding around the ovoo and down off the small promontory. His footage shows us going slowly off into the distance, intermittently wobbling like novices. Looks great though, heading off into the big empty light-tan countryside.

The combination of the difficult tracks and the quicker handling of the Norton soon had Dick biting the dust. That wasn't something that worried

the old fellow particularly. He was up and away before I'd even realised he was gone. Penelope has a much longer wheelbase which makes her quite stable and almost unwilling to fall over, but she's like the Queen Mary and not very quick to change directions. You don't just flick her out of the way of a big obstacle. You plough into or over it. Horses for courses, but both were proving a handful in the sandy going. Both of us were fading in the heat. We were trying to keep hydrated, drinking from our 'camelbacks' as we rode, but it wasn't easy to keep it up.

We saw a group of camels of all ages, and what a thrill that was. They weren't tethered or restrained in any way that we could see. Eggi said they wouldn't be wild camels, they would belong to someone, somewhere. Mongolia is known as the land without fences and also the land of the big sky. Both were evident from this first day. Land ownership outside of the towns is not permitted so there are no boundary fences, you just take your animals where the feed is. It's not a very efficient system. It doesn't really encourage anyone to produce feed but relies solely upon nature. After our camera stop with the camels, Dick took off just as they began to cross the trail ahead of him. This split them and he got a close-up encounter as he rode through.

Seeing those two-hump camels led to some daydreaming. It isn't all that

far away, maybe Iran, that the camels only have one hump. There must be an overlap somewhere. I imagined the surprise of a one-hump camel when it saw a two-hump camel for the first time. There would be the camel equivalent of, "Will you look over there! Boy, is she stacked or what!" What happens if lust of the loins gets the better of them? Does a one-and-a-half-humped camel result?

... But, back to the ride.

The going didn't really get any easier but we got a little braver. This resulted in higher speeds and Dick taking a second tumble. He must have hit a soft patch on an angle or something because he later described the bars being violently wrenched sideways, putting him into a front wheel slide at 60 kph or so. This threw him heavily, with the bike landing on his inner thigh. He straightened the damaged footrest and with difficulty started the bike and resolutely continued on. It wasn't long before we stopped for a break and it was evident that the hard-man was fully spent. He took his jacket off and again his T-shirt was completely sodden and able to be wrung out. He was exhausted and sore. The main damage had been to his right leg, the one he uses to kick-start the bike if he's sitting astride it. We decided that he should travel in the van for the rest of the day and Steve would take over.

Steve had never ridden Dick's bike and his experience on old British singles was limited to the occasional short ride on Bessie, my pre-war BSA. He has, however, raced mountain bikes for years and has great balance, being able to ride a unicycle and also stop stationary at traffic lights on a two-wheeler without putting his feet down (annoying bugger). Steve was only tentative for a short distance and, being used to the slipping and sliding of mountain biking, he wasn't overly daunted by the snaking of the bike in the sandy going. This first day was having more dramas than we really needed but we were resilient and patient, knowing that every turn of the wheel was taking us closer to Ulaanbaatar. We might be slow and clumsy, having a few tumbles, bending a few bits here and there, but we were there and doing it.

The first settlement we came to was a great experience for us as we were introduced to our first meal-in-a-ger. This was to become a standard thing for us all across Mongolia, just like fish-in-a-basket is in the pubs of England. The village of Ulaan Uul might have 100 or so gers. They have electricity and the main road, such as it is, passes through. With far more aplomb than you would expect from a 19-year-old city girl, Eggi soon had us inside a ger and the family preparing us a meal. This is quite normal for travellers, apparently. The only difference this time was that the locals had never had non-Mongolians in their ger before, so it was a new experience all round.

We were expected to (and were keen to) rest while they made the noodles and chopped up the mutton and potatoes and stoked up the fire. Bowl after bowl of Mongolian tea was thrust upon us. It's niceish, well sometimes it's nice. It can be sweet and refreshing, but you can get a bit sick of it and the amount you have to drink plays havoc with your bladder. These gers don't have toilets. We were also a little uncertain of the protocol. Out the back somewhere there would be a long-drop toilet

ACROSS THE GOBI

in a shed. This might be shared by several families and was not always the most pleasant of places. But when all you needed to do was have a piddle, did you just go a little way away, turn your back and let fly? This wasn't something I felt I could ask Eggi, yet. Typically, a meal-in-a-ger might take a couple of hours but the rest and the experience was always nice. So nice that usually within a couple of minutes Cabin Boy would be asleep.

We always enjoyed seeing Eggi and Ganbaatar interacting with these roadside folk. It was impressive to watch how well they were accepted and how skilful they were at coming into these people's lives for such a short time. They might be from Ulaanbaatar but that didn't matter a damn. They'd soon be passing babies around and chatting away, explaining about us, and where we were from. It was also interesting to watch the family dynamics, which often involved three generations. It's the kids and elderly who gather dung for their fires whilst the other adults look after the stock and the more general household chores. Some Western travellers say that the smell of a dung fire permeates the food and taints the taste, but our systems mustn't be so finely attuned, as that wasn't something we could determine.

The ride to Ulaanbaatar was a little bit like the three bears' porridge in the fairy tale. We had a day that was too hot, we had one that was windy and too cold, and we had one that was just right. We were also getting better at riding so we could now get along at reasonable speeds, look at the views and gaze in awe at the fauna. We saw eagles, hawks, marmots, desert rats, hairy cattle, yaks, goats and sheep. I kept missing the eagles but I had the most wonderful race with some gazelles. They appeared to the left of me but a bit ahead. The railway was on that side as a natural barrier and I thought if I could get ahead of them on the right, they would probably stop and Dick could also see them; I knew he was just a little way back. It became an exciting race as I tried my best on a rough road to out-speed some of nature's quickest animals. This went on for a while and I kept thinking that soon I would get a better bit of track or they would get tired. It was thrilling because not only was I racing only about 20 metres behind about ten leaping and jumping gazelles, but also I was going faster than I was happy to go, except of course I was happy, hugely happy and exhilarated. I was fair flying at about 80 kph when suddenly on my left, like a flying rally car, came the Mitsi, airborne over the bumps and rises. I was gobsmacked that anyone would drive an ordinary vehicle like this. I hoped Steve was filming it all although I wondered how he would be hanging on. The intrusion of the flying Mitsi spurred the gazelles to a final burst of speed and with a swerve to the right ahead of me they leapt over the new road that was being built alongside our trail and made off into the desert.

By now we'd realised that Dick's boil-in-a-bag motorbike jacket still had its winter lining in it. Zipping it out and opening all the vents made quite a difference to his comfort levels in the hotter going. The jacket is wonderful in colder climes and is made for the road, with protective body-armour in all the right places which, I kid you not, gives a great level of confidence to the rider. It's just a bit too synthetic when it gets hot. This may have added

to Dick's discomfort and caused the high perspiration rates (and my kids think I'm a sweaty beast – they've missed the champion).

Steve and Dick had both enjoyed some time in the comfort of the Mitsi with Eggi and Ganbaatar. Apart from the air conditioning, the wide range of music available, the plush suspension, etc, there was the close-up contact with our Mongolian guides. These were the first Mongolians that any of us had met. Learning about their lives and their country was a terrific experience. Their background was so completely different from ours, which is largely Anglo-Saxon Christian. Our antecedents came from the other side of the world, as did Dick nearly 50 years ago, and we have grown up reading history books that tell us about that world. Our environment has also included indigenous Maori and various Polynesian and Melanesian races. New Zealand has also had Chinese and Indian settlers for a century or more but the land and history of the Mongol people is barely known to the average Kiwi. Listening to them talking to each other was fun too, as the language is full of unusual sounds. Mongolian is unlike any other language we heard. It's not harsh like Chinese or guttural like German; neither is it melodic like Spanish or Italian. It has sucking and chuffing noises and is quite pleasant to listen to. I suspect it might be difficult to learn, but I think that about most languages.

I was fascinated to watch Eggi, as a 19-year-old city girl, having no qualms about sharing a bedroom with the middle-aged lothario that we suspected Ganbaatar to be. She was to do the same and also to share a tent with our second driver in the next leg of the journey after Ulaanbaatar. Obviously, the company's budget didn't always stretch to allow separate rooms.

We had our first and only theft occur one night while we slept in a cold inhospitable hotel next to the railway station in Choyr, the only town as such between the Chinese border and Ulaanbaatar. With the bikes parked in the dusty compound just outside our bedroom windows we presumed them to be safe, but in the morning we found Penelope was missing one mirror. We hadn't heard a thing. However, this was hardly the crime of the century and amused rather than annoyed us.

The ride from the border to Ulaanbaatar had been a difficult and yet rewarding one for us. We'd seen countryside so barren that all 360 degrees looked the same, with not a hill in evidence. We'd seen semi-nomadic folk living lives that we found hard to identify with. They were a level up from hunter-gatherers, their lives simple and uncluttered, but things would be tough. We'd been shown respect and friendship wherever we stopped and we were quite affected by this. We'd also had a lot of laughs and we all concurred that if the adventure had to end now, it had been worthwhile. We were also pleased in a way that it had been so hard. The Chinese are building a proper road from Ulaanbaatar to the border. They have only done about 50 kilometres so far but within two to three years there will be a ribbon of blacktop cutting through this part of the Gobi. The thought slightly saddened us although we couldn't explain why. Another wilderness partially tamed perhaps?

Riding triumphantly into Ulaanbaatar was a momentous occasion. Ulaanbaatar lives up to its reputation as a Soviet-style city. It has over a million inhabitants; about a third of the population of all Mongolia. It didn't have the crazy flow of traffic of Beijing. It had congestion instead. It's hard to reason why in one city the traffic cascades and bubbles along whilst in the next it dribbles and dams up. Possibly the drivers are too hesitant or not forward thinking enough. It was interesting to see that the cars were both left- and right-hand drive. Nominally they should be left-hand drive but the easiest, cheapest cars to source come second hand from Japan where they use right-hand drive cars, as in Britain and many of the old Commonwealth countries.

Many people are surprised to learn that there are still 75 or so nations (about a third of world) where driving on the left applies. For us on our travels, only Pakistan provided that familiarity. I love imagining the chaos it must create when a country changes over, as Sweden did in the 1960s. I recall reading that so as to avoid people all swerving from the left to the right at the same given hour, endangering life and limb, they chose something like 3 a.m. on a midweek morning so there would be minimum numbers on the road. Did that work? Hell no. Everyone got up so as to be driving at the exact moment of change, and of course good-natured mayhem resulted.

There was only to be a couple of days in Ulaanbaatar as we were still a bit behind schedule. Most of the time was spent resting and recuperating. We stayed in a fairly forgettable, backstreet, budget hotel with only occasional hot water. It was interesting to observe the quite different national characteristics of the folk we had rubbed shoulders with to date. The Chinese were up at the crack of dawn and the cities hummed from an early hour with markets and the like. If you went down to breakfast at 7 o'clock it would be like a scrum. In Mongolia, it was different. We asked what time breakfast began in our hotel in Ulaanbaatar and were told 7.30. Turning up, as instructed, we found the room in darkness. The one poor staff member turned up a bit later, yawning. He then drip-fed us breakfast as he cooked it. A typical Chinese hotel would have had four or five staff and everything would have been laid out.

We had a great day sightseeing with Eggi. It was graduation day for university students and tradition dictates that the women dress in their finest silk dresses and the young men in suits. The women were quite stunning in figure-hugging azure sheaths, each with a colourful posy of flowers pinned to their chests. It was uplifting to see so many happy people having fun and posing for photographs in the public squares and also at the Buddhist temple. Ulaanbaatar isn't a visually appealing city, being quite flat and featureless with lots of Soviet- style concrete buildings, so the fun and colour of the occasion made it much more pleasant.

We were moved by our experience at the Buddhist temple. The place

exists as a monastery where young monks are taught. It has an enormous gold Buddha in a specially constructed building. Memory tells me it was over 30 m high and the dimmed room also contained many thousands of smaller Buddha figures. With the eager youths, we spun many prayer wheels that day and when we later compared notes, we agreed that we'd all found it a special and spiritual experience. This was not something we'd expected. A prayer wheel is usually mounted on a vertical spindle and contains thousands of prayers, so spinning it once is like saying all of those prayers. You always spin clockwise and there are lucky numbers of spins, which I think were mainly uneven numbers up to nine.

We also visited the lookout above the city where a school group on an outing took great interest in Steve's film-making. From the lookout, with its old Soviet tanks honouring the dead of World War Two, we could see the entire city laid out before us, beneath the only forested hills we were

to see in the whole country. The surrounding countryside looked a wonderful playground for lovers of the outdoors. The city itself is a little dilapidated. It hasn't done so well since losing the financial prop of the old Soviet Union in the 1990s. Even the centre of the city was fairly charmless. Kids living under the streets with the heating pipes were in evidence, as were large numbers of despairing drunks. While Dick and I struggled with the vagaries of the local email system, Steve enjoyed a night out with Eggi and her friends. Eggi is from a middle-class background. Her mother is a doctor who had done some of her training in Moscow, and her father is a driver. One brother is living in Spain whilst a sister lives in Japan. We were to become very close to Eggi and admired her abilities immensely.

Our first day's riding out of Ulaanbaatar should have been a doddle. Even though the distance was going to be longer than usual, there would be sealed roads. However, we struck a bit of a hiccup early in the day when Dutch Courage inexplicably stopped, just on the outskirts of the city. Initially, it seemed that the coil had failed. Luckily Dick had included a second-hand spare, but still spark didn't return. A spare condenser was tried before the decision was made for the escort van (which was now a diesel Mercedes 4 x 4 driven by Tubchin, another more than 20-year-veteran of Mongolia's small tourism industry) to go back into town and buy a new coil. This took a couple of hours and it was early afternoon before we were really humming along. Actually the humming had lots of stutters in it as the road, although sealed, had a myriad of humungous bumps and holes in it. Lots of these would bring involuntary gasps of pain. The sudden shock would give you a real kidney punch. Sometimes you could stand on the footrests and avoid the killer blows, but not often. We had endured hour after hour of corrugated roads that shook and pummelled us, but the sudden shocks of the sealed roads seemed worse. In Ulaanbaatar we'd seen a couple of locally owned crotch-rocket sports motorbikes and we'd wondered how much of the country they could ride, as going south wasn't an option. It was all desert tracks. This main road going west would be a killer for their harsh taut suspension. They would be shaken not stirred. We decided they might be rich poseurs who don't take the bikes out of Ulaanbaatar.

This first day was notable for two other things. We saw our first signpost when we had to split south. Also, Penelope decided Dutch Courage shouldn't be the only one seeking attention. Very embarrassingly she blew the flange off one of her exhaust pipes. The pipes are stainless steel which are chrome plated to look like the original. Unfortunately, stainless isn't as good as mild steel for the use it was being put to. The pipe ends with a small flange welded to it that fits inside the screw-on gland nut. This would not be an easy thing to repair without a specialist stainless welder. It was, however, not a difficult thing to jerry-rig at the side of the road. Panthers are a single cylinder design with one exhaust valve letting the gases escape through two exhaust pipes. We could block off one exhaust pipe with no real ill effect. A short walk along the road was all it took to find an empty

beer can. A quick application of the Swiss Army knife soon had a circle cut from the can bottom which became a blanking plate held in place by the gland nut. This was the only occasion when I appreciated the Mongolian approach to waste disposal. These two delays were a little humiliating as this was the first

THE LAST HURRAH

day with the new driver and we were not giving a good example of what we were, and had to be, capable of.

The day ended a bit over 300 kilometres from Ulaanbaatar, off the seal and away 20 kilometres or so to a ger camp. We were the only guests and many of the gers were still being erected for the coming summer tourist season. We had a ger to ourselves, as did Eggi and Tubchin. These gers were very plain and not decorated on the inside to the levels that we saw elsewhere but it was still a thrill to be staying in one. We dined in yet another and there were washing facilities down the other end of the camp. The sunset was quite stunning. A memorable day was ending. Dick and I stayed in camp and watched it go. Tubchin went off to try and source a spare tyre to replace the one that had blown out during the day's travel, while Steve and Eggi went walking and talking in a nice display of the solidarity of youth. The night began to get cold and we were pleased with our stove burning away brightly, making the ger warm and cosy.

A ger is such a versatile and unique dwelling. On my return to work as a technical writer within the building industry, the following article was written.

Mongolian ger – the ultimate sustainable house?

Modern New Zealand houses are mostly spacious, warm, comfortable and durable but this comes at a price – one being the production of about 8 tons of waste from the construction of every large house. Waste is more than the off-cuts of timber, plasterboard and so on. It's also the waste produced in making all the building products. Producing so much waste is something we should be a little ashamed of.

At the other end of the scale is the Mongolian ger which tens of thousands of Mongolians still live in. We probably think of them as round tents but they are much more.

Bought as a kit-set from a 'ger shop' or specialist market, a ger comes with a wooden floor, lattice walls, solid door, two centre poles and a centre ring,

 which takes all the roof framing. The walls and roof are insulated by layers of felt, and the whole thing is covered in canvas with ropes tightening around the belly of the structure to make it structurally viable. The felt insulation is ordered as either 'one finger' or 'two finger' thickness depending on the wealth of the purchaser.

Stoves are not included in the price but are an essential part of the ger, sitting in the middle between the two poles that support the roof centre ring. The stove is used for heating and cooking on and is fuelled by whatever combustible matter can be found. This is usually wood or coal in the bigger towns and animal dung elsewhere, with young calves supposedly producing the hottest burning fuel.

Gers come in three sizes and, interestingly, the medium size is the most popular and the most expensive. Typical prices are US$400, $450 and $500, although more is paid if the second finger of insulation is wanted.

A ger will contain a family's treasures and be colourfully decorated inside, often with patterned rugs on the walls and simple furniture constructed to sit against the curved walls. In the towns there will usually be electricity providing lighting and power for the television. Remote settlements may have solar panels and satellite dishes instead.

Designed specifically for the local environment, a ger is a haven from the often harsh Mongolian conditions. It's a snug refuge in the winter when it can be −40°. In the summer it protects from the furnace-like temperatures that can be well over 40°. Because the canvas outer skin is tensioned up with ropes over quite substantial walls, nothing flaps or moves in a high wind. When it rains and during winter, the vent at the apex of the ger is pulled closed. In spring or summer the walls can be lifted for ventilation.

Often a Mongolian family will have two gers. One for general living,

cooking and dining, and the other for sleeping. Poorer families may only have one. A latrine type of toilet will be out the back somewhere, possibly shared with the neighbours.

As a housing unit a ger makes a lot of sense. The outside cladding may only last about 10 years but is easily and affordably replaced. All the components of the ger come from very renewable, local resources and are easy to inspect for signs of deterioration.

A ger doesn't cost a lot of money and can be erected in less than 2 hours. It is very transportable, fitting on a camel or ute, or in the back of a van. While property ownership is the norm in town and sections are fenced, no one owns land in the countryside – it's a land without fences. If you have the animals you can stop and put up your ger wherever you find some feed for them. Then you can shift when the mood, season or situation dictates.

The ger works well as a dwelling. The alternatives in the region are charmless Soviet- style blocks of flats constructed from reinforced concrete with all the materials often transported 1,000 kilometres or more across difficult desert terrain.

Our night in a ger was to have a drama that frightened us greatly.

The cold, clear night cooled the ger down after we settled, and the fire died away. In the early hours I was awoken by Dick, moaning, mumbling, and quietly calling for help. Dick is a resolute super-tough character who wouldn't be calling for help unless it was vital. Both Steve and I had finished the earlier part of the night by reading with head-mounted LED lights that were quickly at hand. Dick was suffering from severe cramp in both calves. He'd tried to stand and stretch the muscles to lessen the pain, had been unable to do so, and had fallen. We dragged him from his tangled sleeping bag and desperately massaged his calf muscles, which were as hard as rock. I had some Tiger balm™ and we rubbed that on as best we could. The pain was obviously excruciating. No sooner would we get one calf to relax, if we left it for a second it would go back into spasm. Dicks' eyes had rolled up out of sight and all I could see were the whites. I'm not used to medical things so had no idea if this was what happened when a person dies, or was Dick just having cramp? My first thought was that Sharon would kill me if I let Dick die on this foolhardy adventure. My second thought was for poor Eggi. Her first long adventure with a client and one dies on her. It was a huge relief when, after what seemed like an hour but was probably no more than 10 minutes, we managed to get both calves to relax and stay that way. What a night.

By dawn we were cold in our sleeping bags and it was great to hear one of the local staff slip in and fire up the stove. In no time at all it was cosy again. It was a welcome surprise to find that Dick was able to walk with no problem when he awoke. It must have been the Tiger balm™ because a cramp as strong and prolonged as that would normally leave him partially disabled. Dick's cramp was to recur a couple of times on the trip but only ever in one leg and it always went away once he stood up. He also started taking quinine before bed as someone had told him that it lessened the likelihood of an attack. When available, bananas were part of our diet as their high potassium content apparently helps alleviate cramp.

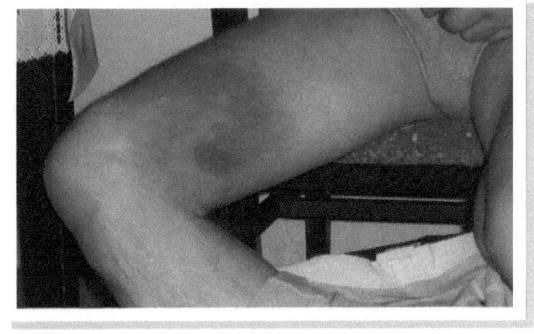

In the days that followed, Dick's bruised thigh was still giving him gyp and the blue and purple hues had become very impressive to look at, if you were that way inclined. Accordingly, Steve did most of the riding. The Merc was nowhere near as comfortable as the Mitsi had been but Tubchin was very proud of it. Tubchin looked gruff and stern, quite dour, yet I sensed he liked us. We could also sense his latent competence and I think he would have loved to take Dick hunting. Most of the guiding that is done in Mongolia involves taking wealthy clients out shooting ibex and wolves, so we were quite different from their normal clientele. I was a little disappointed at not hearing him and Eggi singing together as the others got to do.

We camped out in the desert a couple of times and slept in some fairly basic hotels in the small settlements that dot the southern route across to the Russian border. Our days were always hard and the tracks often rutted and very corrugated. Sometimes the corrugations were so bad they shook you to a standstill. If they were small corrugations you could just grit your teeth and accelerate up to a speed where they smoothed out and you planed across the top in an almost controlled fashion. The big ones however had me almost weeping at times, as there seemed no way of riding them without destroying the bikes. Steve was bonding strongly with the Norton and was very good with it. He needed to be. There were occasions when there was no way in the world I could keep up. This usually seemed dependent on what he was playing on his iPod. Other days and in other conditions, Penelope and I could vanquish him (and anyone else, should they front up). Some days we felt marvellous with such magic feedback from the bikes.

Now we could see the Altay Mountains that dominate the western part of Mongolia. The tops, with their everlasting snow cover, were above 4,000 metres. At one lunch stop we were told there was snow ahead. Our lunch meals were nearly always in a roadside ger. Mostly the food was the same; mutton pieces with noodles and potatoes broiled in a wok. It was quite salty and easy to become a little bored with. Mongolia doesn't have much in the way of fruit, veggies, or eggs and there is no pork. One of the few pleasures was the wonderful fruit juice from Russia.

Whilst it was a little exciting to be riding towards our first hills and snow, the reality of the cold soon set in. Worse still, the tracks were starting to turn slippery and the riding surface became treacherous. Possibly the hardest ride I have experienced followed. Snow is a bugger to ride in. You have to keep wiping it from your visor where it settles, refusing to fall off like rain. I estimated that the snowy ride of about 70 kilometres took us close to three hours. It was every man for himself and there was no way that I would be stopping and checking progress with Steve. We had the Merc as a sweep vehicle, inside which our lucky crew would be warm and cosy, and could help if needed.

Finally coming down off the muddy slopes out of the snow was a

huge relief. I was also bursting for a leak, so at the first opportunity I put Penelope on her side stand and staggered off to try and get my frozen digits to find and free my temperature-shrunken member. Whilst I was doing this Penelope decided she needed to lie down. No one was in sight so I had to try and right her. With luggage on her and in the awkward position she had fallen I couldn't get a good hold, and my efforts were in vain. I had to await the others while she dripped petrol, oil and battery acid. Ten minutes or so later they arrived and we soon got her upright. Steve had mud down both sides of his riding gear so he must have fallen on both sides at least once. However, he carried on into the slowly clearing afternoon and was quickly lost to sight.

As mentioned earlier, the tracks across Mongolia are multiple and sometimes the valleys are wide. After a while, Tubchin caught me up and redirected me as he felt I was drifting away from the best route. A short time later he stopped me again and told me to stay where I was. They had scoured the wide valley with binoculars and hadn't been able to see Steve, so were going to backtrack and try and find him. Although we were much lower, and it was no longer snowing, it wasn't what you'd call a pleasant temperature. To keep warm and occupied I walked off in several directions (not all at once). I would spy out a marker and walk to it, then turn around and look for another, always making sure I could still see Penelope. Meanwhile the others were searching for signs of Cabin Boy – not lost at sea, but definitely missing in action somewhere. The width of the valley was immense and the slightly rolling contour made it hard to spot a lone motorcycle. A couple of hours dragged by before they spotted the Norton on a small ridge with a sleeping lad snuggled down beside it. Phew. He'd done the right thing, once he hadn't seen us for a fair while and the moment was opportune, he'd stopped and stayed where he was. Soon we were all back together and riding in a convoy. We found a small, bleak settlement and had a very cold night in an old bank building. At least we had a fire in our room for a few hours. Our Mongolians suffered in silence, but they're probably tougher than we are.

We were very pleased with our health and fitness to date. Apart from Dick's heavy fall, we felt we were all in peak condition. I couldn't remember feeling as fit for many years. I felt light and strong. We were contented, and pleased with how men and machines were coping with the journey so far. The team had gelled from the beginning and there were always a lot of laughs and optimism, especially now that we had most of Mongolia behind us. We were graphically made aware of how quickly things could change however, when we were making our way into a small hamlet that is renowned only for the fact that the new Mongolian prime minister was born there. As we approached, the Merc had a near miss with a speeding jeep. Then, as we turned onto the main street, an approaching van almost took off my left elbow. A split second of horror followed as I knew instinctively that Steve was just behind, coming in from the left. When the dust cleared, our hearts were able to start beating again. This bloody idiot had managed to miss both of us by less than a gnat's whisker. Shook up, we stopped at the edge of town to take stock and calm ourselves. To our amusement we found a tree, a leafy green tree, which Steve rode around with some ceremony. Apart from the forests above Ulaanbaatar, this was the first tree we could remember seeing in Mongolia. Dick commented that it was probably on the site of an old septic tank or toilet, which had enabled it to grow. We did wonder why the village folk hadn't tried to grow more there.

Three-quarters of the way across the Gobi we were to have a significant health challenge. Dick monitored his sugar levels each day and injected insulin morning and evening. He was also diligent at taking the required cocktail of pills that his condition dictates. He has managed his diabetes for many years and has the health and constitution of a man half his age. It is that strength and strictly disciplined management regime that enabled

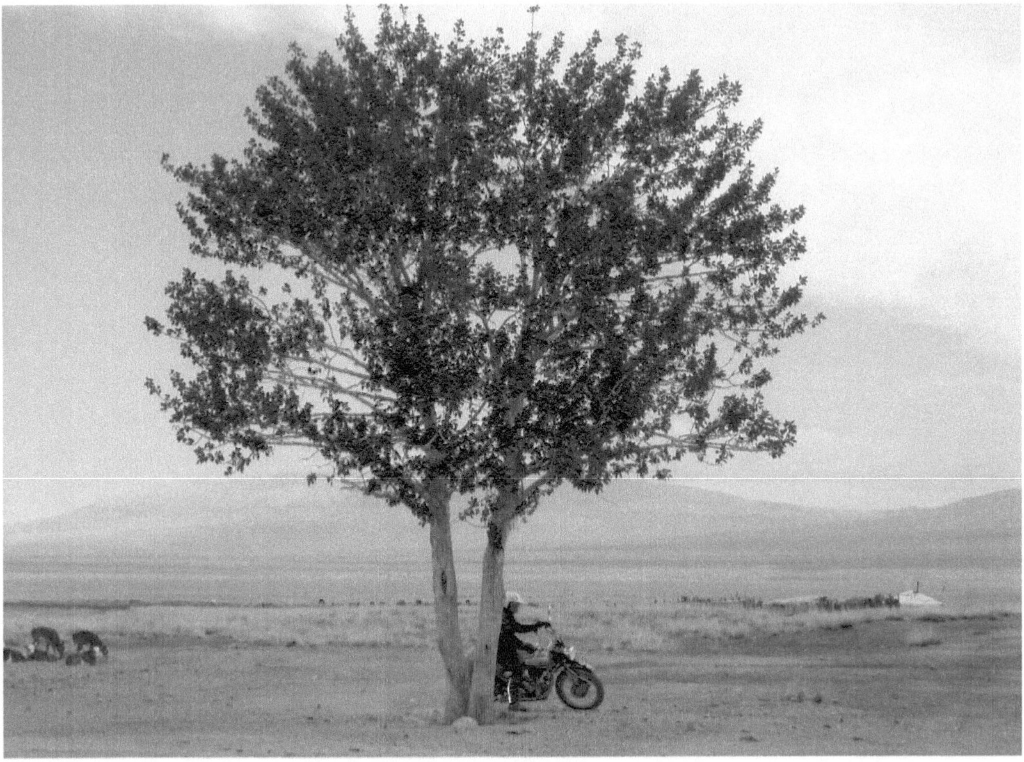

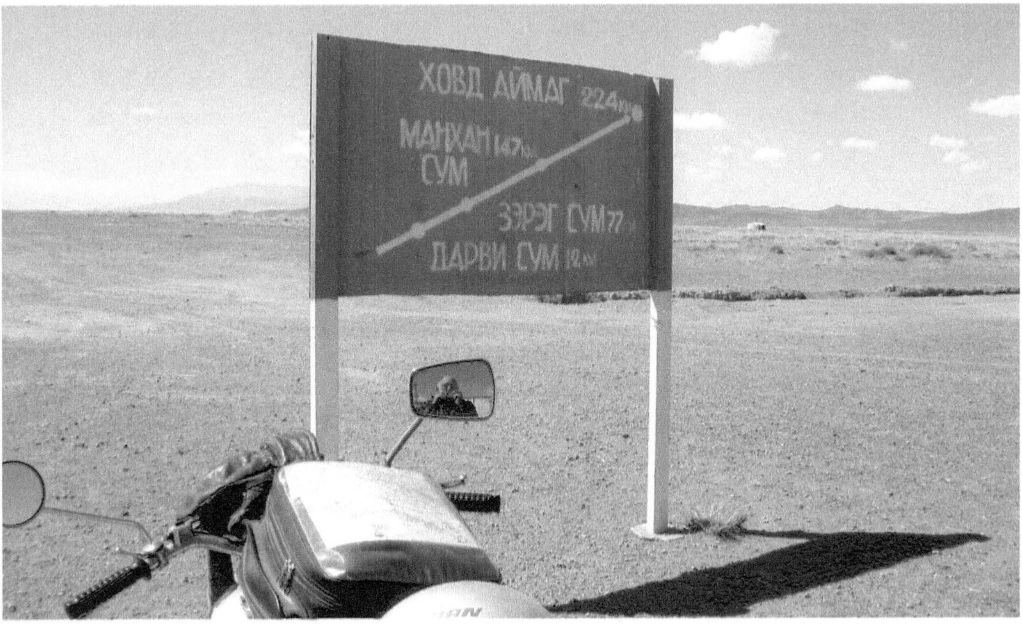
ХОВД АЙМАГ 224
МАНХАН
СУМ
ЗЭРЭГ СУМ 77
ДАРВИ СУМ

him to even contemplate the journey in the first place.

After the usual hard day's ride we had reached the small town of Khovd. The previous night had been an enjoyable one spent camping in the desert. Dick had made a dung fire (animal dung, not his) just to test how hard it was to do. We'd cooked up all sorts culinary delights on Dick's little petrol cooker and under a full moon we'd had a surreal night with our Mongolian hosts in their special country. We'd had a nomad and his hairy pony appear out of nowhere and similarly, mysteriously disappear after a chat. We'd even treated ourselves to fried potatoes for breakfast. Wonderful.

But a night roughing it should be followed by a night of relative comfort. Tubchin had found a friend in Khovd who had also been a guide with him so he and Eggi went off to catch up, leaving us in a reasonably adequate hotel. In the search for a meal we walked the town as we so often did. On this occasion Steve and I chatted away, shoulder to shoulder, while Dick followed a few paces behind. We'd been given a couple of dead-end directions that had us zigzagging across town before finally we found a place to sit and order a meal. It had been a longish walk but was of no real consequence to any of us, or so I thought.

Dick then hit us with the most shattering news. He felt he was unable to continue with the trip. He told us that he'd been staggering along behind us, barely able to keep on the footpath. We hadn't noticed, being absorbed in our own little world. His deterioration had been so rapid it was frightening. He'd had a good day and was fine when we set out from the hotel. We weren't quite sure what we could do, as this wasn't a place where you could just abandon the adventure. It was a forlorn little group and we had a miserable meal.

The walk back to the hotel improved the mood a bit as Dick felt a little better and, amazingly, by bedtime he was almost chipper. But we knew we still had to do something. We couldn't just ignore it. We decided to continue together and try and get a blood test done as soon as we were in Russia. We had accommodation booked for us at a resort in a few days time. So first thing next morning, even though Dick now felt fine, we found the local telegraph agent and rang Silk Road Adventures in Greymouth. After a short delay, we were put through and spoke with Pat, asking her to try and arrange this for us. As always, a calm affirmation reassured us that their agent in Russia would make it happen. We had no idea of what time it was in New Zealand, but it was just after brekkie in Khovd.

The ride from Khovd to Olgii was a special one of about 220 kilometres. We travelled down a long green valley (everywhere else in Mongolia had been brown) and climbed over a pass of 2,600 metres, lunching with a Kazakh family with five kids, including a boy with a club foot. The father was a road maintenance man and was the only adult of the small family group who spoke any Mongolian. We learnt that they had been with the boy in Almaty for a year or so when he was younger and during this time he had several operations. Unfortunately, he still needed more and they didn't yet have the money for this. It was a desolate spot at the foot of the pass where they now stayed and tried to save for these operations. They had just a couple of rooms in a rudimentary shelter. The older kids went to a school about 20 kilometres away. Even though it was well into spring, the nearby stream still had a topping of ice 200–300 millimetres thick. These are the sorts of places in Mongolia that have temperatures in the −40 to +40 degrees Celsius range. We gave them some extra money when we left. They hadn't asked for or expected any, but graciously accepted it. We'd enjoyed the shelter, warmth, nice meal and good company, learning about them and their hard lives.

Olgii was always going to be a special place for us because it was where we were going to visit the degree confluence point 49N:90E, one of the original aims of the trip. We were to navigate to this point on the globe that I had 'bagsed'. There's a project which is trying to collect data from each degree confluence point on the land mass. This is wherever a longitude and latitude line intersects. Dick had made a time capsule from an old metal grease-gun cartridge and our plan was to plant it at the point and make an ovoo over it. We had all sorts of treasures to include: club badges, family memorabilia, information about us and the trip, New Zealand, etc. In a strange Dickism, our hero had brought with him his long-since extracted front teeth. These ugly, yellowing monsters had been kept, for reasons known only to the man himself, and were now going to be put away for posterity. How bizarre, how bizarre.

We were all excited about this little side trip. It had sounded so intrepid when I announced that we were going to go to a degree confluence point in western Mongolia, almost over to the Russian border. Well it is remote from New Zealand and Europe, but I'd studied my topographical maps and it looked like our spot would be out in a valley near some big hills and less than 10 kilometres from Olgii. With Mongolia not having fences or private land ownership, a lot of the potential difficulties were simplified. 49N:90E had been carefully chosen, and 'announcing plans' on the project's web site outlining a visit before 30 May 2005 was one of the first public affirmations that we were really going to go and do this trip.

Sadly, in March, a trophy-hunting Scottish bastard with 50 degree confluence points under his belt went there first. Naturally, we were livid. He'd even had the gall to leave his email address on the web site so I gave him a thorough towelling. He responded that it was the same if you went there first or fifteenth – it was the challenge of navigating to the point that gave the pleasure. I told him what a load of bollocks that was and how I didn't think that Scott would have agreed with him when he saw

Amundsen's flag at the South Pole. Unbelievably, months later, when he was going off after a lot more points in Eastern Europe, he asked that everyone refrain from going to them until he had gone first. Bastard ... I'm not as angry as I was, but he's still a bastard. We decided that 49:90 was still our point and we'd still go for it and no other. Too much planning had gone into it.

Olgii is a sizeable town of maybe 20,000 people and is the region's capital. We found it to be quite different from other Mongolian settlements as the population was mostly Kazakh in ethnicity and many of them were very drunk. We'd seen this before in our travels (and participated enthusiastically in similar behaviour in our youth), so we're not judgemental. It's not always pleasant, however, to be the centre of attention, surrounded by 20 or 30 drunks, many of whom insist on kissing you. This was a little nonplussing. Ultimately, we escaped and found a rooming house, then explored the town a little looking for an evening meal.

Olgii was also the first place where we saw lots of Ural sidecar outfits. They were common as family and work transport, sometimes also being used as taxis.

We'd also seen many of the single cylinder two-stroke Jupiters (or Planetas) in the countryside, often carrying whole families. These sturdy Russian workhorses have long seats to accommodate this practice. They also have crash bars up front to hang things from. They are definitely not pretty but are rugged and practical. Although he'd ridden most of the Gobi Desert across to Olgii, Cabin Boy would now be back in the van in his primary role of camera man. I'd planned 49:90 long before he came on-board and this was to be Dick's and my special moment. A couple of days earlier, coming back from injury, as they say in sporting papers, Dick had struggled in the unusual Mongolian morning light, finding it hard to judge the track surfaces. Following along behind I could tell it was going to end in tears because Dick's lines weren't appropriate for the conditions. A few near misses occurred before he parked the bike horizontally off the track and, in a gentle fashion and uninjured, he retreated to the van. The next comeback would wait until 49:90. Tuesday 25 May 2005 would be that day. Dick's earlier health and balance problems seemed to be aberrations that were behind us now and we all looked forward eagerly to the momentous occasion. Eggi and Tubchin understood what we were doing and even though their time with us was nearly up and we were still a day or so behind schedule, they could see this was an important side trip for us.

Dick and I awoke reasonably early, going downstairs to suss out breakfast and greet the day. We stood outside on the pavement and chewed the fat, but all was not well. Dick had to hold onto the wrought iron fence palings to keep his balance. His sugar levels had seemed OK but now he was clearly in trouble again. By the time the others had assembled for breakfast, Dick was in quite a state and strongly of the opinion that he couldn't go on. This was worse than the episode a couple of days earlier. He was now very tottery and beginning to get confused. Eggi found where the medical centre was and we were seen immediately by a middle-aged woman doctor. She checked him out and declared that he couldn't go on with the trip. Dick's confusion was worsening; there were too many conversations happening at once and his reasoning powers seemed to be slowing. He asked me to make decisions for him as it was all becoming too difficult. He suddenly seemed a confused, shuffling old man, something I would never have thought possible. This was a flint-hard legend, who battled shoulder to shoulder at 200 kph on his race-bike Bucephalus. Only five months earlier I'd watched him get the hole-shot and lead a competitive field in a classic race for a while before being swallowed up by the faster bikes, still finishing a good fifth or sixth.

The doctor thought it might be a side effect from the altitude, although this seemed unlikely as he wasn't short of breath and his aerobic fitness is excellent due to his healthy lifestyle and hill climbing. His blood pressure was very high though and although there was a flight out of Olgii that day, the doctor emphatically said that he could not travel until his blood pressure was down. He had to go to hospital until this was achieved. You cannot imagine how this news sounded. This was the end of the road. The dream was being terminated. There wasn't even talk of 49:90. Dick wasn't going to pass Go and get $200. No, he'd been given the Go Straight to Hospital card. This was a hard break.

Eggi had made numerous calls about flights, about what she had to do with us, etc. The initial plan was for her to stay with Dick until Saturday when she would escort him to Ulaanbaatar. There he might be able to connect either to Beijing then Auckland and back to Sharon in Wellington, or perhaps to Amsterdam where maybe his sister Willy could provide succour. Now both those options seemed appalling for a man in his condition. Eggi wanted Tubchin to take us to the Russian border so their contractual obligations would be met. We declined this in favour of staying put with Dick until we knew where he was going. We needed to be confident he was in a state where he could go unescorted on the international legs. This would create a problem for the tour company, but that seemed a minor hiccup. Eggi needed to be back in Ulaanbaatar for exams on the 30th anyway. But the first thing was to get Dick to hospital. We adjourned back to the hotel to get his gear and do some serious planning. Steve had the room key and was away up the road sending emails, so we awaited his return in the road outside the rooming house ... a fairly sombre group. Strolling past was a scruffy haired, be-stubbled westerner, a traveller. "Do you know if there is a market where I can buy food?", he asked in quite heavily accented English. Eggi explained where to go and I asked him if he was one of the Polish motorcyclists we had heard were in town. No, he was French and he and a mate were travelling in a Russian 4 x 4 they'd bought in Ulaanbaatar from friends. Learning what we were doing, he was thrilled because he'd seen us in the desert a few days earlier. We hadn't noticed a grey Furgon (vans, common across Russia, often of the brand UAZ) with a couple of guys waving, because they all did that. Hearing of the probable demise of our adventure he then uttered the immortal words, "Maybe I can help, I am a doctor". This was in sing-song "Allo, Allo" type English with doctor coming out as docteurr. Of course we said, "Probably not, our friend is a diabetic and must go to the hospital". Our jaws dropped in unison when he said that diabetes was his speciality.

Soon we were upstairs with Dr Thomas and he was reassuring Dick that maybe the trip might not be over. These were dream words that I hadn't dared to utter, but here was a doctor urging Dick not to give up yet. He went away to get his medicines and brought back his imposing friend Greg who was huge and a little scary to look at, as he had lines of scabs on his face and holes in his clothes, a partly shaven head and a bit of a pony tail. Thomas jokingly introduced him as his nurse. Bloody hell. We were to learn later that the scars were from a crazed mechanic rolling their van while showing them how to drive it. Thomas had broken his ribs in the tumble and Greg had battery acid pour on him.

While Thomas had been away getting his field kit we'd discussed the idea of asking if Dick could travel with them, as we'd already ascertained that we were travelling similar paths for some time. It would be better to be in the hands of a specialist who spoke English and we could delay the attempt on those international air flights. I wondered how we could broach the subject. Thomas gave Dick a couple of pills and took his blood pressure. Already it was down to 170/90, which Thomas didn't think was too bad. In a wonderfully decisive move, Dick himself asked if he could maybe tag along in the Furgon. This was quite a moment for me, as only a couple of hours earlier Dick was incapable of making any decision at all and would have been unable to ask this favour. He still wasn't with us fully but he was at least firing on a few cylinders. The boys said "Of course" and plans were made. We even started to talk about 49:90 again. Almost by

the minute you could see Dick's health return. We reckon the pills must have been magic or something, although Thomas assured us they were nothing much at all. Perhaps it was the influence of breakfast kicking in. We'll never know.

The boys were interesting and entertaining characters. They were mates back in Paris, although Greg had been working in London as an arborist, even though his background was in information technology, or was it the other way round? They had a mutual doctor friend who married a Mongolian woman, another doctor I think, and they had been out in Ulaanbaatar for the wedding. After all travelling together for a bit the boys bought their van and were aiming to drive it back to France. They'd brought with them a computer and projector set-up so they could show old movies and international films to local nomadic people they might meet along the way. To enable this to happen they had also bought a ger as a mobile cinema. They would set up the ger and in their words ‚Äúmake movies" for the village people, and Thomas would do a clinic if needed. He had a mountain of medicines with him and proper medical credentials. It was all most impressive.

The UAZ Furgon had been a nightmare; they must have bought the most unreliable one in all of Mongolia. It had been a constant struggle and it seemed they'd been ripped off by most of Mongolia's mechanics. The UAZ is rugged and simple but being Russian, has inbuilt flaws and foibles. There are hundreds of thousands of them running all over Russia and they come in many guises including police vans, post office vans and ambulances. They appear unchanged from the late 1950s when they were introduced. Thomas and Greg's had the standard heavy-duty roof rack upon which they stored the ger frames. It looked great, but watching them start it by shorting out the starter with a screwdriver was a little unnerving. It was intended that Dick would be able to earn his keep by working on the van. The boys asked if he could show them some basic maintenance routines.

Now we were facing a future that was palatable at least. We told the Frenchies about 49:90 and soon we were all planning the visit for just after lunch. We'd stay the night and head off to the Russian border the next day. This would then give Eggi and Tubchin enough time to drive directly back across the northern route to Ulaanbaatar. After a heart-stopping morning, everything was falling into place even if Dick wasn't able to ride in triumph up to the degree confluence point. As planned, we met just after lunch. The boys entered the coordinates in their GPS and took over our video camera to film the event, as Dick wasn't familiar with this role. Olgii was the only town we were to find with a river going through it. This river kept thwarting our attempts to head out of town towards our destiny. Trying to turn two bikes and two vans around in small lanes and the like, resulted in the predictable. We lost each other. Well, we lost the Frenchies but kept on trying to find our way to the one bridge. Ultimately we were successful in finding the bridge and our van, but not the UAZ. Never mind, we were keen to get out and navigate. I knew they had the coordinates and would find us some time. They were unlikely to run off with the camera having just rescued the whole adventure. The arrow on my GPS pointed towards some big hills and we were able to follow a road that passed in front of them. We would then head off across the sloping desert. As we rode along, with me holding the GPS out in front in one hand, lining up the arrow, I could see that it looked like someone was way up ahead more or less where the spot should be, a couple of kilometres away.

Initially I presumed this was Thomas and Greg but it looked like there was only one of them and where was the UAZ? As we closed on where we needed to turn off I kept looking at the figure, now off to the left, because I was sure now that the person had to be very close to our spot. Turning off the road and beginning the bumpy ride across the tussocky desert I could line up the GPS arrow and my sentinel. There was only about 1,500 metres to go and I could tell he was close to 49:90. My amazement grew as we closed on this lone figure. It was like he was a marker. I wondered what he must be thinking as this convoy of two motorcycles and a 4 x 4 van turned off the road and headed his way. He was probably quite scared as I rode up to him and passed by only metres away, to then stop 15 metres on, park the bike and walk a further couple of metres and triumphantly declare we were at 49:90. This was a huge buzz as we'd talked a lot about this moment back in New Zealand during the planning stages. We'd laughed at how ludicrous it really was to navigate to an exact spot on the earth's surface, photograph it North, South, East and West, then go home again. We were going to do a little more but we didn't think we were despoiling the wilderness aspect of this desolate but still quite beautiful spot. We felt that building an ovoo was quite appropriate, as I'd love this spot to be a shrine to intrepid travellers.

It was hard to believe that only hours earlier we were on our way to the hospital and about to abandon the whole adventure. Dick was now so frisky, he almost needed to be sedated. We had a lot of laughs when we found that he'd left the time capsule back in the hotel in Olgii. The boys had found us by this time and it was decided that only Steve and the Mongolian crew would go back to get the all-important capsule while the rest of us collected stones for the ovoo. It was amazing to watch Dick now scampering around the hillside searching out and bringing back the stones and rocks needed. Intermittently, I would get bored and stop to talk with Greg or Thomas, then be shamed into going and searching out more suitable stones. Greg was now wearing a del, the warm Mongolian long coat that he had had made specially for him in purple. He looked like some sort of giant presiding monk with an official role to play. It was great. All the time the shepherd looked on in bemused silence. Well, we presumed he was a shepherd as there were a few sheep off in the distance and we couldn't think of any other reason for him to be there. The boys had shared a cigarette with him but he wasn't a chatty type. This delay gave us lots of time to get plenty of matter gathered. The putting in of the treasures was a lot of fun as we showed off all the things destined for posterity. We included money from New Zealand and China, newspaper cuttings, club badges, postcards from home ...

Dick's teeth were still hideous, but in they went. What future historians will make of them and their reasons for being there still makes me chuckle. Ovoos always have blue rags tied on somewhere but we topped ours off with my blue tripod collapsible stool. It had lived up to its name almost immediately it was used and this was an ideal opportunity to abandon it. We took lots of photos and Steve had the movie camera almost up our noses at times. It was doubly special as we knew that tomorrow we'd be saying goodbye to Eggi and Tubchin. This was one last thing we'd do together. Our ovoo was 800 millimetres high when complete and we were all a little sad to leave it. When we did leave, Steve lingered a little and talked for a while with the shepherd before rejoining me down by the road back to Olgii. I wrote about this day and issued a challenge to others of our ilk, part of which follows.

ACROSS THE GOBI

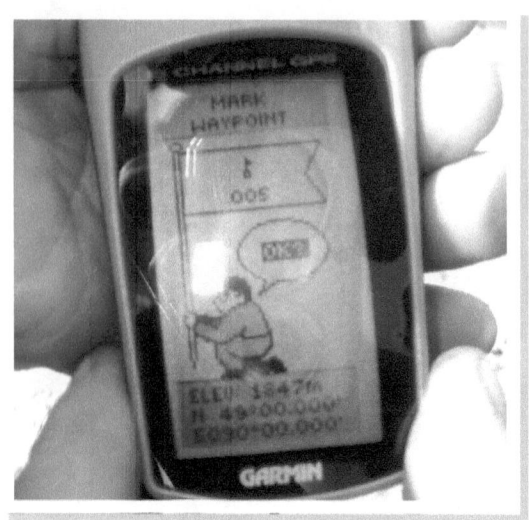

The 49:90 challenge

Classic bike enthusiasts all like a challenge, or they wouldn't ride and cherish the antiquated machinery that they do. For some the thrill is the challenge of recreating what was created in an age gone by. For others it's the ambience and the style of an era they love. For no one is it the easy option. Why make a motorcycle when you can buy one new? Why put up with dodgy electrics, marginal brakes, suspect reliability and usually a complete lack of suitable performance, but I generalise. It has to be said that I'm not one of the world's greatest polishers, nor am I always the best at finishing a project. It's because I'm too much of a dreamer and lack the single-minded focus to restore and then keep pristine. I want to dream an adventure and ride the dream. Life doesn't always let us do this, but sometimes we should stand up and shout, "You just don't understand. I have to do this".

When I was young I did ride my dreams and now in middle age I'm riding another dream

– a crazy dream, an irresponsible dream, an impractical dream, a fantasy. I'm riding across half of the world, the half that no one ever does, from Beijing, through Mongolia and Russia, crossing Kazakhstan, Kyrgyzstan and Uzbekistan to the magical, mystical cities of Samarkand and Bukhara, then back into China and over the Karakoram Highway into Pakistan, and so on into Europe. We're two silly old fools on the world's most unlikely motorcycles. Who would choose a couple of old sidecar-hauling plodders? And how sensible or practical is taking a couple of old single bangers across the deserts of Mongolia etc?

Well, we've done that. That was only 2,500 kilometres of body punishing desert tracks. Sure there were two serious snowstorms, periods of scorching heat, soft sand, mud, gravel, corrugations for hundreds of kilometres, etc. It's probably fair to say that machine and men are performing equally. None of us is in as good a shape as when we left, but equally we're all still going strongly enough.

We've eaten in gers with nomads, we've seen eagles and marmots, wild horses, chased gazelle at 75 kph, camels ... puhh smrrr, we've spun Bhuddist prayer wheels, cast stones on the Shamanist ovoos and toasted with vodka. We've crossed the bloody Gobi Desert on old British singles. This is the ultimate odyssey, a real Boy's Own adventure. Sure, we've had a guide in China and another in Mongolia and we also have the Cabin Boy (second son Stephen) along to chronicle our efforts.

We don't see ourselves as adventurers. We're just normal folk having an adventure. For me it's a midlife crisis without the sex. Not knowing what's around the next corner is exhilarating. Allowing the exotic to become humdrum is wonderful. Every day challenges.

We struggle with maps, strange languages, foods (and don't mention the toilets).

What we've done so far and what we intend to achieve is not an effort that Severin, Fiennes, Blythe, Bonnington and others of that ilk would even admit to. We're The Last Hurrah, a little like 'The Last of The Summer Wine' but with motorbikes. We've got goals to achieve as we go ... just like Jason and the Argonauts from Greek mythology. We've done one already and not only want to share it with you ... we want to involve you.

The Degree Confluence Project is an interesting concept. All the intersections of latitude and longitude degree lines are being photographed and written about. The aim is to navigate to the point, photograph your GPS, photograph North, South, East and West, and write a short note about getting there. We have navigated to a spot just out of Olgii in western Mongolia (49N:90E). We've done the business and built an ovoo on the spot. We left a time capsule with small treasures in it. We hope our offsprings' offspring will one day visit Grandad's ovoo in Mongolia. How neat would that be?

But what about you? A Panther and a Norton have been there and left club badges. Imagine if a BSA group, or a AJS, Triumph, Velocette etc, also went to 49N:90E. This could become like a haj. At some time in your life you have to ride your bike there to leave a club badge or pennant. Soon there'll be Indian, Matchless, Douglas, Greeves, Sunbeam, Rudge and Vincent ovoos, won't there? Who'll be the first? It could be someone on an Indian Enfield. They'd just have to ride over to Pakistan, into China, across to Kyrgyzstan, through Kazakhstan, 1,000 kilometres of Russia and only a day's ride in Mongolia. Easy, when you say it quickly.

Anyway, the challenge is there. It doesn't matter what the bike is or how suited it is. What matters is how suited you are. A huge impression was made on me in 1971 or thereabouts by a series of Motorcycle Sport (or Motorcyclist Illustrated?) articles by a couple of lads who rode from Europe to Cape Town, by moped. Many journeys have been done on what the armchair critics would consider unsuitable machines. A couple of New Zealand nurses rode home overland on BSA Bantams in the 50s and only a few years ago the Smiths rode Tiger Cubs to Cape Town reversing the ride done by Smith Senior 30 or so years earlier. So it's not the machine. It's the desire and the commitment. Who knows, the next visitor to 49N:90E could be riding a Norman Nippy ... now there's a thought.

For the non-cognoscenti, a Norman Nippy is a moped from the 1950s. Back in Olgii, we found the two Polish motorcyclists who turned out to be a honeymooning Belgian couple. An and Mickie had been riding a pair of Kawasaki 650s for many months and they'd travelled to many interesting places. They'd come in from Russia and decided not to ride any further into Mongolia as the bikes proved to be a handful in sand and also in the snow they'd had a few days earlier. They decided to leave the bikes where they were and travel around for a while without them. We had a nice night out together and when suitably replete, Dick and I left the young ones to do young ones' things and walked back to our room in a reflective and happy mood. Our time in Mongolia was nearly over. There would soon be new adventures to face. Dick had decided that his little episode should not be communicated home. After all, there was nothing they could do except worry. I shared this sentiment and relayed nothing but the positive in my next email. Unfortunately, in a text to my daughter Hannah, Steve mentioned that Dick had been sick but now was well! Hannah told Steph who told Sharon. By the time I next checked my email, there were many worried messages from family and friends, all asking me for the truth and telling me to stop hiding things. Luckily, I have broad shoulders.

Our last day in Mongolia saw us ride through the now familiar amazing countryside (if that's not an oxymoron), over a breathtaking pass between snow-clad hills and along some river flats. We stopped near the last town inside Mongolia and while the guides went off for something (I can't

remember what), Dick and I climbed a hill above a cemetery. This clearly showed his fitness was fine and it was amazing to think that it was only a day ago that we were amid such a crisis. We sat on a rocky knoll and I did a reflective interview of Dick with the video camera. Far below, the tiny figure of Cabin Boy waited with the bikes. It was a tranquil moment and a nice time out from our normal routine. When the Frenchies caught up, we all set off for the border together, past a couple of checkpoints and on to the fairly squalid border settlement itself. Here we had to farewell our Mongolian friends. It was quite emotional for all of us. Eggi had looked after our needs for three weeks. This was her longest guiding experience, and a challenging one. We'd bonded intensely. I knew that Dick loved her like a daughter and I knew from her tears that we'd all touched her as well. Wiping away her tears she asked me to look after Dick, for whom she had a huge admiration because of his determination. It was also clear that she had quite a fondness for Steve. We've often talked about her since, as we believe she will have a stellar career. We'd love to see her as Mongolia's president one day. She was so decisive and capable for one of such tender years.

We loaded our excess baggage into the UAZ and started the process of getting out of the country. All border crossings are fraught, tense times. There is always the two-part process. First you have to get out of the country you are in and, for some reason, many countries make that difficult. I wonder sometimes if the penalty for not having the correct paperwork would be to be kicked out of the country. A little bizarre. Thomas and Greg seemed to be struggling with the authorities and Eggi kindly offered to help while we pushed on ahead. Ahead was Russia, the big bad bear that frightened Eggi a bit. She was of the opinion that robbers would be everywhere and we should take care. Funny how people of each nationality seemed scared of what might happen in the next country. After our release from the border officials, our first task was to get through the huge mudhole that began the no-man's-land area between countries. It was fitting that Mongolia should pose us one more difficult task. It was a challenge, but most of Mongolia had been a challenge. It had all been so satisfying that we doubted there would be another experience as intense. Goodbye Mongolia, we wish you well.

*We learnt later that Eggie and Tubchin did a more or less non-stop trip back across the northern route to Ulaanbaatar with Eggie doing most of the driving, as Tubchin got rolling drunk once we'd gone. The route was much shorter but included several river crossings that would have been beyond our bikes' capabilities. Eggi got back in time to sit and pass her exams.

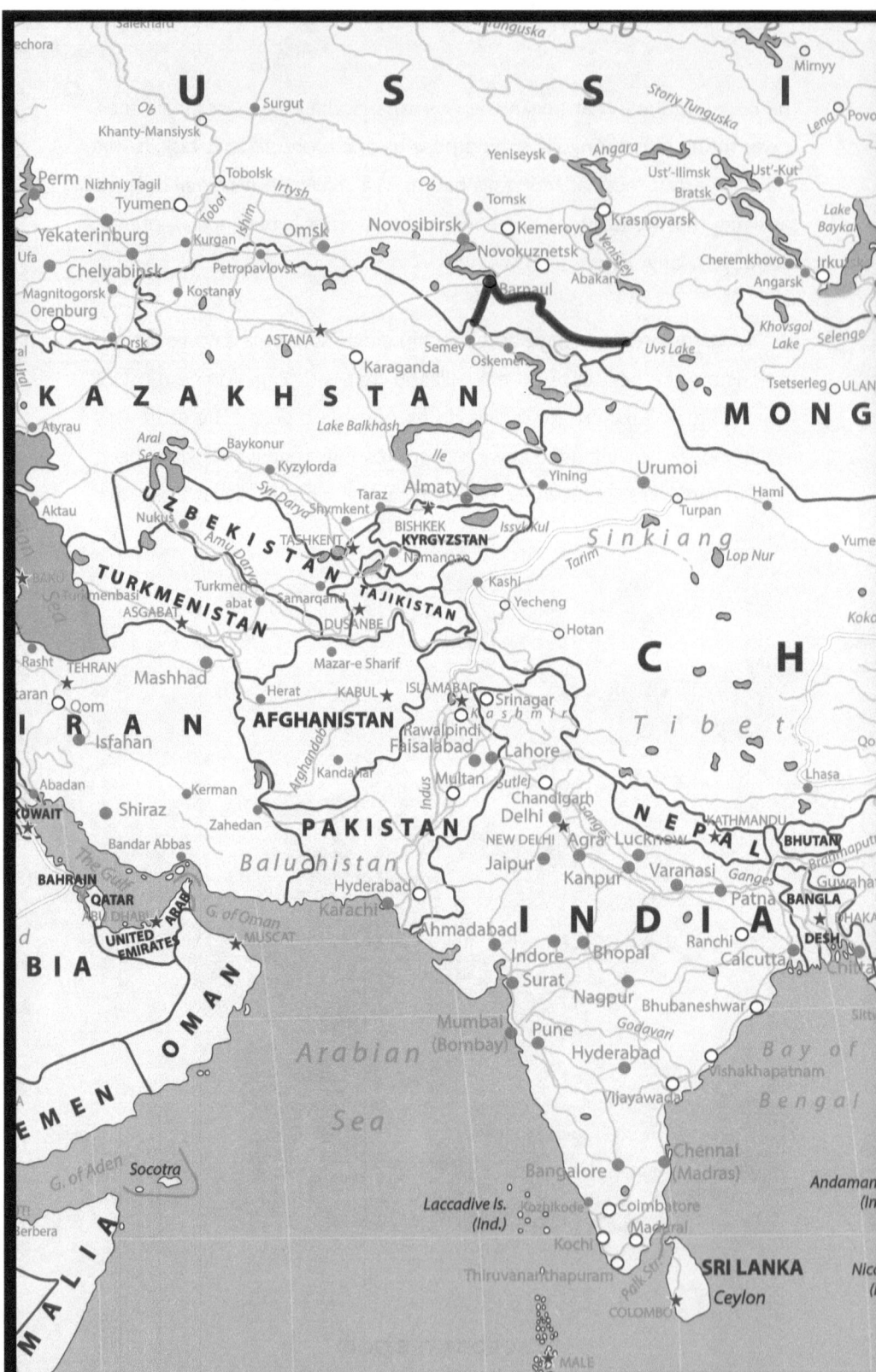

CHAPTER 4

STARS IN MOTHER RUSSIA

Because we seemed to be making a better fist of getting out of Mongolia, Dick stayed with us and rode pillion behind Steve across the no man's land leading up to the Russian border. It was an unusual role reversal; the pupil riding, while master was passengered. It looked even more odd to me as Steve was wearing Dick's riding jacket and vice versa. After the challenge of the mudhole right in no-man's-land we made our way a few kilometres up a hillside to a barrier where a small queue of trucks and overloaded vans waited. This appeared to be the actual border. A soldier took our paperwork away for a while, returned with it and indicated that we wait. And wait we did on this bitterly cold, windswept hilltop, huddled down against a truck's wheel to keep out of the wind. Occasionally the guards would open the barrier for military vehicles going the other way. One of the guards was a woman, armed to the teeth with knives, grenades and a Kalashnikov. We

wondered what these soldiers had done to be banished to this hellhole. It was an incredibly bleak spot. We were slightly surprised that even though we were up there for a couple of hours, Thomas and Greg hadn't turned up. We certainly weren't going to wait any longer than necessary and as soon as we were given the go, we went.

Almost immediately we started to appreciate the difference between these Central Asian neighbours. Even this stretch of road from the actual border down to the document processing point about 20 kilometres away, was sealed. We pointed at the white line and the road signs and the occasional Armco barrier. We were fairly cold but happy, as there was the stimulus of something new. Visiting Russia had been one of Dick's dreams and he was now about to realise it. There was another queue down at the document processing point, but at least it was sunny and quite a bit warmer now that we were down off the tops. I remember the outside toilets as being among the worst of the entire trip, but I won't spoil your appetite with the details.

The border crossing itself was stressful. Even though we had the required visas, letters of invitation and vehicle carnets, it was time consuming and frustrating. In these situations we were pleased to have Steve organising us. He was quick to catch on to the demands of officialdom and personable towards them. The day was beginning to run away from us though and Dick really needed to eat again. It was good to see the boys finally arrive and we got some snack-food from them to allay our immediate requirements. There was a lot of to-ing and fro-ing with various officials sending us from room to room. Small amounts of money were requested in one section but when they realised that we didn't have any Russian kopeks, the official shrugged and stamped the documents. We did have to part with some US dollars for insurance though. We thought we'd smoothed the path for the Frenchies but they were asked for an exorbitant amount of money that they refused to pay. The negotiations appeared to have stalled, and they retreated to the van to try and out-wait the officials. We decided to leave them and move into Russia while we had the chance, agreeing that we would stay in the first town, Kas Agar. If we didn't meet up, we would be in Gorno-Altaysk the next day, where we had a place booked. We'd see them there. So, with Dick again riding pillion, we headed off to seek food and shelter. A lot of our surplus gear was left in the van. Steve and I had most of our stuff but Dick's was in the UAZ.

The first village we came to had nowhere to exchange money, stay or eat. It did have an interesting grocery set-up in an ordinary house and if we'd had local currency we could have bought the makings of a meal. We were still carrying our back-up army rations and our dehydrated meals and could fish those out if nothing better was on offer. We carried on to Kas Agar and found a small food store on the side of the road. We'd heard that there was a restaurant in town and we were trying to get directions. Steve did his usual skilful reconnoitring and ascertained where the eatery was

but, better still, the lady who owned the store also had a small cottage that she rented out and there was a room spare.

The good fortune increased when some of the border officials arrived in a jeep. They were now quite friendly, in marked contrast to their demeanour at the border. One of them had fascinated us earlier because he was in a blue uniform whilst the others all wore green. He also stood out because he was a huge, blonde, Greek God of a man. He had film star looks and moved like an athlete. If he'd told us he represented Russia at the Olympics in the discus or something we would have nodded with a grin. We never did find out the significance of the blue uniform. Our first guess would have been that he was in the air force, but we didn't think such troops would be stationed there. He was affable now and had a smattering of English. When this was used in conjunction with Steve's tiny bit of Russian, our needs could be communicated. The oldest guy, with the most gold braid, soon had a big roll of money out and we exchanged US dollars for roubles.

Our spirits were rising. In one fell swoop we had solved the problems of accommodation and money. The military and the shopkeeper led us up a backstreet to a small dwelling where we were instructed in the use of the kitchen and shown where their toilet was, around the back in the next street. We asked if it would be a good place to leave the bikes, inside the gate, just by the front door. The military all fell about laughing, indicating that by morning there would be nothing left, not even the padlock. This led to more local folk being involved in joyful chatter and much gesticulation. In no time we were pushing the bikes down the road to another house and along a plank into a front room, where they would be safe for the night. Steve went back to our landlady's store and bought some delicious bread, cheese, tomatoes, salami and jam. We also broke out our rations and cooked up a storm, having the most wonderful yet simple meal. There was another room partitioned off from the kitchen and it seemed someone must have been sleeping there during our tenure. Around midnight, a car stopped outside and tooted. There was a bit of crashing and banging and our unseen fellow guest left, presumably to go to work. We never saw him. It could have been Elvis, alive and well and living in Russia.

Friday 27 May dawned clear enough for us to see the snow-clad hills. In the early morning we could hear kids playing outside, even up on our roof. It was fascinating to see the Russians starting their day. Their houses looked different, their clothes looked different, their lives seemed different, yet there was a similarity. Just like the life I'd put on hold, they had a work routine. Each morning the big fishing rod of our employment reels us in for an 8-hour work stint. When our day is done, the ratchet on the winding spool is disengaged and we run free for 15 hours or so before the line tightens and the process is repeated. Some are dragged in fighting each morning whilst others go meekly, feigning willingness. Half a world away from home, it was the same. I empathised, and wondered about their lives. They were quite different from the Mongolians, lacking the Asiatic features and dark skin. I hadn't expected to see such a dramatic change. Sure, there were lots of Kazakh-looking people but most were pale skinned, often blonde and tall. I thought this surprising, seeing we were so far from Moscow.

We indulged in a slow start to our first real day in Russia. Climbing over the hill that straddled no-man's-land had brought us into a different world. Suddenly there were hills everywhere and snow-fed rivers. Dick was put back in his rightful place on the mighty Norton and Steve was my burden for the first time on the trip. We'd originally planned to get a third bike in Mongolia or Russia. There hadn't been time in Mongolia, and it had suited us to have the spare rider as it meant there was no pressure on Dick to ride whilst still out of sorts. It would have been a time-consuming operation to get the papers needed to export a bike. Going from country to country was complicated enough; arriving without the full complement of papers would definitely ensure failure.

In the late morning we had a few speckles of snow and we were glad to find a primitive but warm roadside café We'd been following a wide valley in the shadows of impressive alpine scenery. It was so different from Mongolia. There were road signs (we'd only seen two in all of Mongolia), the road surface was good, there were bus stops, and private cars on the roads. It was almost sophisticated, not 'Europe sophisticated', but after where we'd recently been it was quite advanced. The afternoon's ride was one of the most uplifting I could recall. The valley had forested sides and we rode alongside a river past villages of wooden houses with blue trimmed doors and windows. Steve sat facing backwards, filming Dick riding through this wonderland. We had a few more snow flurries but generally the sun shone and we were all positively glowing with just being there. Here we were, riding our old darlings in Russia.

I'd been pretty damn proud of the fact that I hadn't really fallen off Penelope in all the difficult riding in Mongolia. There had been a 'parking' incident with a bank in the Gobi but I hadn't hit the ground, so to speak. Caught on film is Dick riding off down the valley, then there's a yelp from me and the last couple of tumbling rolls captured forever as I overbalanced, my leg unable to hold the loaded bike on the down-side. My leg wasn't long enough, or the ground wasn't high enough and rumble-tumble, there I go, roly-poly down the bank. This was embarrassing, and the old girl took quite a lift to get her upright. The ride continued past massive forests of very light green trees. I think they were elms. What a contrast to the week before when Steve had ridden circles around the only tree we'd seen in Mongolia. There appeared to be no such difficulty growing trees in Russia. There were millions of them.

We'd been fair eating up the miles on the tarseal, even taking into consideration the slow start and a good respite in the warm café. We slowed down a bit in the late afternoon, however, as more snow flurries banished the welcome sun. This time the snow seemed determined to stay. I didn't think it could be as bad as the snowstorm we'd endured in Mongolia, but as time went on I began to be a little irritated. We weren't sure if we'd get to Gorno-Altaysk. The snow got thicker and thicker and it became difficult to keep our visors clear. I had my balaclava on and wasn't too cold but visibility was a problem. Lift the visor and you exposed your face to the snowy blast. Put it back down and you couldn't see through it. We were travelling along a section of the route that didn't seem to have many settlements. Whilst I'm sure none of us were too alarmed, I know we were all concerned. Just when I was thinking we should have a conference about maybe hunkering down for the night or giving ourselves a set length of time to find shelter, the heavy snow forced us to a standstill. We could no longer determine the sides of the road.

To our amazement we had slithered to a halt by a stopped truck. We were lucky not to have ploughed right into it. Apparently there was a turn-off nearby and we were advised to take it. We didn't quite understand the directions, but found the turn-off and slowly made our way through the swirling gloom. Less than a kilometre on we came to a cluster of buildings and made for the nearest. I'd spotted one off to the left, while Dick went towards one straight ahead. As I was making my way towards my one, we heard Dick yell. His bike was down and he needed help getting it back up. This done, Steve set about finding someone in what appeared to be an abandoned village. Eventually he did, and we learned we were in a ski resort which was more or less closed for the summer. After receiving directions, we paddled along as best we could. Fortunately the snow stopped for a while, making things far more pleasant and achievable. Yet again Steve captured footage of me going arse-over-kite, as we sophisticates say. He filmed me making my way down to the front of the main accom- modation building and when passing a tree, I suddenly fell over. The tree roots had caused my downfall. Bloody things.

THE LAST HURRAH

The accommodation block was warm and reasonably welcoming. We would have been OK outside in our tents, but hell this was lovely. We cooked up our own food for the evening meal and had a comfortable night. In the morning we ventured across to another building for a good cooked breakfast. The winter scene could have been off a postcard. Our home town doesn't experience snow so this was fascinating. We'd put the bikes under my tent fly and soon had them exposed to the thin sunshine now bathing the countryside. Arriving, while we prepared to leave, was a group of what we would describe as the new-rich of Russia. Young, attractive, in smart gear and smart cars, they'd set off the night before for a weekend of playing in the hills on their highly spec'd mountainbikes. This wasn't the old Russia of communist times but a new affluence, something we were to see quite often in modern Russia. Not everything has gone well since the break-up of the Soviet Union but for some it's been great.

We knew we'd done about 330 kilometres before being forced indoors, so had only about 100 kilometres left to reach Gorno-Altaysk, a resort area. Steve took over riding the Norton and Dick pillioned again. At the junction with the main road we passed a confusing road sign that we were to see several more times in Russia. It appeared to show a car with its roof being blown off. We didn't have a clue what this might mean but we'd look out for them anyway. The roads had been cleared of snow and the ride was lovely, as we passed through small hamlets on our way down the lush valley. We stopped at a small roadside market where we indulged ourselves with hot coffee, hot dogs and a rest in the sun. An English-speaking teacher interviewed Steve in front of a movie camera and they swapped email addresses. Other people came up to us, expressing their interest in our adventure. Many of them had gold teeth, prominently displayed. It wasn't just the older folk either. I was surprised when an attractive young woman ran past, flashing a golden smile at me as she went by.

Already we were in love with this picturesque area of Russia. The

scenery was exquisite. It was spring and all the cottages in the villages we passed through had substantial gardens of dark, almost black soil that had been freshly turned and planted. Hens scurried about the place, such a change from Mongolia where they are almost unheard of (Mongolia has no chickens, pigs, fruit or vegetables). This looked like a part of the world where we could bring our nearests and dearests to holiday. It wasn't as harsh as Mongolia. They'd love it. As we neared Gorno-Altaysk it became a bit more commercialised. Big roadside hoardings provided unwanted visual pollution. We missed the turn-off to the lake and our resort and hit Gorno-Altaysk right on lunchtime. We tried to find a bank that was open, and waited until 2 o'clock just in case, but had no luck – it was Saturday. Whilst Steve and I went looking to exchange money, Dick remained with the bikes. He later admitted to falling asleep standing up, leaning against a wall for comfort.

On our way back to the turn-off we spotted a bank we'd missed on the way in, and we doubled back to use its hole-in-the-wall facility. In what turned out to be one of the trip's mysteries, the machine would only allow a few dollars of money to be exchanged and the charge for doing so was as much as the amount we changed. We presume that someone somewhere has programmed the decimal point in the wrong place.

After passing over a huge one-way humpbacked bridge we made our way alongside a beautiful stream, looking for our resort. When we did find it, we were disappointed that it was not completely in working condition. What was wonderful, was the news that Thomas and Greg were waiting for us. A spunky young thing with tight jeans hung low to show her lower back tattoo took Steve to them. Soon we were all together, sharing experiences. They'd only just arrived, having sat at the border for a couple of days before capitulating to officialdom. The bad news was that they were actually under guard, in the process of being escorted across this part of Russia to the Kazakhstan border. A couple of soldiers in a Lada were at the camp with them and would accompany them the next day. It seemed that their paperwork was deficient so the Ruskies were shovelling them on to Kazakhstan, at a cost. They told stories of the nights at the border, fraternising with the guards with much vodka, drunkenness and singing. It was sad that they were being pushed on ahead on a different route from the one we would be following.

Fortunately, Dick's illness was now a past memory. We weren't worried about the lack of medical support as all the signs and his performance since Olgii had been good. We were disappointed to be parting because we'd quickly bonded with these two characters and we would miss the regular contact with them. There was always a sense of fun when they were around. There was the hope that we might catch up with them somewhere along the Silk Road. But now they were running short of money, and felt it would be impossible to get the UAZ home to France. They were considering selling it in Tashkent, Uzbekistan. This would be a shame, as they had dreams of using it and the ger as a market stall, to sell wares from this part of the world.

So, we had only an afternoon and evening to celebrate our friendship and shared experiences. The boys thought it might be fun to have a movie show that night but their generator had been giving trouble. They had it apart and in a lot of bits, and started to clean it after some advice from Dick. Meanwhile, Dick and I went off on a walk up to the country store that serviced the area. It was here that we really saw the advantages of travelling in this part of the world. Both China and Mongolia had been cheap but not always very modern or with many services. At this lovely little store I bought five icecreams, three big 600 ml bottles of beer, two loaves of bread, a salami and some cheese for the princely sum of $3.50. Add to this the low cost of petrol, the lovely Anna Kournakova lookalikes that seemed to be everywhere, and you can understand why it appealed to us. The generator was made to generate but we didn't get to make movies. We talked too much and had a few more beers. It was a poignant moment when next morning our saviours bade us farewell and, with their army escort, disappeared. Dick hadn't got to ride with them but we'll be forever grateful to them that the Last Hurrah didn't fizzle in Olgii, Mongolia. We liked our little log cabin chalet and the peacefulness of the region so much that even though we were behind schedule, we decided to stay another day to rest and play with the bikes a little. We also rationalised our luggage a bit as now we had to carry everything ourselves. A few surplus things were given away to local workers who had shown an interest in us, including a very nice Ducati bag that Dick couldn't find room for. I'd already done my bit by accidentally leaving a bag of unwashed clothes in the Mongolian support vehicle. This meant that I had only one T-shirt and then it was into the merino Icebreaker™ gear. From here on most photos show me in my Whangamomona Hotel T-shirt. This could be seen as good promotion for them, but as they're reputably New Zealand's most remote hotel, I wonder if the exposure did them any good.

The weather was sublime, warm enough for the pretties to shed a lot of their clothes and yet not too hot to enjoy the day. It was tempting to hole up there for a while and just enjoy some time doing nothing. Sadly, the need to be at given spots on given dates was prescribed by the countries we were travelling through and by the fact that we had lives waiting for us to return to. In my youth I had just wandered, going where the mood took me, taking as long as it took. We didn't have this luxury and, after only one day of leisure, we were back on the road. We'd not seen or heard from any doctor, which wouldn't be the last time that our Russian agent was to let us down. We were just fortunate that Dick was as fit and hardy as ever.

The ride to Barnaul was just another day at the office. Often people assume that we're just cruising along, whistling a happy tune. Well we did that, but it was work as well. It was what we did, almost every day, just like work. We got up, had breakfast, rode until morning smoko, rode until lunchtime, did another session after lunch, had another break and went out to do it again. It seemed relentless at times. There were days when we didn't want to do it and our resilience was challenged. But here we were riding in the shadows of the snow-topped Altay Mountains. This was southern Siberia and the reward for our persistence was Barnaul.

We knew nothing about Barnaul and the name was hardly inspiring. We were only going there because it was the turnaround point. There is no direct route from Mongolia down into Kazakhstan. You have to go into Russia for a 1,000 kilometres because those Altay Mountains block the way and you have to ride around the top of them. We suddenly came upon this large city of more than 600,000 people and even at first sight we could tell it was a magic place. The river makes Barnaul look impressive and there are big bridges and tall buildings.

We had no map, so on the outskirts we pulled off the dual carriageway onto a roundabout and stopped precariously to get our bearings.

Whilst seeking directions from a woman walking by pushing a pram, a car stopped and a jovial character demanded to help. Soon Steve was in the car and Dick and I were following. There were trams in the streets and the buildings were often very imaginative and modernist. The main roads were wide and busy, the footpaths thronged with stunning, very European-looking people. You could see the students among them, for this is a university city. What surprised me most was the colour and diversity of both city and inhabitants. I had travelled throughout the European communist block in my youth (with the exception of Russia). I knew what to expect ... what a laugh; that was then, this is now. The drabness had gone, the almost uniformity of clothing had gone, the sameness of everything being government-issue was no longer evident. Our guide, Dimitri, located our hotel and seemed to have an inexhaustible supply of beer in his car. He insisted that we drank it right there on the footpath outside the hotel, while Steve booked us in. Despite our paperwork showing a booking, the hotel denied all knowledge of us. Eventually, with Dimitri's help we were accepted as guests. As usual, we'd attracted an interested group of bystanders, but they weren't intrusive or annoying. It was nice to be standing around in the sun with a beer in hand, revelling in the attention. In our heart-of-hearts we knew we were nonentities, but here we were almost celebrities. We'd ridden from China across Mongolia to get to their city.

Dimitri didn't have a great command of English but he had enthusiasm and vision. He left Dick and I with some beer and whisked Steve off to places unknown. They weren't away for long and when they returned they had in tow one of the coolest dudes you could imagine. This was our first meeting with Evgeni. He was wearing cool shades, black jeans, a soft white shirt, a leather vest with a few small patches, a Nazi-style helmet.

His bike was a big vee-twin Kawasaki, I think, dressed up like a high, wide and handsome Harley. It was huge, with tasselled saddlebags and tassels everywhere else, including some from the handlebar ends that reached the ground. It also had four speakers booming out pounding rock'n'roll music. There were lurid graphics on the bike, an overpowering statement. Evgeni was introduced as the owner of the Biker Bar, that the spunky tattooed girl back in Gorno-Altaysk had told us about. Soon some Ural-riding motorcyclists had also gathered around. We were road-soiled stars from an exotic land they knew very little about. Dimitri seemed very proud of us. Evgeni insisted that we didn't leave the bikes at the hotel, but follow him to his friend's bike shop where they would be safer.

It was quite a thrill to be riding in convoy through Barnaul behind this flamboyant character, his speakers blaring out music whilst our old single cylinder bangers contributed their distinctive thudding accompaniment. Soon we were in a back alleyway courtyard meeting with another Evgeni, and Michaelov who ran the MotoCentr, a motorbike shop that specialised in Japanese imports. It had some quite impressive big sporty bikes there; not a Ural, Dneiper, Jupiter or Planeta to be seen. We admired their bikes and photos. Their riding year is so short that it's treated like a season and has a season opening rally which apes everything that is done in American biker circles, right down to the wet T-shirt contests and babes baring their frontal charms.

With no choice in the matter, we were adopted by the bike-riding fraternity of Barnaul and showered with hospitality. We were collected from our hotel on our first night and taken by taxi to the Biker Bar. Unfortunately, we didn't take our cameras with us, and so have no pictorial record of the most amazing bar I've ever been in. It's no wonder that the place has a spreading international reputation. Outside, setting the scene, is a giant stylised Ural motorcycle. Inside is the most imaginative fit-out, with real bikes coming through walls at you. These have been cast into the concrete

THE LAST HURRAH

walls so a figure might have only the front of their helmet and their arms showing on one side, attached to half of a bike which protrudes from the wall. They seem to be bursting forth. There are photos and memorabilia everywhere. Parts of motorbikes make up the furniture. Videos play in the background. Here we were introduced to many of the people who made our stay in Barnaul so special. We met Anna, the diminutive daughter of a couple of university professors or teachers, who stayed at home during the day working on web design and playing with her computer. She had many friends, quite good English and she facilitated a lot of what happened over the next few days. She had a friend in the bar who looked like a smiling punk rocker. We were told she was doing a high-powered degree in nuclear physics or some such. It was hard to believe. I drank a lot with Anatoly, a folk singer, whilst Steve played pool with a group of youngsters, including an American on a university exchange. We didn't pay for a single beer or for the meals we ate. It was a memorable night.

We felt at home in Barnaul, in our comfortable two-star hotel. One of the enjoyable things for us was the daily interaction with a kids' soccer team from a distant regional city, who were in town for a tournament. They were cheeky and lots of fun. They all had a smattering of English and the energy of youth. One kid had red hair, like I had in my days of hair, and we laughed about this as I tried to convey we were related.

Quite early on our second day, a knock at our door signalled the beginning of an intense period of celebrity. A woman journalist and her male photographer wanted to interview us and photograph our bikes. This entailed us all going down to the bike shop, where we were going anyway to do maintenance. Hardly had we arrived when a TV crew turned up. It didn't stop. Another two TV crews came. We rode up and down the road for one crew while the photographer ran about taking photos at the same time. These were to feature on the front page of the paper, later sent to us by a friend who had a friend in Barnaul. One crew got us to ride out onto a big bridge and stop in the middle, whereupon they conducted an interview – a bit like stopping on the Auckland Harbour Bridge. Crazy. One of the crews had an extremely attractive front-person and she convinced Steve to go back to the studio with her so they could download some of our footage. He didn't seem too reluctant! In the midst of all this we tried to do a bit of maintenance. I arranged for my toolbox lugs to be re-welded to the frame and Dick did an oil change. Apart from being minor stars, we were also enjoying the sights of a bustling city.

One in particular that made me laugh was seeing the latest Lada Niva badged as a Chevrolet. It was a little more rounded than the usual Niva, but it was still obvious that it was one. Detroit, what have you been up to? We were told that it wasn't even as good as the older models as they had chosen a particular engine that wasn't rated at all by the local cognoscenti. Ladas have always been the butt of jokes in New Zealand as they were incredibly cheap and you got what you paid for, e.g.,

"Why do Ladas have heated rear windows?" "To keep the pushers' hands warm." "What's on the last page of the Lada owner's manual?" "The bus timetable." "How do you double the value of a Lada?" "Fill it with petrol."

"What do you call a Lada on a hill?" "A bloody miracle."

The New Zealand Dairy Board imported them as a swapsie deal where the Russians bought our milk powder and paid us in Ladas. I don't think the rumour that it was one car for one carton of milk powder was true though.

Dick and I enjoyed several walks just exploring the streets near our hotel. It seemed so exotic yet familiar. We marvelled at the numbers of tall and beautiful women. No wonder Russia does so well at basketball and volleyball. We shopped in a small supermarket, laughing at our inability to understand the purchasing processes, although we eventually managed a bag full of fresh produce, breads and cheeses. In the late afternoon sun we stopped and chatted with a young woman who appeared to be selling beer from a trailer-mounted tanker. A sign proclaimed the brew had been made for a few hundred years. We tasted her dark, murky wares, which we didn't much like, and lingered in the warmth, watching folk coming to her with all sorts of containers. When we saw her selling to young kids we asked if the product was alcoholic. Her answer was no. Dick and I could remember the yeasty taste from somewhere but couldn't put a name to it. We were to see these tankers throughout the region, all the way to Uzbekistan.

We felt quite at home here; we were comfortable at the hotel and were enjoying our small sorties into the city. The food was good and Russian fruit juices are all wonderful, whether they are orange or peach or pineapple or mango or combinations of all of them. They seem so flavoursome and thirst-quenching.

We laughed and whooped with enjoyment when we saw ourselves featured on the main TV channel. Steve's footage looked great. There in front of us was Dick riding between camels in Mongolia and panel-beating a footrest after a fall. We thought we looked fabulous but had no idea what was being said about us. A last night of beer and kebabs topped off our stay perfectly.

Now that we were well into spring, with the higher regions of our trip behind us, we decided we wouldn't need our warmest gear and could

abandon the surplus. It was now consistently warm and we were heading towards even warmer climes, down through the 'stans'. We made a big parcel of goodies and prepared to attempt to post it home. MotoCentr Evgeni offered, and in fact insisted, on accompanying us to the post office, so with Steve up on the back of his big sporty Kawasaki, he led the way. They disappeared inside while Dick and I stayed with the bikes. When I say disappear, I mean disappear. We didn't really take much notice of where they'd gone, and they didn't reappear. An hour went by. What we didn't know was that they had to unpack everything and then repack the things that the Russian postal service decided could be sent, into a new box. All this took a hell of a long time.

Coincidentally we saw Biker Bar Evgeni who was now in his business suit. It turned out that as well as owning the Biker Bar, he owned the Diesel Jeans franchise and also Nike. These favoured foreign brands were sold through two linked boutiques that would rival any in Europe. He took us in and arranged drinks. One of his sales staff was so stunning she wouldn't be out of place on the catwalks of Paris. I couldn't help but make an excuse to photograph her because I knew people back home would accuse me of exaggerating. There didn't seem to be any customers but the shops sure looked good. Dick and I felt a little out of place, all togged up in our bike gear, but being celebs we were accepted and fawned over. Suddenly it started to rain quite heavily and then Penelope fell over. Quick as a flash Evgeni was out helping the guy he had posted as watcher. His immaculate pale suit, shirt and trousers combination that had looked so posh minutes earlier was now a sodden mess. He didn't seem to mind.

It was after 3 o'clock when we finally rode from Barnaul in the wheel tracks of MotoCentr Evgeni. He took us to the outskirts of the city and just before a checkpoint he gave us back the Cabin Boy, and farewelled us. The big Kawasaki had no number plate and we presumed that he must have known where the checkpoint would be. We had a 300 kilometre ride ahead of us but the roads were good. There was a bit of precipitation but it never became intrusive or really to the point when you would call it rain. We'd missed the heavy rain while we waited in the boutique. The wind was quite unpleasant though. Despite these minor adversities, the afternoon went well and we all seemed happy about the ride. We stopped and sheltered in the late afternoon at a roadside café and ate heartily to warm up, laughing about the irony of sending away all our warm gear. At one stage the sun came out, and as we were riding at right-angles to it, Steve tried to film our shadows as we rode through a countryside of huge collective farms. This scale of farming was beyond anything we'd seen before. There were no farmhouses for quite large distances and then there would be a small cluster. The freshly sown fields stretched almost as far as you could see. There were no settlements of any substance along the route that was to take us to Rubthoske, the last town before the Kazakhstan border. Rubthoske has a reputation of being less than charming and an area of high drug usage. We were only to spend one night there, and as it was pre-booked we didn't worry that we'd arrive at nightfall. All we had to do was locate the hotel, find some food and fall into bed. Now that we were on our own without a guide to find us somewhere to lay our heads, this was one less hassle for us to face. Our Central Asia itinerary had us staying in a hotel here, then again in a few days time in Almaty, then Bishkek, Tashkent and Samarkand. These were all the big cities and in between we'd probably camp out or just see what came along. Of the 80 days or so that Silk Road Adventures were looking after our documentation, they'd booked us into two-star accommodation for 30 days.

For the other 50 days it was up to us to find shelter as best we could. It was just getting dark when we reached the outskirts of town and I ran out of petrol. Oh, joy. I'd thought we could probably do 300 kilometres on a tank and was proved to be almost right. The fuel from the one litre bottle we kept for filling the cooker got us to a gas station. Then, in the gathering murk we rode into the medium-sized, uninspiring town. We found the big square where our hotel was located quite easily and Steve went to check us in. There were a lot of young people fooling around and we were an obvious target. They surrounded us and bombarded us with questions. They also played with whatever parts of the bikes they could get their hands on. Our helmets were particularly popular and they took turns trying them on. Then several said it was their birthday and we should give them presents, suggesting the helmets would be ideal. It was obvious by now that they'd been drinking. Their high jinks wore thin quite quickly and Dick and I couldn't believe that our Cabin Boy could be taking so long. He came out at one stage and a student who spoke a bit of English went back in with him. What a surprise – there appeared to be a bit of trouble with our booking!

While we waited and smiled through gritted teeth, we noticed among the group surrounding us that there were a number of deaf people – some youngsters and a guy of about 40. They were signing to each other, trying to find out about us. They seemed the nicest and most lucid of the group by miles. I thought how neat it would have been to be able to sign. We wouldn't have needed to know Russian. I resolved to learn one day.

Steve reappeared with the news that we couldn't stay there even though our documents showed a booking. Why? Because we weren't Russian. Well, we knew that and couldn't see what difference it made. However, they were resolute, so Steve and a couple of students went off to find another hotel. This was a setback but we'd had worse and a town this size would no doubt have several hotels. The main concern was getting a meal for Dick. We'd probably eaten at 4.30 and now it was after 9 o'clock. We were tired and getting increasingly sick of the drunks. After another interminable time, Steve came back with his little entourage and more bad news. He'd been to two more hotels and neither would have us. We were getting significantly pissed off now. Our last hope seemed to be a big hotel along the main road a bit. Dick and I fired the old girls up and followed the group who surrounded Steve and his student guides. We'd let them get a little way ahead then we'd catch up, or we'd just chug alongside with the gaggle, who were still swarming around and sometimes running to keep up with Steve.

The group didn't diminish in number and it was obvious from a couple of things that Steve said that he didn't think this was a very 'nice' group of young people. Some of them had been trying to push drugs on him. It was hard to know who to trust and who was in for an opportunist adventure. There were a couple of students who were helping but the rest were drunken yobbos. If only we could just ride away.

The new hotel was about a kilometre away and appeared to be what was needed. It looked like a westerners' hotel that would soon give the young people the elbow. It had bright lights and was blaring out loud music, although that might have been from the place next door. While Steve and his henchmen went in, Dick and I again waited with the bikes. Here we met Alexander, a middle-aged biggish fellow who had a reasonable command of English. He also had quite a presence, something I appreciated, especially as some of the kids finally buggered off once he appeared. When Steve returned it was with bad news that the hotel was full, but someone had rung someone else who would give us somewhere to stay. A couple of the students wanted to take us there, saying it wasn't far and as it was now late, we should push the bikes not ride them. We were soon in darkened streets and feeling a little uneasy.

Alexander was tagging along but it was all getting a little unnerving. When travelling, sometimes things can appear safe and aren't, whilst some situations appear dangerous and are harmless. Unfortunately, it's hard to determine which is which. I'm a naturally trusting person and I was surprised when Steve warned us that he wasn't totally trusting of our helpers. I knew Dick was concerned but I was still feeling OK about things, for now. The dark backstreets were sometimes only alleyways and we became increasingly more nervous as we went further away from the bright lights of the main road. Suddenly, in the shadows ahead of me, I saw Steve fall over with the Norton. My heart jumped a beat but I was close enough to see that he had only over-balanced and the student with him was helping him up. Dick was a bit further back and his immediate interpretation of the situation was that Steve had been knocked down. Because of the heightened expectation of danger, the reaction was predictable. Already on edge, Dick thought we were going to have to fight our way out of what looked like a dodgy situation. He had his trusty Mercator knife out in a flash, the blade quickly locked in the 'don't meddle with me' position. The moment passed, but our hearts were still pounding. We seemed to be getting into darker, scarier places and were getting even more nervous as there didn't appear to be an end in sight. Soon after the Mercator incident, Alexander indicated that he would get his jeep and we should stay where we were. It was hard to know if he was a benefactor or not but we didn't have much choice.

Ten minutes or so later Alexander was back, so the students and Steve piled in with him and Dick and I followed along behind. As we zigzagged through the dark streets between darkened accommodation blocks I was trying not to recall Eggi's warnings about the dangers of Russia. I wanted it to be neighbourhood paranoia, not a real happening. At one stage we passed a wild-looking man, waving to us in a demented manner. Alexander continued on and around the back of one of the imposing accommodation blocks. The man appeared again and was flagging us down. This turned out to be our contact. We think he was the caretaker of the building and we were to sleep in his spare room. He had no English but obviously wanted to help. There was nowhere to put the bikes and Alexander wanted us to follow him to a friend's lock-up. Tired and hungry as we were, we didn't have much choice so away we went. I tried to memorise the 'left, right,

right, straight ahead, left, past the old church, right ...' but gave up, thinking, "Oh God, I'll never remember where the bikes are". The compound where we put them contained a few buses and a couple of huge Rottweilers. Alexander then took us back to Pietr, our new benefactor, and indicated that he would see us in the morning. The saga was almost over.

However, before they left, the students wanted some money. This irritated us a bit, but the amount wasn't much, it was now after midnight and they were a long way from where we had met them. It could be said that they brought it all on themselves but we gave in. We wanted to be alone to get the meal that we desperately needed.

Pietr may have been a bit simple. It was hard to tell. He grinned a lot. It seemed he had given up his room and would be sleeping in the spare room or lounge. The flat was at the bottom of the main stairs leading up to the other apartments. We were still cooking when there was a disturbance outside the door. Pietr excused himself and popped outside. Bumping and crashing followed, which sounded like a full-on mugging to our heightened senses. Steve rushed for the door and I followed, popping out the blade of my Swiss Army knife. I've never done this sort of thing before, never had to. As we got to the door, all pumped up and scared, Pietr came in smiling, indicating it was just some drunks. Possibly he handled this every day. By the time we'd cooked up some rations and eaten, it was after one in the morning. It had been a long day. We didn't really know where the bikes were and we didn't know if Alexander was a goody or a baddy, but we needed sleep and now was the time.

I heard Pietr creeping around early in the morning. When we arose, there he was grinning away at us, patiently waiting for us to ge t up. He was extremely hospitable. We never knew why he was contacted to give us a roof over our heads but we were glad he was.

The square outside the apartment block had other apartment blocks on it and was very Third World, with horses and carts tied up. This wasn't sophisticated like Barnaul, more the Russia we had imagined, with not many sealed backstreets and not much colour. The day was pleasant enough, being neither hot nor cold. I spent a little time standing outside with a son of Alexander who had ridden his bike over with a mate. They chatted while we awaited the man himself. Alexander's business card showed him to be an agricultural inspector although we later wondered why he would need to carry a pistol in his pocket if that was his job. The Cabin Boy had been adopted by Alexander and his voice would boom out, "Stefan, we go find exchange" and "Stefan, we go get bikes". We did both of these and Steve was always made to go in the jeep so Alexander could boom out his short, loud utterances. If you were discussing a central European, you would say that he didn't have much of a command of English but as a Russian, he was right up there with the best we'd met.

I'd thought about our drama with the yobbos of the day before and like Baldrick from television's Black Adder, I'd come up with a cunning plan. The problem was that we were exotic and interesting and the bikes were ditto. Put us together and the throng assembled; we seemed to feed the frenzy. So when Alexander took Steve away to try and exchange money, leaving Dick and I in a shopping car park, I put the plan into action. Normally, in a prime spot like this we'd be mobbed. This time we parked our bikes together, then quickly walked away 30 metres or so to sit on a wall. We could see the bikes and how people would walk up to them, look at them, look over at us but decide not to detour over to talk. This was wonderful. It worked a treat. No one came over to see us, and each group that stopped to look at the bikes only did so for a minute or two, then walked on. No more annoying pushy crowds.

Alexander had demanded to take us out of town and to the border, which was less than 50 kilometres away. Navigating through cities is often a pain in the neck and we love not having to do it, so didn't put up much resistance. Not that arguing with Alexander did much good as he just boomed out instructions and swept all along with him. As we followed his jeep across town, I knew he was going the wrong way and sure enough, he'd taken us to be interviewed by local TV, radio and the newspapers – all at once. This turned out to be quite a bit of fun with Dick responding to the question: "Are you just a motorcycle traveller or are you a biker who listens to rock'n' roll music?", by uttering the immortal words, "I listen to the birds in the trees and the wind in my ears".

We told all sorts of porkies about how much we liked Rubthoske, and how nice Alexander and Pietr had been to us. At least that bit had been mainly true. I got in a quip about the cops being very prevalent with roadblocks when the weather was fine but when it had been cold, like the day before, they were nowhere to be seen. As usual in Russia, there were some charming stunners among the journos and hangers-on who did the al fresco interviews. The main TV interviewer would chat away in Russian, then an interpreter would relay it to one of us and we'd respond and the process was reversed. Each of us was interviewed in turn. While one had the camera in front of them, the others would be replying to the group questions from all around.

Despite being flattered by the attention, we were pleased to finally get out of town and head away towards the Kazakhstan border. Again we passed through areas of massive cultivation. This area was all flat and the day was now quite pleasantly warm. Around lunchtime we reached the border and dined at a café attached to a gas station. It was fairly primitive but OK. As usual we were excited by the thought of another country. This was another of the biggies. In his inimitable fashion, Alexander escorted Steve through the process of getting us out of the country. It seemed that he knew one of the customs women and could oil the wheels of officialdom for us. I don't know why they make such a big deal about letting you out of the country when you aren't one of theirs. It's always a drama. It took a couple of hours before we finally farewelled Alexander and pushed the bikes across to the Kazakh processing-booth about 100 metres further on. We'd been grateful for his help but were pleased to be left alone again to do things at our own pace and in our own way. There was a danger of him ending up like Vegemite – too much spoils the flavour.

This should have been the end of our sojourn in Russia and it so nearly was. Processing our way into Kazakhstan had involved a bit of pushing and shoving. The people trying to get processed wait outside a couple of windows that open occasionally, and everyone clamours for attention. At times it looked like a rugby scrum. You go from one window to the other and ultimately you have the right stamp and get released into the country. Both the Russian and Kazakhstan border processing facilities demonstrated the worst of officialdom. They were incredibly arrogant towards most people and especially so if you weren't one of their own. It was particularly sad watching the efforts of one family group trying to get into Kazakhstan to bury a family member who was in a crude box strapped to the roof of their Lada. The Russians treated the Kazakhs like shit, and vice versa at the other border.

As usual, Steve acquitted himself well in the squabbling throng and finally our papers had all the stamps needed. We pushed the bikes through to the guy at the barrier and it was at this last hurdle that we fell. A vigilant official spotted that our visa didn't give us access until the 5th of June. It was only the 2nd of June.

We didn't see this as a problem as we had the letter of invitation to the country that had enabled the visa. They wanted us to go to their country. It was hardly the crime of the century to be a few days early. The embassy in Beijing had made the cock-up, as we'd wanted it for an earlier date but this was what we ended up with. It was a classic opening for a pay-off. We asked nicely for an 'express' visa. How much would it cost? Amazingly, we had happened on the only non-bribable border official. The man in charge would not budge. We would have to go back into Russia. Usually, in this instance you just refuse to go back. We figured that if we ignored them they would come to their senses and let us in, as in three days everything would be fine. Surely it wasn't worth the effort to cancel the paperwork and make us go back into Russia. What if Russia didn't want us back? We sat around for a while but lost the argument and we had to retrace our steps. Predictably, the Russians weren't all that impressed at having to process us into the country when we didn't have a letter of invitation or visa to make this backward step happen.

We couldn't face going back to Rubthoske, so, celebrities that we were, we camped in the rubbish at the side of the road outside the Russian customs post. We made our way off the road and put up both tents and a cover over the bikes. Oh what fun! There was the gas station 150 metres up the road and over the other side was a small eatery run by what looked like a mother and son combination. That was it. There were no houses that we could see, there wasn't a border village. Just when we thought we'd pulled back a couple of days on the itinerary, we were set back three. We looked at the pictures in the Russian motorbike magazines we had been given. We read, we talked and took turns at going off for long walks in pairs. We watched long trains (often of more than 60 carriages) go by on two sides of us. On the second day we had a guy come over and ask us to sign a cassette tape. He'd heard us on the radio and suddenly, there we were. We must have looked fairly down and out for famous people. It wasn't a popular border and I don't think a tourist crossed in the three days we were camped there. A local lad came by on his tatty old two-stroke bike with a couple of friends aboard. His bike was like the sort of

thing I remember having at his age. It was a wreck, with no brakes, and wires that you twisted together to get ignition. Everything that stuck out was broken or bent, but it went. A day later he came by with a sidecar attached, probably just to show off.

We would dine at the eatery across the road a couple of times a day, cooking up our rations for the other meals. It wasn't particularly unpleasant, it was just boring. The boredom was momentarily eased when two pretty young things came mincing through the long grass from the cafe at the gas station. Their footwear was in no way suited for the trek, but obviously we were of such interest that they would risk a turned ankle to check us out. It was a short interlude that probably disappointed both parties. They looked and smelt good, but our conversation was hardly an in-depth analysis of Chekov or the performance of the big bear since the breakdown of the communist dynasty. It didn't take long before they became bored with us and minced off again. From where and to where, we never knew.

The temperature was in the low 30s with a humidity factor of 25 percent, so even the weather was OK. It could have been worse, we just couldn't think how at the time. Finally, our time was up. On the night of the 4th some Russian guards came over and asked if we wanted to start going through at 11 p.m. We wondered if this was a joke, or perhaps a reaction to me asking the Kazakh officials if they were open at midnight because I would be there at one minute past on the 5th. We declined their offer, partly in preference to having a full night's sleep but mainly because they were only the Russian part of the deal. We'd gone through their side before and look where it had got us.

Russia had been such a combination of good and not so good for us. Visually, it had been a treat with the magnificent forested valleys in the early part of our traverse and the quaint little villages springing into spring. Even the huge collective farms on the plains had interested us. It had been so cheap, yet in places very sophisticated. Barnaul had been exhilarating and Rubthoske challenging. A fair deal. In the main, the people had been friendly and a sight for jaded eyes. It had been a good example of what travelling away from the tourist trails should be like. I made all sorts of embryonic plans to return one day and hire a sidecar outfit to explore this corner of the world. Mother Russia had not disappointed.

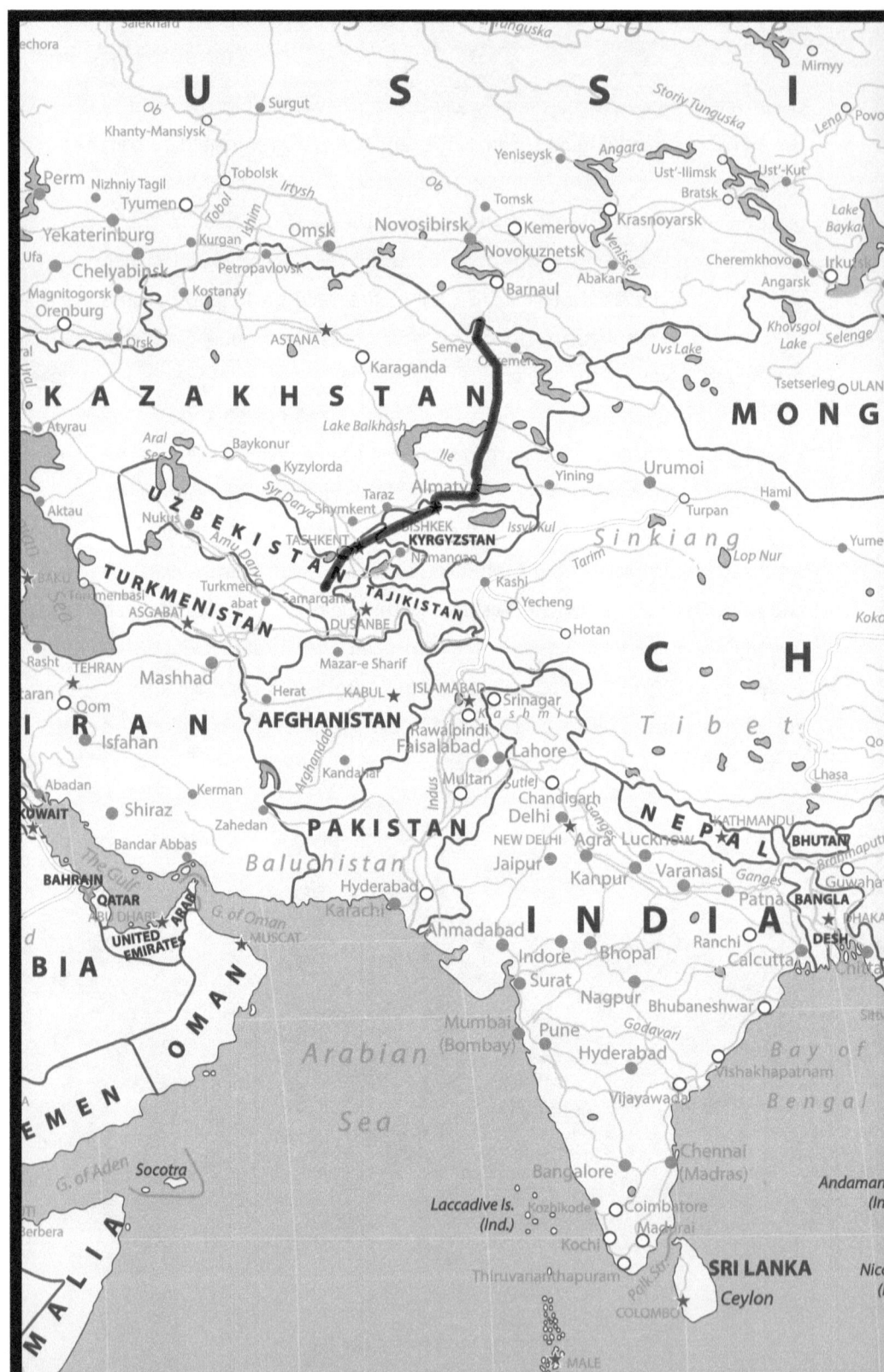

CHAPTER 5

THE 'STANS'

The Kazakhstan border officials were all smiley when we returned. They knew we'd camped at the border only a short distance away. It all seemed so pointless now, and we were relieved to finally get through the first stage and move from the border point itself. A few hundred metres on we had to do some more documentation and there, to our surprise, was the Frenchies' UAZ. More deficient paperwork, so the vehicle had been impounded. This was staggering, as we knew they didn't have lots of money, had paid too much for it, had spent a fortune on keeping it going and were dependent on selling it for a good price in Uzbekistan. Yet there it was, abandoned. There was no sign of the ger. We wondered if they'd somehow managed to transport it on with them, but we doubted it.

Despite this sad thought, finally riding away from the border was a happy moment for us. Steve was on the back filming, and life seemed good. Sometimes these feelings overwhelmed us. It's hard to describe being somewhere so exotic when we always felt so ordinary. Dick would articulate it with his oft-repeated refrain that he was "just a boy from Antico St". That said it all for us. The sun was shining, the weather was kind, and we were heading for Semey or Semipalatinsk, depending on whether you were Russian or Kazakh. We didn't have any Kazakh money; that would be our first task when we reached Semey. All the more reason not to muck about.

The roads were still OK but quite bumpy – sealed, but bumpy.

Semey proved to be a modern city but we weren't going to stay there. It's notorious for being near the site of 467 nuclear tests. This is the main reason for its relative affluence (and the continued contamination that has been identified). On our way through we couldn't see anywhere to exchange money so we parked outside a small general store. After advice from the shopkeeper, Steve took a taxi into the central city to find a big hotel or bank. Dick and I mucked about waiting for his return. A poignant photo shows Dick guarding the bikes, sound asleep, sitting on the kerb.

Although Steve was the acknowledged champion, both of my travelling companions are awesome sleepers. Whenever we stopped for a rest, they would immediately fall asleep. This was often just beside the bikes on the side of the road. If there was nothing happening, they would stack up the zzzzs, in case they needed them later I suppose. My array of photos of sleeping guards is quite amusing: the boys guarding the bikes in Russia, the boys guarding the bikes in Kazakhstan, the boys guarding the bikes in Uzbekistan. One day Dick even went to sleep standing up. What a great skill to have when you're travelling. I'm not too worried about not sleeping, if perhaps the ground is hard, the wind howling, wild dogs are circling or for whatever reason. My philosophy is that you'll be so knackered the next night that you'll sleep like a baby. There's usually a reason for being awake;

you're worried about something. Equally, there's a reason for being asleep; you're tired and the body needs a charge-up.

Steve returned and we headed south, aiming for Almaty or Alma Ata, again depending on whose map you are reading. A thunderstorm briefly caught up with us as we left Semey, although the rain more or less missed us. We only had half the afternoon to ride, and our aim was to get to Almaty as soon as we could. As we passed small towns, we could see on the outskirts of each what looked like a miniature middle-eastern village. I thought the first one I saw was an attraction, like some sort of Lego Land. Then it dawned on me that they were ornate cemeteries. They had miniature minarets and mosque-like tombs.

Although Kazakhstan was quite different from Russia, it showed the stamp of having been part of the old Soviet Union. In the early evening we rode up behind one of the cemeteries and decided to pitch camp. The tents would be out of sight of the main road and the town was a few kilometres away, so there was a low likelihood of foot traffic coming by. We cooked up a passable meal and before dark my left and right hand men were both inside the tents looking at the insides of their eyelids. I wanted to do a small private inclusion on the video camera so went over to a wall that faced the setting sun and set up the tripod. I talked to the camera for a bit, reflecting on the days that had recently past. With my back to the wall, I sat and waited for the sun to set. It seemed eerie to be sitting with other folk's loved ones when we were so far from our own.

As I thought of family at home, I wasn't maudlin or sad but was enjoying recalling them to the front of my consciousness. I then experienced something odd. Friends and family started to clearly appear to me, one after the other, in quite quick succession. I had no control over this and found it a bit spooky. I didn't want to interrupt it, so just sat, letting it happen. At times I was quite surprised who came into my mind. Workmates appeared, people I had only had fleeting interaction with popped in. It was like a flipchart where every page was an acquaintance. This slightly unsettled me, but the experience wasn't unpleasant.

The sun was setting in gently spectacular fashion. In the half light I walked through the cemetery looking at the monuments and their embellishments. Among the tombs were shrines to young men who had been killed in Afghanistan. A flock of doves was disturbed by my intrusion and flew away from one substantial memorial. I caught sight of a bushy-tailed red fox scurrying away. Many of the tombs included finials with the bleached remains of horse's heads tied to them. Kazakhs love their horses but it was sad to think the horses were slaughtered because the owners had died. Maybe they constituted the funeral feast, or maybe later when they died of natural causes they were reunited. It was a thought-provoking night.

The following four days riding to Almaty were hot and hard as we made our way across the brown, arid plains. We camped out three nights in a row and enjoyed each different campsite. We travelled over some hills through fields of poppies and lavender. We could now see the huge Tian Shan Mountains that separate this region from China. It seemed strange to be crossing such hot plains when the snow-clad peaks weren't far away. Each session out on the plain was a challenge because of the heat and

THE `STANS`

the still bumpy road. The stops were always homely and enjoyable; usually a simple family unit would be running what we'd probably call a truck stop café, often in a settlement of only a few houses. Sometimes there was petrol sold at the café, but often not.

One stop in particular we enjoyed immensely, although it didn't start so well. Having bought some icecreams and drinks, we asked a shopkeeper if we could sit under her shadehouse area. Initially her husband said no, as it wasn't finished. The day was hellishly hot and we were fairly desperate for some shade. Steve went back a few hundred metres for a plunge in a river, but Dick and I didn't have the energy. We probably also thought we weren't due a wash, it being only mid-week! However a little later, we were not only invited to share the shady shelter but were treated to tea and biscuits, fruit and all sorts of special things – this time as honoured guests, not customers. There was a small toddler who seemed to be the centre of everyone's world and the grandfather was in evidence as well. The wife had a small smattering of English that she'd learnt at school but never used, and she did a lot of the shop work while the husband did outside chores. They had a hose going and several people came over and used it while we were there. Interacting with three generations of Kazakh country-folk was quite special. We lingered for a considerable time. We liked these personal experiences far more than any visit to a tourist attraction. We also watched another small family trying to arrange transport out of the village. It was like hitch-hiking but seemingly with more rules on both sides. There would be payment from the hitchers but the driver would need to deliver them as directed, if at all possible. It was a fascinating afternoon and produced a treasured memory of people whose lives so briefly touched ours. It's funny how you can intuitively like and enjoy some people even when it appears you have little in common.

As we closed on Almaty the roads improved. We had a nice overnight stop in a town called Taldy Corgan. The night was balmy, and we wandered about looking at the numerous places selling rotisserie chicken before settling on an outdoor restaurant where we had kebabs and beer. A beautiful but drunk Russian girl tried to tell us her life story. She removed her dark glasses to reveal a gruesome black eye. Despite her intrusion, the night was relaxed and slow. Even though we'd been on the road for quite a while, we still enjoyed each other's company and nights like this were special.

Dick has lived a full and varied life. He's a natural raconteur with a lurid turn of phrase. People in Dick's tales "fart like a draft horse" or are "as pissed as a pelican". His bike doesn't have lots of torque. No, it "pulls like a schoolboy". Most of his descriptive gems are far more suited to a campfire with a beer in hand than publication. I've heard many of his tales before but, as they are told differently each time, it doesn't matter. Steve quite obviously enjoyed listening to outrageous stories about outrageous people. These adventures are often from the years when Dick was a professional hunter, or from his early motorcycle racing days. They aren't the tales of a blowhard, it's just that interesting things happen to interesting people (which is probably what makes them interesting in the first place).

The night back at the hotel was less than relaxing as people in the room next door were having an all-night party. It was hot so we had our door to the balcony open, but so did they. At times I was sure the frivolity was just at the foot of my bed. Still, it's not a lot to complain about, is it, the occasional loud party? It was hardly going to affect the rest of my life and my sleeping champions were sleeping as though their lives depended on it; or maybe it was the beer. The last morning on this leg of the journey took us across the usual hot plain, with the heat haze obscuring the hills. At one café and rest stop I saw a small kid shooed away from what I thought was a paint pot. But no, this was whitewash. When I looked in the pot it was boiling like a witch's brew. Talk about hubble, bubble, boil and trouble. This was one scary looking pot. Dick then recalled from his childhood in

Holland that a girl from the village had died or had limbs amputated after falling in some fresh whitewash. Adding quicklime to any moisture creates intense heat. I have since read about it and it must never be made in a plastic bucket – the heat is such that the bucket will melt.

A welcome respite before the final stretch across to Almaty was at an oasis of green among a few small hills. From there you could see a straight line of tarmac going off to infinity across a shimmering, flat expanse. All travellers stopped here for a refreshment break and most plunged various bits of clothing and anatomy into a stream running from a standpipe. Just above this was an outside brazier where two women and a man constantly cooked kebabs. Above this again was a café with a long verandah where we sought refuge for an extended break. Our tall and elegant waitress bore an amazing resemblance to the striking Bernice Mene, a recent New Zealand netball captain. Behind us was a table of four women, two of whom were in military uniform. One was clearly a Russian, the remaining three had the darker skin of the Kazakh people. We watched them eat their way through an enormous array of food. The helpings were massive and they seemed to have double ordered most things. They kept on talking and laughing and eating until it was all done. We didn't do badly ourselves with the generous lamb kebabs or shishlaks, as they are known in this part of the world.

Suitably replete and rested we went back out into the heat for the last leg across to Almaty. It was hot and hard, as usual. We passed a horrendous car crash at one point, which shook us all a bit. The cars had hit each other head on. One was a modern Mercedes Benz and it had suffered, as you would expect, from a front-on impact, being shortened and with doors open and airbags exploded. Further down the road was an older unrecognisable Russian car, possibly a Volga or a Moskovich, on its roof where it had cartwheeled over the top of the Merc. It was so badly squashed that we presumed there would have been lives lost. We'd seen amazingly bad driving everywhere we travelled but this was the first accident we'd actually come upon.

Shortly afterwards we stopped and rested among some trees and thought about the crash, each of us knowing how much luck you need on these roads to stay alive. I always laugh at home when someone pontificates about how New Zealand drivers are "the worst in the world". Have they ever travelled? Certainly not in the Third World, Latin America, China, or Mongolia. Russian roulette is played on the roads here, or is it Kazakh roulette? Drivers were just as bad in Russia. If the only opportunity to pass is on a blind corner, then that's when you pass.

About 30 kilometres from Almaty we passed a couple of lads fooling about on a Ural. They soon gave chase and flagged us down for a chat. Alex and Archom were students and they led us into town in a bizarre ride. They would speed up and go past showing off as only the young can. Both of them would shoot their hands in the air. Or they would stand up. The bike was missing and farting but looked quite good. The lads, with a bit of a struggle, managed to find our hotel for us and we chatted for a while. They were working at night as security guards and as university was closed for the holidays, they'd gone into the country to play.

The hotel was a bit flasher than we were used to, even having hot water, but then Almaty was a bit flasher than we were used to. In fact it was bloody smart. There were an inordinate number of up-market European cars in evidence. This wasn't a city full of Ladas, Volgas and Moskovichs. Instead, it had more Mercs, Beemers, Saabs, Porsches and the like than we would ever see back home in New Zealand. This was the first hotel we'd stayed in that had tourists. The strangeness of it made us shyer than usual. We made contact with none of them. The voices we heard were American. I wondered whether that encouraged our silence. There didn't seem to be any travellers in the hotel, just tourists. There's quite a difference and travellers will know what I mean. It was nice however, indulging ourselves with this bit of luxury. We all need pampering occasionally, even those of us naturally attracted to squalor.

Almaty was to be a visa stop. We were scheduled to meet with our local agent from Central Asia Tourism (CAT) who would take us to the Kryg Embassy on Friday morning to help us get an 'express' visa. The visas were normally only processed on a Wednesday, and would take three days. It seemed to be the usual rort, but in these circumstances you have no option but to play their silly games. Rima was middle-aged, elegant and dressed in smart clothes that wouldn't disappoint a well-heeled Euro-madam (this isn't intended to describe her as someone who manages a bordello). Her English was good and she was informative, telling us all about the city as we were driven to the Kyrg Embassy. She was friendly and obviously a tourism veteran. We all felt less warm towards her after she'd vented her spleen a couple of times about the gypsies and beggars we'd noticed. They were all Uzbeks, she proclaimed with unexpected scorn. She had no sympathy for them or their plight. She was good with us though, and managed to get the ambassador to agree to give us a visa on his day off. We just had to pay him a significant amount of money. Rima also arranged for us to have the driver take us across town to the auto market where Dick could seek out a 19-inch tyre for the back of the Norton.

The market was a bit oppressive in the heat but it was fascinating, and we were ultimately successful. Dick had brought a spare rear tyre with him but the original was wearing out. By buying one now we would still have a spare that would fit both bikes. Our bikes both have 19-inch wheels front and back. Whereas Penelope has interchangeable wheels, Dutch Courage uses a slightly narrower front tyre, so it wouldn't be ideal to use the same size tyres front and back. It's only the rear tyre that wears significantly. The fronts should do the distance in one go. My plan had always been to start with two brand new, identical tyres. When the rear one became worn, I'd swap the front one to the back. This should occur about half way and get me all the way on the one set of tyres, touch wood.

In the early evening we had a call from hotel reception to tell us a gentleman wanted to see us. This was Marat Buzubaev, the young director of a motorcycling-based tourism venture. He'd heard about us from CAT and had to come and see for himself. Marat was a Kazakh gem. He was relaxed and congenial, with genuine warmth. He also spoke good English and loved what we were doing. He offered to show us around Almaty the next day and take us up into the mountains. He wanted to do this in admiration of our effort. He wasn't on the take for money. This was so nice and we accepted graciously. Steve then went out into the busy streets of Almaty and experienced the nightlife while Dick and I had a quiet night in.

Almaty is a large city of over a million people. It's no longer the capital; that role has been transferred to Astana, a few thousand kilometres to the west, nearer Europe. Almaty lies in the shadow of imposing mountains that dominate the view and were now in the process of snow-melt. The city slopes gently away from the mountains and the deep gutters lining the inclined streets constantly ran with the results of the spring thaw. It seemed incongruous to be experiencing temperatures in the mid 30s when we were just below an alpine scene which could be from a Swiss postcard. Here we also observed another ethnic progression, with the tall blonde Russians now being in a minority.

The Kazakhs aren't too badly off after a slow start, following the break-up of the Soviet Union. They have oil wealth in the Caspian Sea and they have hopes that the wealth will slowly spread through the rest of their huge country. There's a dispute raging over whether the Caspian Sea should be classified as a lake or an inland sea. It makes a huge difference to those countries that share its shores. If it's a sea, the countries that line the shore each have a distance offshore that can be included in their territorial area. Any who have found oil in this area can claim it as theirs. If it's a lake, the countries lining the lake share its resources. Of course those who haven't found oil want the area to be declared a lake so they can share in the spoils.

In all the 'stans' it was interesting to find that the middle-aged and older people often felt that things had been better under the old Soviet Union. Everyone had jobs, houses, education, social services, and four weeks holiday each year. The younger folk have greater freedoms, like the independence, and of course now there are western goods for sale in the shops, if they could afford them. A result of the loss of the Soviet umbrella was the emergence of overt poverty. The beggars that could be seen in the big cities were something the older folk found scandalous, whereas the young grew up with it. The young we met were often like Marat, hard-working and industrious. Our impressions were coloured by meeting solely those who were doing OK. Those who weren't, we could only observe from afar.

Saturday was particulary pleasant as we weren't under pressure to achieve anything special. I tinkered with Penelope and the other two wandered about before our rendezvous with Marat after lunch. We had a lot of chuckles over the succeeding weeks as we recalled this day because it gave rise to Dick 'doing a runner'. Steve had given Dick a suitable sum of money and told him to go off downstairs to the outside café and bar where we had fed the inner man a couple of times previously. Subsequently, I finished what I'd been doing and joined the group, arriving just after Steve and Marat. Steve got me a coffee, paid for it and popped upstairs for something. We then all went out for an afternoon with Marat. This afternoon was quite a highlight as first we were taken around the city just looking at the sights. We had a walk in a beautiful park. Everywhere we looked, there were brides in stunning white gowns. They all seemed to be being photographed and often there wasn't a groom in sight. This apparently was the norm in the springtime. Every Saturday there are hundreds of weddings and the brides all go to the prominent places for their photos, a bit like we had seen the graduates

doing in Ulaanbaatar. Of course there were the other entrepreneurs who had doves and balloons to release in the spirit of the moment, for a small fee. The park also had enormous Soviet war memorials, almost grotesque in their overbearing presence.

We had a short visit to a spectacular yellow and white Russian Orthodox Church before heading to the skifields above the city. The alpine resorts above Almaty look as though they are part of the Tyrol. We passed over the enormous dam that protects the area below from the mud-slides that had been so destructive in earlier times. At every vantage point on this

scenic drive, brides were being photographed. We probably saw several hundred that day. We also saw a lad with an eagle perched on his shoulder, and his mate who was dressed in a bear costume. If you paid him some money he would put on the bear's head and pose threateningly. Somehow this struck a sour note with us and I agreed with Dick when he said he wouldn't have been sad if a hunter had mistakenly taken him out with his Winchester. Oddly, we weren't so offended by the eagle on a chain.

After a coffee at a resort, high above the plains, Marat took us back to his clubhouse and workshop for the motorbike tours he leads around the Tian Shan Mountains. This embryonic tourist venture had a few recent setbacks as a result of the unrest in neighbouring Kyrgyzstan. Lots of people cancelled their trips because of this and the coming summer was looking a bit grim. Unfortunately the Silk Off-roader's Motoclub, as they are known, hadn't insisted on deposits being paid when the trips were booked. The trips looked to be well organised, with good back-up, and

a range of bikes were supplied to the paying clientele. These were mainly Japanese semi-trail bikes, sourced from Turkey. They also had a trio of old Ural sidecar outfits that were going to be replaced with new ones. Steve was very taken by the thought that for $500 he could get one and have his own transport. Bearing in mind what we'd seen happen with Thomas and Greg's van, we knew we'd have to be sure that the paperwork was sound and export of the vehicle was assured. We simply didn't have time to make all this happen. Marat dropped us back at our hotel late in the afternoon, telling Steve that he might see him later in a nightclub. He also wanted to show us the way out of town, and would escort us on his bike in the morning until we were clear of the city.

Steve decided on a nap before going out and Dick and I ventured out again on our own. This could be a little risky, as we'd already had our moments of 'almost' being lost on several occasions. However we always felt that we'd just been seriously misplaced! It's funny how foreign cities

can have so many similar looking streets. It doesn't help if you don't take much notice while you chat away during the perambulation. Wise travellers always at least note the name of the hotel they're staying in, but no one said we were wise. (Years ago, I remember having a hell of a laugh at the expense of some female flatmates when we met in Munich and I asked where they'd left the Combi. "Einbahn Strasse" (one way street) one read from her carefully transcribed address book.) We felt we were getting better at not getting lost and besides, we knew where we would go for our evening meal.

All was well – we had a pleasant night, dining well and looking at the world going by. This wasn't our world but it was a nice world to look at. Many of the women were stunning-looking and dressed in an almost provocative way. There were lots of bare midriffs, plunging necklines and tight clothes. This was a big city trend we had first seen in Russia and it brightened our days and nights considerably. (Nobody could accuse us of being politically correct or sensitive, new-age guys.)

Dick and I had enjoyed the evening and were reluctant to let it go. Accordingly, we decided to have a beer or two at the café below the hotel, where Dick had eaten at lunchtime and I'd had a coffee. We were just about to leave when a waitress came and asked if we'd eaten there. We said no, but she was fairly insistent that we had, and that Dick owed her for a meal. This woman wasn't our waitress. When ours turned up, she shooed the other one away with some difficulty, telling her that we'd only had beer. It was almost a sour end to the night. It was only next day that we thought to ask Dick if he'd paid for his lunch the day before. You can guess the answer. For some reason Dick thought that Steve had paid for him when he paid for my coffee. We thought this a big joke and made fun of Dick and his tactics of doing a runner to get a free meal. We even introduced a zimmer frame into the tale. How bold was that, returning to the scene of the crime?

Next morning at a reasonable hour, Marat turned up on his bike with his wife Roman on the back. They'd been up all night but would get us well on the way before going home to bed. We were glad to have them as guides as Almaty was challenging to ride in. The traffic was aggressive and determined. It was with some sadness that we farewelled them once we were well out of town. The day was alternately hot, then cold and occasionally drizzly. We hadn't yet had any serious rain on our trip. We'd had snow twice and we'd been on the edge of a thunderstorm, but no significant rain. The most significant things about the day were the long detours, and roadworks that lasted for 10 or 20 kilometres at a time, making the going hard and tiring. We also had a minor delay when Penelope stopped dramatically at the side of the road.

One minute we were purring along on a smooth piece of road, the next there was silence, just the rustling of the chain whizzing around and the tyres humming on the tarseal. There had been no missing and coughing as a precursor. A couple of minutes' examination determined the fault to be a stripped thread, which the lower of the points screwed into. This could potentially stop us dead, as my magneto spares didn't include this piece. Fortunately, my spare lower points' assembly was longer than the old one. With fresh thread it screwed to the right place and was able to be locked in place with the lock nut, without it slipping. It seemed a little dodgy, but there was no alternative. This stop was intriguing in another way. We'd coasted to a stop about 10 metres from where a farm worker was doing something fairly inconsequential. He totally ignored us. This amused us but actually disappointed us a little too.

This little delay plus the detours meant that the day was nearly over when we finally rode into Bishkek. There was no big road leading into the city, or if there was, we missed it. Consequently, it was a slow ride in, twisting and turning through minor streets. We flagged down a taxi once we got to the city centre, and Steve went as a fare-paying passenger while we followed along to our hotel. It was a well-appointed tourist lodge with a pool. Bishkek turned out to be a visually similar city to Almaty, but a tad smaller. It too was overshadowed by the enormous snow-clad mountains, but it seemed a little duller somehow. It was like Almaty's slightly less stunning but still-beautiful sister.

Bishkek was another place where we had to get bloody visas. Here we had to get the second Chinese one, another rushed 'express' process, again taking three days. The embassy had moved out to the edge of town and the driver we had hired spent a hell of long time trying to find it. It seemed that none of the locals knew where it was either. We finally got there right at noon (closing time) but just managed to get the applications in place, even though Steve didn't have the passport photos required. Of course, once they had our passports we couldn't get the Uzbekistan visa, so we had to wait and enjoy the city.

We discovered a great eatery called Fat Boys that also had a lending library. We indulged in some western food with chips, and loved it. Later Steve and I revelled in the delights of the guesthouse swimming pool. Dick is a committed non-swimmer and he filled in the time in other ways. In the pool we met a Frenchman who was going home the next day. When I asked him about going "back to work" he laughed and said "No, back to holidays". He'd been doing a scouting job for the travel company where he worked as a guide. They'd been considering doing guided trips through the mountains of Kyrgyzstan so he'd spent a few weeks checking it all out. Now that he'd finished his work, he'd go home for a holiday.

Because of the delays in Beijing and at the Russian border and in Bishkek, we were struggling to catch up to our schedule. We weren't going to be able meet with the Silkriders in Tashkent after all. They were already there. We'd also received an email from Murray of Silk Road Adventures warning us that we now couldn't ride our bikes into Tashkent. The government had passed an ordinance banning them because of the likelihood they'd be used as terrorist vehicles. The Silkriders had to have their six bikes trucked

into the city and later they paid the police to escort them out. It was time for some serious, detailed revision of our plans. For us to get to Europe in time for Willy's birthday on the 24th of July we needed to be a week quicker than my agreed itinerary. We were falling behind, not gaining on this. We were tired but OK, the bikes were tired but OK.

There was no way that I could see of gaining time on the route. We had the added complication that our entry back into China had to be through the northern Torugat Pass not the more southern Erkistam Pass we had originally chosen. This meant additional backtracking and more days. We needed to more or less come all the way back to Bishkek before heading across to China. After poring over the maps and some lateral thinking, I decided that we should leave the bikes in Bishkek, fly to Tashkent, take a train down to Samarkand, and omit the leg out to Bukhara. We'd then retrace our steps back to the bikes and head inland to the Chinese border.

One of our biggest problems was having hotels and services booked ahead of us. We needed to rearrange these to fit with our ever-changing schedule. Our type of travel shouldn't be rigidly constrained. Sometimes we went faster and sometimes we went slower. Sometimes we wanted a rest and sometimes we didn't want to linger. We needed flexibility and that was something that couldn't easily be provided. The revised plans were agreed to and we set about trying to make it all happen. At least flying to Tashkent wasn't going to be expensive. Steve and Dick could both get discounts by being either a student or a geriatric. They would pay around $80 and I would pay $100. This was a good deal, and would catch us up a day or two. It would also save us the frustration of two border crossings.

We did nothing special in Bishkek and enjoyed doing it. Like Barnaul and Almaty before it, it was a nice place to observe the beauty of nature, or the nature of beauty. The propensity towards obesity, now prevalent in our western culture, is yet to show itself here. We wouldn't see fat, waddling, plain people until we were back in Europe. (Those who have seen me in the flesh will know that there is plenty to see. I'm not dismissing or denying my corpulence, I'm just observing others.)

The procurement of the necessary visas for China and Uzbekistan meant an extra day in town. Unfortunately our guesthouse was booked out for that additional day. Management agreed that we could leave the bikes and our gear there if we were to return after Samarkand for at least another night. They also arranged for us to transfer to another western tourist-oriented guesthouse. It was clean and friendly but lacked character. After gaining our Chinese visa, we made contact with our CAT's agent and she helped us get the Uzbek one. This was the usual time-consuming trial, but Aiagul was a pretty young thing who made it all quite enjoyable. She told us about the Easter coup d'etat and how it had been a little scary for them, their office being near the big square where the main skirmishes took place. Kyrgyzstan was still in the throes of unrest, with some country areas being deemed a bit lawless. Aiagul also rearranged some of our accommodation up ahead. We were to have CATs as our agents for all three Central Asian 'stans' that we went through.

We had another 'doing a runner' episode when we returned to Fat Boys on our last night in town. Almost immediately a waitress pounced on the Cabin Boy and accused him of not paying the last time he'd been in. She told him where he'd sat and what he'd eaten. Yes, he had come in later and ordered separately. I thought I'd paid for all the meals when Dick and I left together, with Steve staying on to finish reading a magazine. We coughed up and had another good western-style meal. We'd finally become a little sick of the big lamb kebabs that we usually indulged ourselves with. These were often eaten at outdoor facilities and were always washed down with delicious and ample amounts of beer. We considered the accompanying tomatoes and raw onions our veggie intake. Our supporters at home may

have had images of us dining every night on rice and gruel but the reality had been far from this, with us eating well and keeping well.

The last day in Bishkek was occupied with the trivial. We sent emails to our families. I emailed Rollo in England to get him to send some rear suspension bolts ahead of us to Pakistan. Under the outrageous load now being carried by Penelope, the rear shock bolts were showing signs of bending. This had happened to her in South America and we really should have re-engineered to eliminate the potential problem. I also wanted to send a CD to Rollo with some of the trip photos on it. I'd tried the local DHL office but had blanched at the $64 asking price. This meant a visit to the main post office – an amusing if frustrating experience. Although there was only one family in front of me sending one parcel, the posting of my little CD was to take the staff of three, one-and-a-half hours. Each process was sooo slow. The goods weren't packaged by the sender but by the post office worker, who made a box and then a calico bag to suit. This was sewn behind the counter on a treadle sewing machine. The top seam was then hand stitched. Then there was an elaborate hot wax sealing of that last seam. I've done car trimming and upholstery work in my day and I was impressed at how well the calico bags were finished. There was a further delay during my turn, as the tiny young girl attending to my needs spilled the hot pot of wax on her arm. She barely flinched, but was obviously debilitated by the accident and needed help in carrying out the remaining steps of getting my parcel finished. During this time the boys were waiting patiently, then impatiently, outside, wondering what on earth I was doing that could take so long. Finally, all was accomplished and we had a peaceful night in the new guesthouse.

As we waited in the airport at Bishkek the next day, we looked at the substantial gathering of menacing looking American military airplanes. The United States uses this as a base for missions to Afghanistan. It always triggers a shiver when I see the sinister-looking weapons of the air. It's not just American planes that have this effect, the planes of all air forces look equally sinister and frightening. Perhaps it's their colours, or just my imagination running wild. However, there was nothing frightening about Uzbekistan Airways, and the flight down the edge of the Tian Shan mountain range was awe-inspiring.

Our first task on arrival in Tashkent was to fight off all the would-be taxi drivers who wanted to take us to town. Steve had them sussed; he'd read the all-important Lonely Planet Guide and we were alert to their double-the-price requests. We soon chose a driver (even if we had to walk quite a distance from the terminal to get to his car). These freelance non-taxi drivers were often very aggressive in their marketing, with many people finding it hard to say no to them. This one wasn't too bad and quickly found the Pakistan Embassy, something that we would struggle to do in the future.

Our main reason for coming to Tashkent was to obtain a Pakistan visa. But it was Thursday, and of course visas are issued on Wednesdays. There was a roadside window in the side of the embassy building where the punters were dealt with, or more accurately, dealt to. When someone finally came to the window we were told about the Wednesday visa issue but then he relented, and said we should come back Friday, or maybe Monday. We tried to cajole the guy further, telling him that we were going to Samarkand tomorrow and we needed the visa today. He then said to come back after 2.30 in the afternoon. This was good news. We set off with another driver to find our agents. This proved quite a task, and included three telephone conversations with them at different places along the way. By going everywhere they weren't, we finally found them. They were warm and welcoming and had changed our bookings to suit our current plans.

All day, we struggled to get anywhere or make any progress. It was a problem finding the one bank that would exchange money for us and it was a problem finding our way back to the Pakistan Embassy. The city seemed huge. It was bigger than Almaty and Bishkek added together, having a population of about two-and-a-half million. Most of the taxis we flagged down were just men hopeful of making a buck or two taking us places. We always negotiated the rate first. We would have been having a good time if it hadn't been for the day slipping away from us. We didn't get back to the hole-in-the-wall window until about 3.30 (which we would have thought was after 2.30) but the ambassador had gone and we couldn't get a visa. It was hot, and we were irritable and quite pissed off. This was not our best afternoon. The fact that the city has changed the street names in recent times to reflect the move away from the Soviet yoke only added to the confusion of trying to find anywhere.

There were more gypsies and beggars in Tashkent than elsewhere and the city appears to be a little poorer than Almaty, or even Bishkek. There was water flowing in the streets and fountains everywhere. The young seemed to be frolicking in every pool we saw. It's still a major capital, with attendant levels of sophistication and lots of flat bellied, hipster-wearing beauties.

Our hotel for the night wasn't two star as originally booked, but a four-star tourist trap. This had us well out of our comfort zone. We didn't have the nice clothes or appearance of the tourists who were staying and we felt uneasy. Our appearance by this stage was one star. I went for a long walk on my own in the early evening, enjoying the warmth and watching the locals going about their daily rituals. Later still, Steve and I ventured forth again and obtained tickets from the railway station for our trip down to Samarkand. We opted for the luxury of first class. It was air-conditioned and cost the princely sum of $10 each for the six-hour journey. We had a beer on the way back to the hotel and judged our sortie to be a success. There would be no drama next day, we knew where the trains left from and we had tickets.

The train was modern and we had a nice cabin to ourselves. We were waited on by pleasant attendants who brought us meals and drinks. It was relaxing and stress-free, watching the countryside roll past. It was also interesting to watch the digital signboard in the corridor that showed the speed, temperature and time. When we boarded at 7.30 in the morning, it was already showing 36 degrees. Soon we were loping along, often at about 115 kph. By the time we reached Samarkand it showed 21 degrees inside and 42 degrees outside. This meant a wall of fire-like heat when we stepped forth from the train.

Immediately, we could feel the difference in the people as well. There were now almost no pale Russians in evidence. They were all swarthy and often quite stocky. Samarkand has a new part to it but the reason travellers come here is to experience the old part, the historic key part of the old Silk Road which linked this corner of the world with the traders of Europe.

Our guesthouse was a haven from the bustling city. Another Marat came into our lives here as our interpreter. Silk Road Adventures had booked us someone for one-and-a- half days and CATs had given us Marat, who was young, slim, of medium height and by background an Osettian from the Ukraine area, a couple of thousand kilometres away. He spoke Russian and was also fluent in Uzbek. He was a local, even though he didn't look like one. He had none of the Central Asian features or olive skin. Nor did he have Slavic features and he could have passed for a German, a Frenchman or any European. His knowledge of the city was great and he was friendly and skilled at his job.

He set some ground rules about how we were to listen to him and then he took us out to visit antiquities. What a fabulous afternoon. The jewels of Samarkand are many, varied and breathtaking. There are a lot of historical buildings that date from the time of Christ and beyond (remembering that Alexander the Great proclaimed it the most beautiful place three centuries earlier). However, it's the time around Tamerlane (or Timur as he's called locally) that was the most productive and enduring. Mr Timur was a tyrant in the Jingis Khan mould (Jingis Khan had wrecked the city in 1220). Timur roamed far and wide, subjugating peoples everywhere he went, up to Russia, right down into India and across to the Mediterranean. Thought to be responsible for 17 million deaths, he brought back literature and treasures of all sorts. He assembled numerous architects and artists to make this the capital of his empire and magnificent monuments in the way of mosques, madrassahs, minarets and palaces were built in the golden period of the early 1400s.

Every place Marat took us to was magnificent. This is a style of architecture I find stunning. As a former construction site manager I always try to envisage the construction and its difficulties. The shapes are complex and the scale huge. These structures would be difficult to build even today. The thought of doing it without a tower-crane taxes my imagination. The architects even used optical illusions to compensate for the eye's willingness to distort shapes as they get further away. Grand entrances tilt slightly to make them look bigger. The engineering challenges are staggering. The colours are striking, with blues and greens being dominant. The cladding is often glazed tiles and the numbers of tiles per structure must be in the hundreds of thousands. The quantity surveyors must have had to be on their toes when measuring and pricing these behemoths.

There is also the remains of Mr T's grandson's observatory, dating from 1437. In that year Ulugh Beg compiled his atlas of over a thousand stars and calculated the length of the year to within a minute of what we know it to be. His star chart survives in Istanbul, but the remainder of his work is lost. Only part of the large sextant's running track is evident today. Typical of the brutality of the day, Ulugh Beg was beheaded by some dervishes and his observatory was torn down.

We marvelled at all of the antiquities we saw. It didn't matter that many had been restored in more recent times. We admired a door that was 900 hundred years old and still using the same pivots. There were heaps of mausoleums and the like being restored. We wandered among the construction areas and I talked with one worker to get his 'favourite tool and favourite tip' for the 'Blokes on the job' section of a publication I'm involved with. I liked that his tip was to "always be respectful". Although he was working with steel, his favourite tools were timber hand tools.

The town was hot and our stamina would only enable us to do a half-day at a time. We released Marat after the second half-day. He'd been great and we'd learnt a lot. After lunch, feeling all touristed out, we went to a nearby café for a snack and a beer. While still adjusting to the lack of light in the dim room, we noticed a patron taking an excited interest in us. To our surprise and joy it was Thomas, the French doctor. We'd thought that he and Greg would be all but in France by now. Our meeting was boisterous and affectionate. Sadly, Greg had succumbed to a bout of sciatica and the

THE 'STANS'

THE LAST HURRAH

THE `STANS`

big fella had been repatriated to France, courtesy of their travel insurance policy. We had a wonderful afternoon catching up and learning of the dramas surrounding the impounding of the UAZ and the selling of the ger. We also went out that night and imbibed enthusiastically at a local brewing establishment. We dragged along a French girl who was working at our guesthouse. She seemed unhappy and under-occupied at work – an exchange of some sort.

The warmth of the night had nothing to do with the temperature. Easy companionship made for a lively time that included a lot of laughs, some as a result of Thomas uttering the immortal words, "Where are the bimbos?" We knew exactly what he meant. Suddenly the women weren't wearing tight and revealing clothing. No longer could we clearly determine that the young lovelies weren't wearing grandma's bloomers. The handsome women now were wearing ankle-length winceyette nighties (like Steph would wear in the winter, when my hairy pelt wasn't there to keep her from the cold). They were colourful and varied but oh, so demure.

The local market we went to on our last morning was colourful. Every

type of produce was for sale. There were also carpets, clothes, spices, paints, toiletries, tools, ropes, and meat – almost anything you could imagine. Dick bought a snappy pair of lightweight trousers for $4. (He bought a similar but nicer pair later in Holland for $120.) One odd sight that made us smile was in a big busy area where watermelons were sold. Despite the cacophony enveloping us, fast asleep in the middle, in proper beds, were a man and woman. They looked so peaceful in a world of chaos.

After seeing all there was to see at the market, we hired a driver and went out to the village of Hoja Ismail. It was quite different from Samarkand in that the predominant colours of the ancient structures were green and ivory. There were beautiful domes and minarets and it was far away from any tourists. A local wedding was taking place so there were a lot of people adorned in splendid finery. It was a good couple of hours where we also interacted with some of the religious teachers, one of whom spoke a little English.

Our guesthouse was a quiet and shady haven from the searing temperatures thrown at us. There was a courtyard with a small pool and

lots of lounging areas under verandahs. There were bed-like structures with tapestries to lie about on and forms to sit on. It was charming. A bus group came and went during our stay but there was never intrusion from these fellow travellers. We'd see a few at breakfast and might see a few more at night. They were Brits nearing the end of their travels. They weren't quite exhausted but they were certainly looking forward to getting home. Mainly middle-aged, they were friendly but group-orientated.

One morning I breakfasted alongside two couples who were your genuine jolly-hockeysticks English toffs. They were immaculate in tailored safari suits in subtle fawn colours with all the pockets ironed flat. They looked so amazingly crisp, without all the usual travellers' bulges of money belts and spare hats, sunscreen bottles, drink bottles, cameras, or guidebooks. I suspected they were big-noters from the British Embassy. This suspicion was reinforced when the luxury Toyota Landcruiser with the intriguing flying saucer construction on the roof and constantly winking red lights, that had been parked outside, disappeared when they left.

All too soon it was time to leave Samarkand and head back to Tashkent to get the Pakistan visa. It been enjoyable and was undeniably the visual highlight to date. We were all quite happy to be going back to Tashkent by train. It's such a relaxed and easy way to travel. You can read, you can sleep, you can even look out the window; all while someone else is magically whisking you closer to your destination. Someone else will come along and give you food to eat and fluids to drink. On our return journey we had to share our cabin, but that was entertaining and enlightening for us.

I'd noticed Alton at the guesthouse, a wiry man with swarthy good looks, possibly in his forties, who spoke good English. He impressed me as being one of those adventurers whose lives are scarcely believable, yet check out completely. Alton had worked with the Americans in Afghanistan and the Russians in Turkmenistan, Uzbekistan, and Tajikistan. He was a local 'fix-it' man, someone who made things happen for others. He had spent time in deserts, was familiar with guns, yet he professed to not liking them. There was no menace to him, but you did get the sense of extreme capability. He was accompanied by an immense young Russian lad. Vlad was only 16 but his size and shape belied that. He had huge powerful arms and hands. Alton had taken Vlad to Samarkand where they'd buried Vlad's father. He'd died a few days earlier in the mountains of Afghanistan, after his jeep rolled into an abyss. Alton was a family friend and had known Vlad since childhood. It was a sad scenario. Completing our cosy little caboose-full was Ruth, a sturdy middle-aged German woman who was teaching in Samarkand and who was going off home for a couple of weeks' holiday. She spoke Russian and English so could interact all round. The six-hour train trip sped by with much to talk about and share.

We knew we'd be arriving near midnight and had no accommodation booked. Our trusty Lonely Planet Guide advised that there was a crappy hotel more or less at the railway station, and it was right. Hotel Locomotive proved to be extremely grotty, with no running water. We took some jugs of water up to our room but the night was pretty forgettable (except for Steve perhaps, who spent quite a bit of it vomiting, but that's OK mama, he was hardly sick anywhere else).

We were back at the Pakistan Embassy as early as we thought fit, waiting for the right people to arrive. We tried to be charming each time someone spoke with us, even though this was becoming harder the longer we waited around. Finally, we were ushered in to as near to the inner sanctum as we were going to get. We filled out forms and chatted with the underling who was dealing with us. It's fascinating dealing with men from the subcontinent. You can use cricket as an opener, but it can be embarrassing; they always know more about your own cricket team than you do. We talked cricket and wished them well for the forthcoming games with England. They were looking forward to those immensely. It was bad luck for us that the ambassador was very busy, but they would do their best to get our applications processed. We were left to look through the brochures and maps available. We also read their side of the Kashmir conflict, which was very damning of India.

After an eternity we had documentation to enable us to proceed. We then rushed from the building leaving Elvis behind, and grabbed a cab to the airport. We hadn't booked a flight back to Bishkek because of all the uncertainties with timing but we knew there was one at 1.45 p.m. We explained our needs to the driver and sped to the airport, where we rushed around like headless chooks trying to get through security and find the booking counter. The driver had picked up on a possible opportunity. He was sort of helping us, but maybe not.

We got to the right place but they refused to process us, as they didn't think there was time. It was an international flight and although there was still 15 minutes before take-off, they were resolute. This left us stuck in Tashkent. There wasn't a flight the next day and there are no trains anymore. Normally this wouldn't have been a problem, and probably a pleasant interlude would result. Our concern was that it was already Monday, and we had to meet our Chinese guide at the Kyrgyzstan border on Friday, before it closed for the weekend. We really needed to be riding out of Bishkek on Tuesday to make that rendezvous happen.

The only option seemed to be to hire drivers to take us back to Bishkek. Our previous driver had hung around, and he took us the 50 kilometres to the Kazakhstan border. We were there by 3 o'clock but we felt he ripped us off for the fare, despite our negotiations. Luckily we had double entry visas for Kazakhstan, or we would really have been stuck. It was 650 kilometres across to the Kyrg border and we negotiated with one of the wide-boys who'd come across to the Uzbek side to get the early worm. He helped us through the border process and although it was obvious he was only an agent, we were OK with the price we agreed on. The car and driver both seemed satisfactory. This was one hell of a long taxi ride. The road was sealed and we made extremely good time even though there were huge potholes and bumps. The speeds were high but it was reasonably comfortable (although not for me, for reasons that will become apparent later). We had a break for a meal in a small roadside café not long before it got dark. The driver had family connections there and it was a pleasant interlude. Later I wandered among the old car wrecks watching small tame rabbits hop about the place, and some small kids came over to watch me watching the rabbits. With some jovial backslapping, we took our leave from the proprietor's family and some other diners who we think were also related but were going the other way.

Because the road was largely straight and there weren't many towns to delay us, we pulled in to the border area at midnight – 650 kilometres had taken us eight hours. The border was a forlorn sort of place in the early hours as we went through the usual painful process of gaining admittance. Even so, it only took us an hour-and-a-bit to get across and find someone to drive us the remaining 100 kilometres or so. This driver was a bit flaky and his car suited him. It had to be push-started as the battery wasn't being charged by the alternator, but the fare was cheap enough. His problems weren't our problems. We crept into Bishkek at 3 a.m., 12 hours after leaving Tashkent airport. We were fairly knackered, but back on track. A few hours' sleep would revive us and we should be on the road to China before lunch. Arranging to meet at nine for breakfast, we fell into our respective beds. I drifted off with a great deal of trepidation, fingers crossed for a miracle.

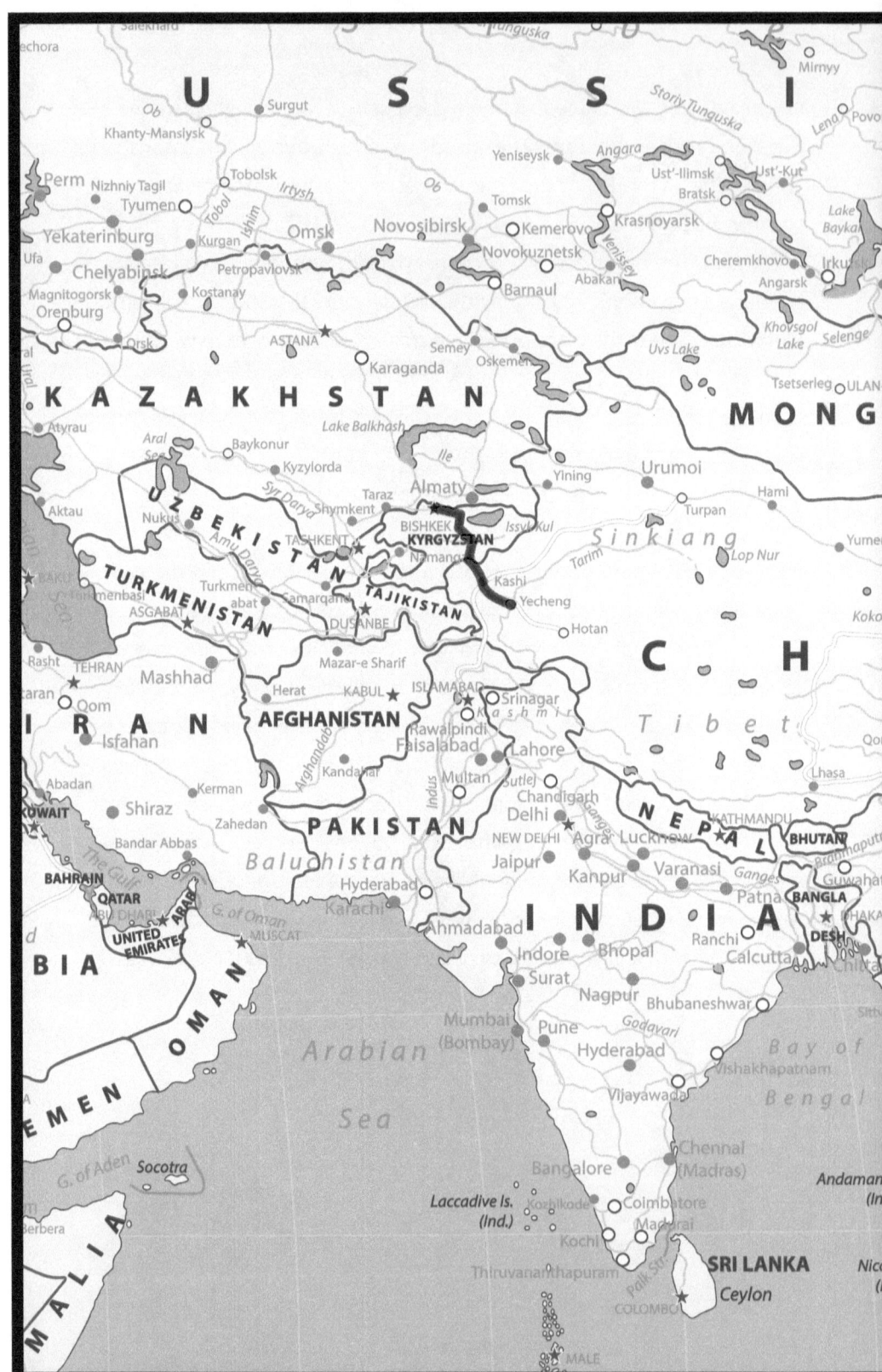

CHAPTER 6

BUMMED OUT IN BISHKEK, CRUELLY CURED IN KASHGAR

For the three days since last seeing Dr Thomas I'd been experiencing a burgeoning medical need. My timing had been unfortunate, as the symptoms didn't manifest themselves fully until after we'd said goodbye to our medical Samaritan. On our last night in Samarkand, snuggling down into my usual semi-foetal position for slumber, one hand under the pillow and the other between my thighs, I noticed something was not as before. Between my two 'ums' (beginning with r and s are the clues) was a lump. Mmmm, I thought, I hope that goes away in the night. The morning brought the realisation that it hadn't. All our medical kit was back in Bishkek. I had hoped my good health would overwhelm any infection. Sadly, this wasn't the case and the subterranean lump grew like Topsy. It wasn't a boil or a pimple; it was a deeply rooted lump that seemed to be enlarging by the hour. By the second day there was some discomfort and when we were racing across the plains of Kazakhstan in the taxi, I was hanging on by the skin of my teeth. I even slept, after willing it to go away. I was clinging to the hope that once we made it back to our medical kit and the antibiotics it contained, all would be well.

But all was far from well. Later Dick and Steve were to remark that they should have picked that something was wrong; they'd never seen me asleep before. Both had noted it as unusual. Back in Bishkek I confessed that I had a problem (the growth was now impressive) and that I needed drugs. We had several antibiotics, so selected the one that sounded the strongest; I took supplementary painkillers and tried the bike for size.

I reckoned I could tough it out on one cheek until the good guys started beating the bad guys. I needed a lie down after this to prepare myself. Steve asked if I would see a doctor. He'd found out where to go and felt it might be wise to show what antibiotics we were using and ensure they were the best for the job. Leaving Dick ready and champing at the bit and the bikes loaded, we went to a medical centre. The middle-aged woman doctor and a male medical interpreter, after nodding heartily when they saw the drugs we had, then took a look at the affected area and immediately referred us to the proctology department of the national hospital near by. They didn't think that antibiotics would win the war that was going on down there.

Finding the proctology department wasn't too hard and we made our way upstairs in a slightly run-down facility that reminded me of our own fading Wellington public hospital. We found a common room filled with laughing and chatting medical personnel. The language barrier made this initial approach difficult but we managed to find an intern who spoke a little English. She was short and vivacious, with flashing eyes and a beguiling smile. She explained that Steve would have to buy rubber gloves before anyone would look at me. I was a little apprehensive that they didn't have their own gloves, but on the other hand I was relieved that they wanted gloves. Of course this confused the hell out of us, but delightful wee thing that she was, she took Steve off downstairs to the chemist within the hospital. This meant that at least someone would look at my problem, although I didn't really want to show it to anyone. It was an awkward spot to 'air'. You can imagine the gymnastics involved. I didn't see any of the medical staff drawing straws, but it wasn't long before I was in a room being examined by a senior-looking man wearing a white uniform and a funny hat.

The prognosis was that the antibiotics didn't have a show. I would need immediate surgery and seven days in hospital recovering. This wasn't acceptable. We had to be at the Chinese border on Friday. It was already Tuesday. After a bit of discussion they offered plan B – immediate surgery then two days for recovery. We refused that too and reached a compromise. They would operate immediately and Steve would take over my care under their instruction. But for this to happen, they would have to do the deal outside the hospital system because the proper care that they were charged with giving would involve the seven days recuperation. They would do the job as a 'perky', a bloody PJ, a private job! All the responsibility would be ours because, in effect, we hadn't been there.

A smallish amount of money was handed over and a team of medical personnel was assembled. The young intern reached up and put her hand on my shoulder and said, "Don't worry". She paused for a second then repeated it before breaking into the song, "Don't worry ... be happy, don't worry ... be happy ... doooo dooo do dooo". She and her smiling mate broke into a swaying dance in the corridor, bringing much-needed levity to the situation. I don't know what I was scared of most, the operation or the now almost constant showing of my probably less-than-attractive nether regions to any stranger who showed any interest.

One of my worries also concerned the area of expertise of these medicos. I worried about the medical pecking order. Presumably, the best surgeons got the brain surgery and, possibly as a result of their skills, escaped to America or Europe. Probably you also had to be pretty good to get the open-heart role. I could even see that doing your bit cosmetically for vain women with lots of money would attract some. Augmenting, altering and generally playing with women's breasts might attract some of the brightest go-getters. But the dark, shady parts that the proctologists inhabit couldn't be described as glamorous. You couldn't show off your clientele or work on television. It's not an alluring spot and the working conditions can't be appealing. I worried that all these people might be the Med School dropouts; the ones banished forever to the arsehole of mankind (or in my case, nearby) because the other parts were beyond their level of achievement.

When the team assembled, I was pulled into an unnatural position and trussed up so I couldn't move. This was necessary because of the placement of the problem. It was in an area that faced down, and you can't expect the surgeon to crouch down and work overhand. The equipment involved pulleys and wires and total humiliation. I was mortified. Talk about being out of your comfort zone! Young flashing-eyes told me that it was OK as they were all medical people there, as though this would reassure me in some way. I couldn't see what they were doing and wouldn't have wanted to, but ultimately the deed was done (the team was like something out of the television programme ER). Steve was given a box of drugs and syringes and various instructions. The instruction they emphasised most strongly, chilled me in an unimaginable way, making the hairs on the back of my neck rise. "No paper!" This was like being told I had a terminal disease. My immediate thoughts were, "What do you mean, no paper, there is no alternative!" In our western world there is no other way to complete one's toileting. The thought of the consequences made me tremble. We over use the words culture shock, but I believe at that moment I was indeed suffering from it. Maybe most of the world doesn't use paper, but I do. I won't disturb you further, but I'll understand when you come up to me and wordlessly pat me on the shoulder in support.

I rested back in the ward, delighted to have a visit from most of the team players before they went off duty. Flashing-eyes was even more stunning in her leopard-skin miniskirt. The older anaesthetist was also a fine looking woman, about six feet tall with the light tan of most Kyrg people. She was another Bernice Mene lookalike, or had I had too many drugs? I was released at about 4.30 p.m. Steve had postponed our leaving of the accommodation by a day. We could still leave Wednesday morning and make the border on Friday ... just. Three full-on days were needed.

That night Steve braced himself to go places where no man should go, and pulled off the dressing. Expecting a neatly sutured wound to clean, he didn't gasp in shock. He coolly commented that he needed a second opinion and went for Nurse Huurdeman. They stood at my lesser end and didn't say much, just that it wasn't what they'd expected. I didn't like the sound of that and kept repeating, "What do you mean, what do you mean?"

They'd been presented with what looked like an abandoned sex-change operation. There was an open 'pocket' filled with wadding. They didn't know what to do, but Steve cleaned me and with a lot of difficulty (and a few painkillers) I made it through the night. We all rose early on Wednesday morning. I wasn't comfortable (to say the least) and at this stage I still had no idea what was down there, as my attendants hadn't seen fit to inform me of the gory details. Steve removed two lots of wadding, with me whimpering like a dog. It seemed like he was pulling a slowly unfolding scarf out from deep inside me, twice. Because of our absolute bewilderment and lack of medical knowledge and confidence, we went back to the hospital. Initially we could only find flashing-eyes' smiley mate, who didn't speak any English. Lots of amusing drawings of my bum and its treatment followed. It would have been funny if you weren't there and it wasn't your bum.

There was a little confusion over whether Steve would have to try and repack the scarves back into the wound each day. I blanched at this and a senior man was brought into it, agreeing that this couldn't be done. I was to be cleaned and dressed a couple of times a day and I was to have a nightly soak in a salt bath. We farewelled all our new friends, including flashing-eyes who had now turned up, and headed off to face the next challenge. It had been quite an experience. We'd walked in off the street and organised a same-day-service operation that cost only a small amount of money. We doubted we could have managed this in many places around the world. Of course now I couldn't get on a bike.

We scoured the town and found a plastic bum-sized bowl for my salt baths, a few pairs of jockeys to hold everything together, some sanitary pads, a driver and a 4 x 4 van. By 1.30 p.m. we were ready to roll for China. Bloody hell, that sounds impressive, even writing about it months later.

I later posted a dispatch on the web page which Kitty and Hannah said contained "too much information, Dad".

... In many ways my bum has dominated our travels since. What I've been left with has been described as a 'kebab pita-bread pocket'. It has also been suggested that I use it for smuggling gold watches or even for keeping our passports safe. We don't know how it's going to close up. This concerns me a little as having the genitals of both sexes might be a drawcard at a freak show, but I'm not that much of an exhibitionist ...

With me awkwardly resting sideways in the van, we headed for the hills, literally. The travelling was great for the others, with interesting countryside as they climbed into the eastern hills of the Kyrg Republic. We stayed in the small village of Koskor in a community-based tourist venture where you stay in a local's house. It was great. A bonus was having the 19-year-old daughter home from university. Ermek spoke quite good English and she made our night even more delightful by being able to explain things to us in her charming, almost coy way. In the morning she posed arm in arm with Stephen for a photo. He hummed "here comes the bride" under his breath as she did so. She, her mum and her sister were all lovely and we would have liked to stay longer.

A 10,000 foot pass was easily traversed. I had all the gear with me in the van so the boys flew along unhampered. We were on the way to Naryn to stay in the wonderfully named Celestial Mountains Homestay. En route we had a break at a little settlement high in the hills and drank fermented horse's milk. I remember getting grumpy as Steve put Penelope on the side stand. Even from afar I could see that the angle was precarious. She toppled over in slow motion and broke her headlight. Steve had been enjoying her and dutifully praised her and her ways, even though it was evident that his true love was Dick's Dutch Courage. I remained chatting down at the small settlement and filmed the boys riding off into the distance, up an impressive hill and over the top, out of sight. I was unaware that at the top, enjoying the view, was a bus-load of Dutch tourists heading the same way as us. Soon Dick was chatting ninety to the dozen in his native tongue. By the time I arrived they all seemed conversant with my problems, including their location! They were a jolly group and the boys had had fun telling tales. They were preparing to leave and as the last

of their group headed back to the bus she said something like, "Good luck, I know what it is like to have a sick traveller, I am the nurse that looks after this lot". Almost immediately I was running after her. No, let's be realistic. I waddled after her like a lame duck. But desperation lent speed to my leaden heels. I intercepted her just before the front door and quizzed her about my newly constructed secret smugglers' pocket. Phew! She knew of the operation and the recuperative process needed. It should be kept open so it could heal from the bottom and it would slowly close up, she assured me. This seemed fairly improbable, but she seemed to know what she was talking about so I was relieved. I was still sore, but a lot happier.

The last day involved an early start if we were to reach the border around lunchtime. This meant getting to and crossing the 12,000-foot-high Torugat Pass. As you can imagine, if the pass is at 12,000 feet then the mountains overlooking it will be a lot higher. The ride towards and into these towering mountains was possibly the most striking of the trip to date. The last 50 kilometres to this milestone ranked with the worst roads of our journey. My driver called it the "Road from Hell". This knocked me around a bit. Recovery from surgery is best done horizontally in hospital attended by sweet-smelling nurses, not bouncing up and down on your wound on a bumpy road. Up ahead I could often see the boys taking big hits. I felt for them a little, but I was mostly wallowing in self-pity. I was sore and miserable. The bland facts show that we met our programme and passed into China on Friday 25th. Our driver had done a great job, managing to be cheerful most of the time even though the last section was so hard on man and machine. Of course he had to drive back over the same awful route.

The border was near the top of the Torugat Pass, where the Dutch contingent was also waiting. Our driver wouldn't go quite to the delineating line. Neither would our Chinese guide's driver bring his van up to it. This meant the vans were probably nearly 100 metres apart. All the gear had to be carried in armfuls from one to the other. For some reason Dick seemed unaware of this and remained animatedly talking to one of the Dutchmen, back-on to the task. This irritated me as I struggled to and fro, puffing away in the rarefied air. At one stage I went over and waited while the conversation came to an end. The Dutch guy asked if I understood Dutch. I felt sure that Dick had said, "Well, he understands fuck off". I turned on my heel at their laughter, livid at what I saw as a dismissal. I finished helping Steve and our new guide with the loads, still fuming. We said goodbye to our driver, who was going to attempt to drive back to Bishkek more or less non-stop after one sleep. Dick was oblivious to all of this, still engrossed in his native-tongued interaction.

The Chinese half of the border crossing was a bit of a scrum which took a while to get through, and we were pleased to have a rest and a meal and beer before the final burst to take us through to Kashgar. This was only a few hours away, but it seemed a hell of a long way when I was sore and grumpy, stewing over my mate's insensitivity. I'm not a normally moody person or one to hold a grudge, but I sustained my anger for the rest of the afternoon. At the hotel I let fly, and regretted it immediately. Dick told me my hearing had been incorrect. He'd said something quite different. I sensed then that he was about to respond, probably to rip shit out of me and my inadequacies. He then big-heartedly bit his lip, I believe in deference to my condition. I walked away, admiring his holding back on this occasion as it hasn't always been his nature to do so. He has been known to 'bite off his nose to spite his face'. His passing up the opportunity to give me a serve enhanced my admiration for him, and saved us both from a moment we might have regretted.

The day that had started early had ended 12 hours later with the boys absolutely knackered, but euphoric. They'd done a magnificent ride. They were dirty-faced and in need of a prolonged rest. It had been a hard couple of weeks with constantly changing plans and challenges but it had been a fantastic time that we wouldn't have missed, except for the last bit in my case.

Our hotel was once the British Embassy. It still had a grandiose entry with fountains and a circular driveway. It looked flash, but appearances were deceptive. Like Wang, our guide Joseph was young, spoke good English and had an intimate knowledge of the area. He was good fun and always organised. The driver complemented him.

Kashgar is in the far west of China and is an Uiygur stronghold. These Muslem folk make up a large percentage of the population and use their own written language, which came from Arabia 1,000 years ago. Signs always show both scripts. Eighty percent of the townsfolk are involved in handcrafts. Joseph took us to see some ancient mosques and to the quaintly named and slightly mysterious 'All Dancing Fruit Garden'. We have

no idea what it was for but the name alone is worth a mention. Later we explored the old Uiygur part of town on our own. It was as exotic and interesting as anywhere in Central Asia. The narrow streets were lined with tiny stalls selling wares from the workshops, which often backed onto them. It seemed odd knowing that we were in China (according to a map), yet there wasn't a Chinese face to be seen. An attractive young adolescent girl hawker tried to sell us locally made knives. She demonstrated their solid construction, five rivets, blah, blah, blah, by bashing them hard as anything on the ground. They were impressively decorated but we didn't need any more knives. I had my Victorinox Swiss Army knife and Dick had his trusty Mercator. We were looking forward to the famous Sunday market and

we'd timed our visit to correspond with it.

Both animal and handcraft markets were amazing. Joseph took us out to the animal market where all sorts of stock are traded. This was another place where there wasn't a Chinese face to be seen, the traders and buyers all seem to be Uiygur or from the neighbouring Tajik region. The big-bummed sheep intrigued us. These sheep have what looks like a woolly human's buttocks grafted on the back half of a reasonably normal looking sheep. This isn't just a fatty flap, it's a fair-dinkum pair of laniferous cheeks. Upon seeing a photo of these most unusual ovines, a friend decided that they had probably been created for lonely Aussie drovers. We also saw some big sheep (not the endangered huge Marco Polo sheep though) and unusual looking goats. We watched a massive donkey or mule being shod. It was tied up to a couple of poles and two hooves were shod at once. I suppose it's hard to kick anyone when two of your four legs are already tied up in the air. Dick refused a cut-throat razor shave. It would be a brave non-Muslim who asked a Muslim to shave him while the Coalition of the Stupid were still forcing democracy on Iraq with armed soldiers in Hummers. The temptation to do something for Allah might become too

THE LAST HURRAH

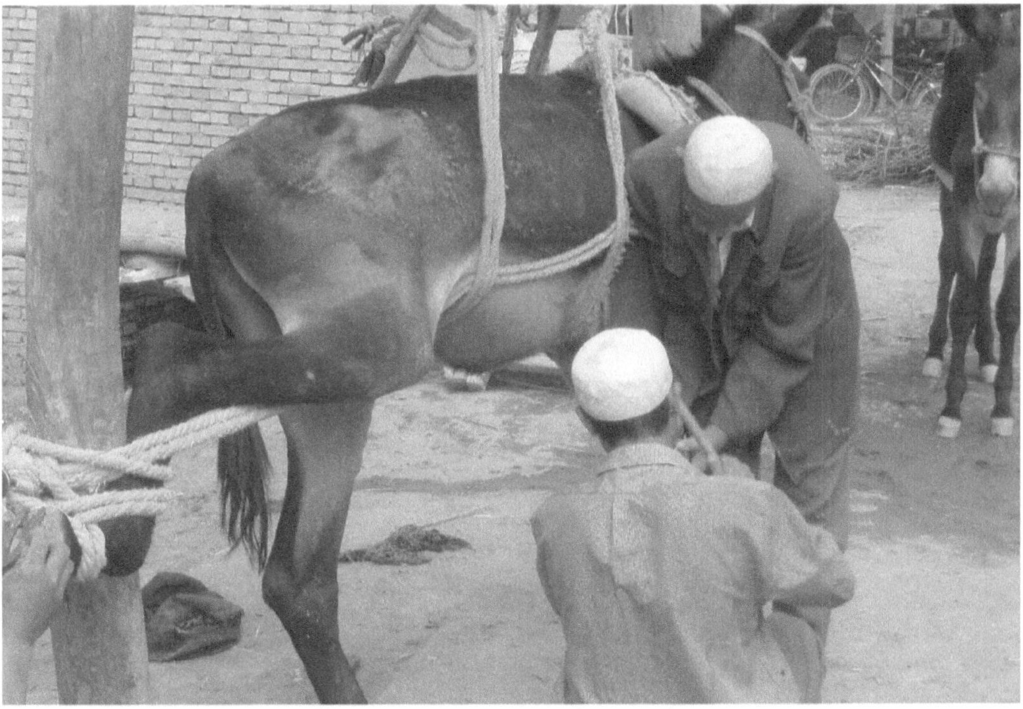

BUMMED OUT IN BISHKEK, CRUELLY CURED IN KASHGAR

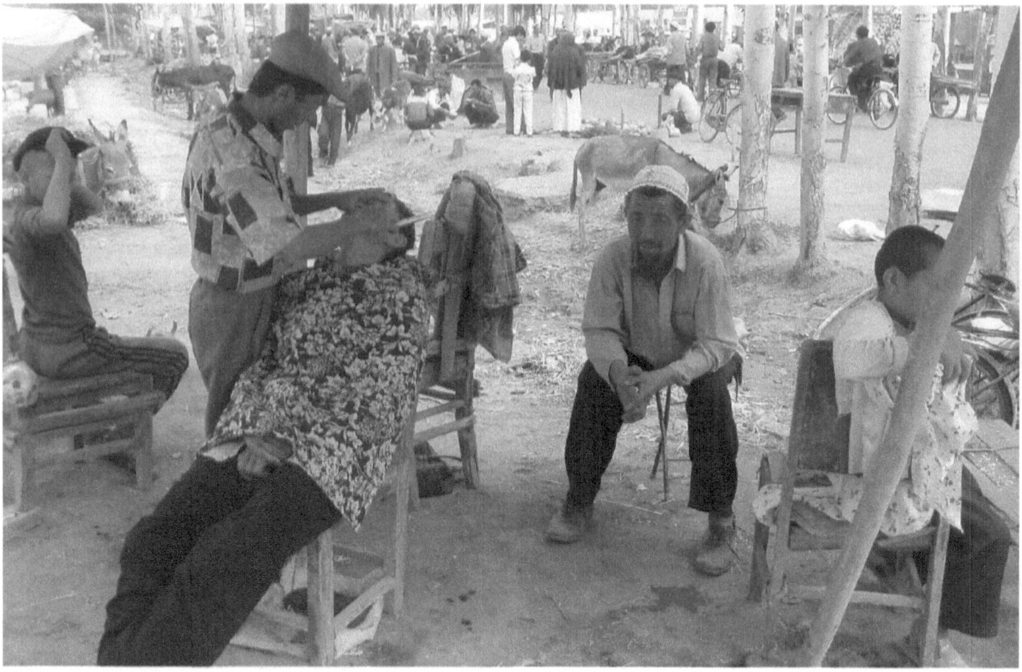

THE LAST HURRAH

overwhelming once the infidel was in the chair.

The market was full of exotic-looking people, and the colour, smells, and noise were all fascinating. This was the real deal. We saw the young knife-selling girl again but now she was selling beads, just as enthusiastically. I bought a few to reward her persistence and general endeavour. We also spent an hour or more wandering through the covered market in the town itself. Dick tried on a fur hat. Animal skins of all sorts are for sale and mostly you can see why. They're often soft and warm, able to be made into useful garments or just used for adornment. What we couldn't comprehend was a stack of hedgehog skins on a skewer, like a crazy kebab of some sort. Was this some wierd flagellation device or an advanced sackcloth and ashes sort of thing? Maybe you stitched the prickly skins into a suitable garment, and when you had impure thoughts you slipped it on to help with the penitence. Maybe it was something to wear to toughen up, to be suited to the harsh life of this part of the world. We never did find out.

Talking about harsh life, Steve was magnificent; doing things twice a day that he must have found repugnant (I know I did). We'd promised

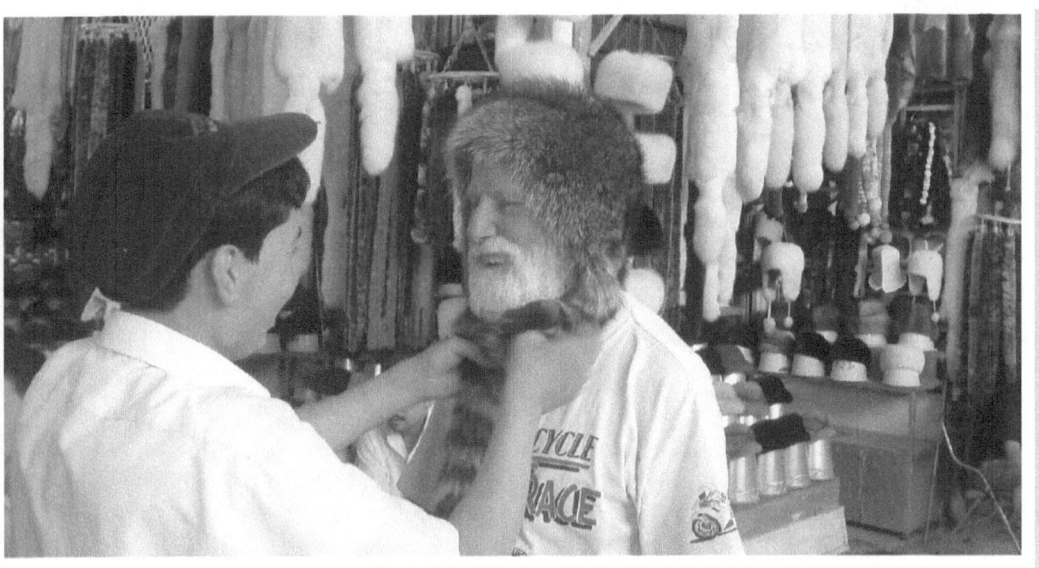

the Proctors in Bishkek that I would go to a hospital as soon as we reached China. So in the afternoon, we went to the First Hospital, boldly stepped up to reception and tried to explain our situation. Confusion reigned for some time, then an older guy with a little English took us in hand. He wasn't even an employee of the hospital. His wife worked there so we went to see her first. She laughed and sent us away. It was obviously the wrong part of anatomy for her and her offsider, but we had a few giggles. We went to another part of the hospital, but the older doctor was leaving on his motor scooter and didn't want to see us either. Finally, the equivalent of an Accident and Emergency doctor had a look and I was sent off upstairs. All the time our new friend was escorting and explaining for us.

We finally arrived at their version of the proctology department (if the gruesome photos on the wall were any indicator). A couple of young doctors with white coats and rubber gloves then went to work on me. Nobody had told me it would hurt. I don't know if they both worked away at the other end, I was too busy clenching my teeth and trying not to scream. Steve hugged me tight. I know it was warm, but perspiration flowed from my every pore. Steve then filmed discretely, asking me if I had any tips for travellers. My agonised response was the old favourite of being nice to your mother and not telling any lies. Steve and our civilian friend then had a jocular interplay.

God, the men in white coats were brutal. Their bedside manner was nil. No patting me and saying it will all be over soon, no pain relief, no assurances at all, just silence while they plunged into the abyss up to their elbows. Lucky they had long gloves on. They seemed to scrape and clean for an interminable time before I was released, completely drained mentally and physically. They prescribed more painkillers and we bade our guide a fond farewell, then I tottered outside for a drink. I felt my progress had been set right back to square one. It was five days after the original operation and now I felt miserable and sore, unlikely to be riding in 36 hours time. What to do? I had to stay close to my nurse so I couldn't take the easy option of flying to Islamabad. Where Steve went, I went. To think that only a few days ago I didn't even know what a proctology department was. Now I was a regular customer. I may have promised to go and see another one in Pakistan, but it's all a bit of a blur.

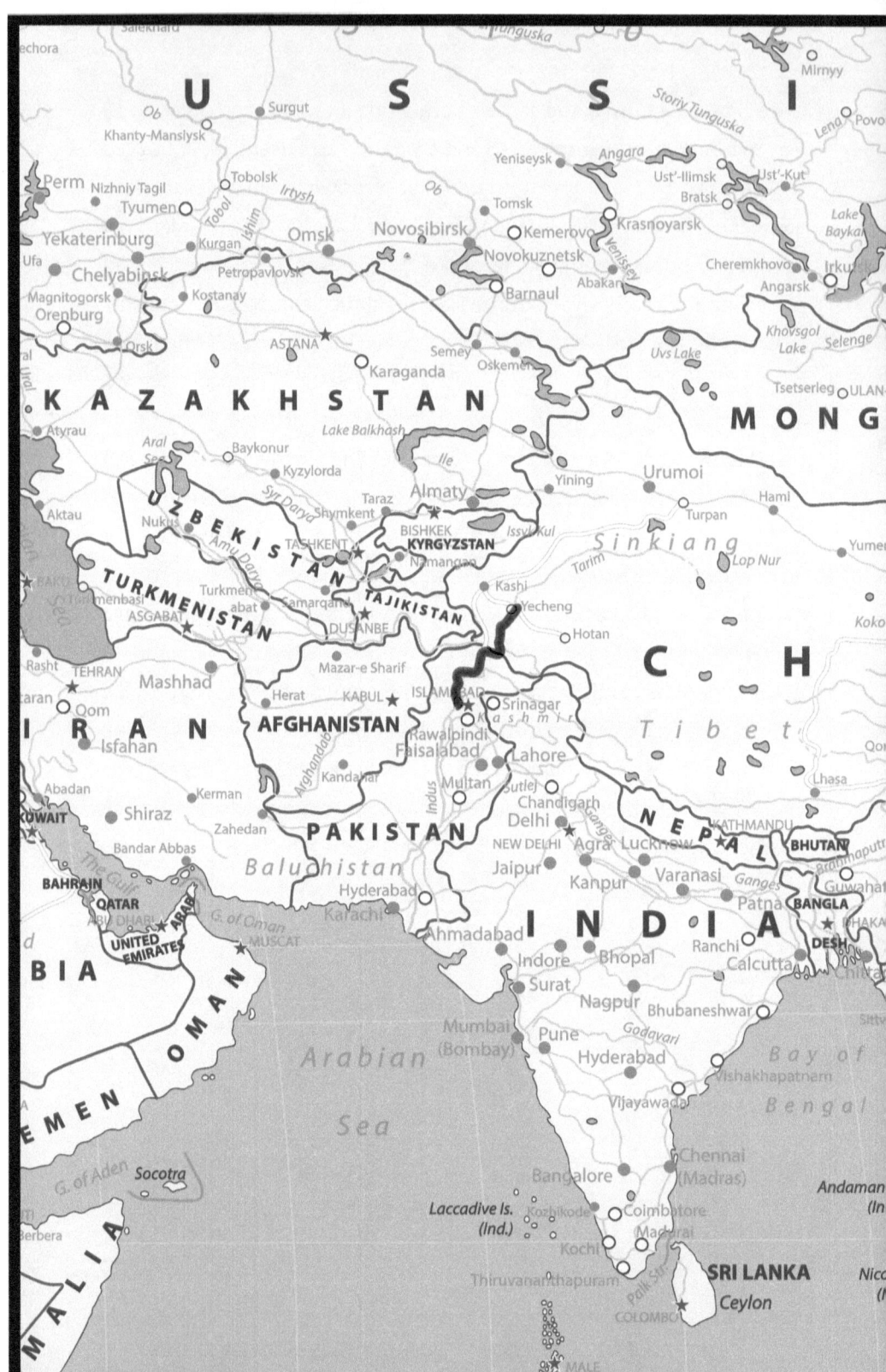

CHAPTER 7

KKH TRIUMPH

Late on Sunday we had our last look around the Chinese part of Kashgar. It was just like Beijing with many of the young wearing outrageous fashions. There was a Chinese sports car being promoted at a shopping precinct. It was called a Geeley and was smartish without being notable in any way other than its name. We'd had a short respite and generally our batteries were recharged. I was still sore, but mentally prepared for the push on to the Karakoram Highway (KKH). The Dutch contingent was heading home and one of the women donated me her leftover incontinence pads. She'd been badly struck with diarrhoea at one stage earlier in their travels. Now she was fine and almost home, so she wanted me to have them. They were the best that I tried during my time of being trussed up, which lasted nearly all the way to Europe.

It seemed unnecessary to have a guide for our time in this part of China. Although we'd used Joseph in Kashgar to take us about the place, our ride through the country consisted only of the half-day from the Kyrgyzstan border and the day upon which we were about to embark. We'd do a big ride on Monday and then on Tuesday morning he'd help us through the border processes. That would be it. It seemed crazy and wasteful as Joseph was based quite a distance away in Urumchi. But I suppose we should have been grateful to be doing something that many others have tried but failed at.

The distance to Taxkorgan was about the maximum that we could ride

comfortably in a day. Joseph warned us that although there was some good road, there were also some bad sections and heaps of roadworks. The urban areas around Kashgar and the settlements we started passing through were fairly chaotic. Drivers all used their horns to warn people of their presence. Penelope's horn, which we hadn't used for a while, sulked and went on the blink. Despite Penelope being her own audible warning device, Steve felt he needed to further warn others of his presence and rode through the busy streets blowing enthusiastically on a whistle.

On reflection, it's hard to take in the enormity of all we saw in one day. The sky was a murky grey-white colour, just like Beijing, but now we were told that it was dust pollution from the surrounding deserts. It looked like an early morning mist that would burn off, but it didn't. The first part of the road wasn't exceptional. We passed through some villages and bypassed others. The roadworks were massive; typical of programmes that are taking place all over China. Late in the morning we encountered the new, good bit of the road. It was fantastic. The road surface was the equal

of the best in the world, the traffic was light and the scenery sublime. We were climbing through hills on a winding road, giving Dick and Steve the opportunity to fully enjoy the freedom and beauty that two-wheeling is all about. Motorcycling can make you feel like you're dancing when the road snakes ahead of you and you're constantly flicking the bike from side to side. I think the French have a description of it, something like 'piff paff'. If I'm wrong about that, too bad. For years I've 'piff paffed' through the flip-flops of a winding road and I'm not going to stop now. I knew the boys would be loving it. Even in the van it was inspirational. At one stage we encountered an amazing Swiss couple who were on their honeymoon and had been cycling for a year! Later, when we fully realised where they'd come from, our admiration grew. They would have taken at least three days to ride between Taxkorgan and Kashgar. I've done a bit of cycling and it's hard work, mentally, physically and organisationally.

Surprisingly, by the beginning of the afternoon I was feeling a little better, despite my earlier comments about the Chinese doctors. Their work was

THE LAST HURRAH

assisted by my liberal and regular quaffing of painkillers. At one of the breaks I agreed to have a crack at riding the bike, as there wouldn't really be a choice when Joseph left us. Gently sitting on one cheek, I found it tolerable physically and tremendously stimulating on a cerebral level. I fair raced along. At some point I caught up to Dick, whose eyes widened in surprise when he saw who was riding. His joy was obvious – I was back! At late-lunchtime, Dutch Courage punctured and some time was lost while we made a repair. This was no huge drama, but Dick did comment that it was lucky it was the back tyre, as the front one on his bike was a pig to work on. This is unusual, as most front wheels are the easy ones, the back being dirty and obscured by drivechains and brake drums.

Our beautiful alpine road was too good to last. Soon we were back to rough unmade roads with detours and creek crossings – the normal obstacles. At the larger, more formal sections of roadworks there was usually a signboard with an instruction in English to accompany the arrows pointing in the direction the road-users were to take. We fell about laughing when we found the arrows pointing to the right whereas the sign said "Go left". That would've put us in the river. My posterior was taking the hits OK although I suspected things might be a little messy, as I was still oozing at the best of times. I was about to call it quits when we stopped for an afternoon tea break and rest.

It was now hot and Dick was pretty buggered. He'd been riding all day and the rough sections had taken it out of him. Steve was quite keen to get back out on Dutch Courage so they swapped. Apart from my sensitive end, I should have been reasonably fresh. I wasn't, but I wasn't going to let on. Not far from that stop, we came to a wide river crossing that looked challenging but achievable. It proved so. The video footage shows me away in the distance having to get off and push, with the submerged silencer blowing the exhaust out in a plume of water as I keep Penelope revving, rear wheel spinning. The one thing that old British bikes like ours don't like is water. If the water gets too high it will get to the ignition points and the bike will stop. Our preparation for river crossings involved a quick spray with WD40 water repellent before venturing in. Steve plunged in quite a bit faster than I did and luckily, apart from a bigger, riskier wake, the result was the same. Both bikes made it through OK but the van encountered troubles and needed work done on it midstream.

Since Steve and I could do little to help, we pushed on ahead, climbing through some rugged terrain. We rested atop a big promontory near a checkpoint delineating an autonomous Tajik region. Here we could see almost for ever down the wide, pale brown valley. We talked happily in the afternoon sun, well rugged up against the altitude-induced cold. We held the camera at arm's length and took photos of us together – a couple of dirty-faced scruffs but nice father-son portraits all the same.

The van was delayed more than half an hour, but then we were all together again, facing more river crossings. The snow-melt of the late spring meant the rivers rose quickly during the day but could also fall quickly in the evening once the sun went down. We reached one river with a

KKH TRIUMPH

small truck stuck in its middle. It seemed that although this was blocking everyone else from having a go at crossing, the occupants wouldn't pay to be towed out. It looked unlikely we could get across safely so we were forced to negotiate for a lift in a large 4 x 4 ute. The truck in the middle was towed off-centre a bit so it was out of the way, although still in the river, then the van was towed across with one bike in the tray of the ute. At one stage the van was swept a little sideways and we were glad to have wimped out and chosen the paid assistance. Although it was a time-consuming process and physically demanding, eventually our little convoy of three vehicles ended up on the right side of the river. There were a few others who were waiting for the water level to drop. That might take one hour or four hours. We had to get on to Taxkorgan and inside, as we'd been climbing all day and were getting up towards 10,000 feet.

Some hard riding followed. Both Steve and I were pushing the old girls as fast as we could safely manage. Actually that's a little exaggeration and safely probably isn't really an accurate description. Nearing dark, the driver took us on a short cut involving a newly made but as yet unused road. This sped things up and we fair raced along the good surfaces. In our experience so far, many such short cuts were fraught with danger but somehow we managed to get off the new, back on to the old. On finally cutting between some imposing craggy bluffs, we came upon an almost hidden town. We were shagged out and hungry. It was cold as well as dark and the altitude was having a significant effect on us for the first time. We felt weak and were puffing noticeably. It was a blow to learn the town was without water, as the mains or pumps had failed. Fortunately we got fed, and we went to bed slightly apprehensive about the next day. We would be leaving China, and our aim was to beat the buses and trucks by being at border control when they opened at 8 a.m.

You know the story of the best laid plans, and I'm sure you remember the mice and men bit. Yep, after breakfast we started to transfer the surplus gear from Joseph's van onto the bikes and Dick spotted the dreaded flat tyre on Dutch Courage's front wheel – the one he'd said was a nightmare to change. He was right of course. It seems to be the one flaw in Dick's home-built front end with its two brake drums. The reassembly needs the patience of Job and a lot of manual dexterity. On this morning, neither was present. An interested throng gathered around. This made Dick nervous and angry, especially when they picked things up. Worse was the assistance that they tried to give when it was obvious things weren't going well. Being at an altitude of over 10,000 feet also meant we weren't functioning as well or as quickly as usual. Dick was having some trouble with his eyesight as his close-up glasses were scuffed and worn. It was some time before we were able to get things to fit and get back on the road out to the customs post.

By then the yard was filled with buses and trucks heading over to Pakistan. The numbers going through each day aren't great but the no-man's-land is close to 200 kilometres long. Once in that zone you aren't allowed to stop and the going is hard, so any traffic tends to pass through customs as early as possible. The Pakistani buses had enormous loads stacked up on their roof racks. There were a few western travellers who seemed a little fraught. Everyone seemed to be shouting and demanding things, usually all at once. We had to carry all our gear through the processes demanded, then load up the bikes again. It doesn't sound much now, but at the time it was quite debilitating as we huffed and puffed with the lack of oxygen. We always seemed to be on the edge of having a headache. It was a relief to finally get through and under way, after saying goodbye to Joseph and giving back our second set of Chinese number plates.

Now it was just the three of us again. We were a good trio and preferred being on our own, in control of decisions about how far we needed to go and how fast. The bikes had been performing relentlessly well. Penelope had a few peripheral items (including toolboxes) fracture their mounting brackets, but the actual engines and transmissions had been performing flawlessly. We hadn't even done the tappet clearances on either bike. Everything sounded OK and they always started on command, so Dick saw no reason to touch them. We were damn proud of them.

The no-stop area is a bit like a no-go area in reverse. There had been big signs in English: we must not stop, we must not pick up anything, we must not deposit anything ... I think there were 10 'must nots' on the list. We were quite happy to follow these instructions because we were keen to get over into Pakistan. The actual border was at the top of the Khunjerab Pass but the Pakistani border town of Sust was another 72 kilometres on. This was going to be the day that I fulfilled the dream from 1981. We were going to ride the Karakorum Highway. We weren't going to do the whole 800 kilometres in one day, but today we would cross the highest road in the world. We were going to climb another 6,000 feet. Our excitement was somewhat tempered with trepidation, as we were already very aware of the altitude.

The Chinese are building many bits of new road so from time to time we rode on nice new sections. They usually hadn't been sealed but they had been formed up with sub-grade so often were smooth to ride on. But the rest of the time we were zigzagging along the rough tracks, slowly climbing towards more fabulous snowy peaks. There were numerous streams and rivers to cross. The riding was quite challenging. Early on Dick put his bike into a bank with a little more vigour than he would like so he swapped with Steve and rode behind me as pillion.

In the late morning we came to a braided river. We spent a long time going upstream and downstream checking it out, and found several routes that would take us almost all the way across. Always however, there was one section that looked a bit too deep and a bit too fast flowing. It was tempting. Steve and I had half a mind to have a crack at it. But knowing that Dick had crossed more rivers than we'd had hot dinners, I gave him the casting vote. He wasn't keen, so we decided to stay put. There was no one else around, although there were signs of the telegraph men having a tent camp nearby. It was a long time before any vehicles appeared and they came from the opposite side.

Into the river went a jeep Cherokee. Almost immediately we were glad we hadn't attempted the crossing. It was indeed deep, and the jeep quickly got stuck. After a bit of backing and forwarding the driver got it going forward, only to get stuck again. The water would have been inside the cab by this stage. After a bit of playing around, he cranked the truck along using the starter motor to slowly turn the wheels. This was quite impressive and we were surprised to see it succeed. It was a heavy vehicle to crank out of a rocky riverbed. A 4 x 4 Toyota went in next, and soon found a deep hole to bury itself in. They tried loading the back with people but it didn't look as though they would get out under their own steam. Getting across this river was becoming a major production, and one that would be dictated by the snow-melt. It seemed we'd have to wait until a big truck came along, even though our bikes are not easy things to load into big trucks.

As so often on our trip, however, the good Samaritan eventually arrived; this time in the form of a monster front-end loader. It had been doing some road construction about 10 kilometres away. It soon had the Toyota out of the river, graded the riverbed a bit for other vehicles, scooped us up in the front bucket, one bike at a time, and waddled across the watery divide with bike and rider held high and dry. Phew! We'd been a little depressed about the river crossings. The previous day had caused us problems and today we'd come to a halt for a while. We'd all watched the Long Way Round DVD and knew that the rivers in spring had also stopped Ewan McGregor and Charlie Boorman, who required big six-wheel drive army trucks to get them across rivers in Russia. What if this were only the first of many such rivers? Luckily, there were some English-speaking students among the folk coming the other way who could assure us this was the

THE LAST HURRAH

biggest river they'd encountered. They were also pleased to learn from us that it was also the largest we'd met. This enabled all of us to face the road ahead with some confidence.

It's always a great feeling when the going is tough, but you are even tougher. There's a tangible sense of satisfaction. After all the off-road riding we'd done, first across Mongolia, then in Kyrgyzstan and China, there was now a synergy between bike and rider that enabled great feats. We were as one, and tricky stuff was just tricky stuff. It was useful having the spare rider as a pillion. On numerous occasions Dick would walk through streams to see how deep they were, and often push us through when needed. The third person wasn't just a spare part. I especially liked getting a little pat from Dick after a challenging bit, with the accompanying shout of "Good riding!" This from someone of Dick's experience made me feel as good as an All Black when he scores a try.

All afternoon we climbed through the brown, grassless landscape, creeping ever closer to our goal. The late start and the couple of hours delay at the river meant the day might end up also being half a night, but there was no option but to keep riding. The bikes were performing remarkably well, despite the altitude. Mid-afternoon I paused and asked Dick where he'd last seen the Cabin Boy. One of my mirrors showed me some lopsided luggage and the other was filled by Dick's bulk. Neither of us had seen him for some time and, whilst that wasn't unusual, after a quarter of an hour had passed we began to worry a little. Often he stopped to film or to change his iPod tunes. There could be any number of reasons for him to not be in sight. After a long half-hour we turned back, and were soon flagged down by a 4 x 4 with the news that Steve was 20 kilometres behind. Bugger! We wound the old girl up, taking all the challenges thrown at us in our stride. We fair flew along the dusty trail for 45 minutes before we found Steve with a small gathering of shepherds in attendance. He had the back wheel out and had patched the tube, but was making heavy weather of getting it all back together. He'd done well considering his only experience with punctures has been on mountain bikes. A team effort soon saw us heading back up the big wide valley.

I half remembered one particular river as being demanding. As we approached it for the third time I thought, "Shit, that looks deep and it looks swift!" But we'd been through it twice in the last hour and a bit so I put that thought aside. Dick rationalised the same way. Neither of us thought it serious enough to stop and have Dick dismount and investigate. I mean, why would you when you've just been through twice? As we rode in further and further I realised it really was deep and swift and it wasn't going to be easy, or even successful. We finally bogged down in a deep hole and were swept off-balance so our downstream legs were trying to support the loaded bike. The saddlebags obstructed, then pinned, Dick's leg. I couldn't keep Penelope going and neither could I hold her upright. Dick was unable to get off and help me and we slowly lost strength and balance, succumbing to the strong current. Water was flowing over the bike's engine and only the handlebars and some of the tank were above the surface.

The rescue mission took some time. Once Dick and I were upright, and Steve was with us, we needed to get all the luggage off the bike and onto the riverbank before attempting the salvage. This took an age to accomplish. At the high altitude our strength was pitiful and stamina negligible. We pulled Penelope backwards in one-metre bursts. It was only after we got her out that we noticed she was still in gear. Finally we were all ashore, absolutely knackered. There was no alternative but to camp out for the night. I wondered if the authorities would mount a rescue mission when we didn't turn up at the border, but presumed not.

Slowly, over the next hour or so, we dragged the luggage 50 metres away to a slightly smoother camping spot. Penelope was pushed away from the river. Before turning in for the night I removed, drained and dried the magneto, alternator, carburettor and exhaust system before taking out the spark plug and kicking her over as fast as my oxygen-deprived lungs would allow. This pumped out the water she had ingested. It also gave rise to the 'kids know best' episode. Steve was filming and I told him to film the water coming out of the spark plug hole, warning him not to stand too close. Footage shows me lunging on the kick-start lever and a jet of water shooting out, covering him and the camera lens. Later I sprayed WD40 around and we settled for the night. We heated up some of our dehydrated food and although we were struggling for air and strength at the 12,000+ foot altitude, we weren't overly despondent. We were confident that in the morning we'd get Penelope running again. Dick had put a stick in the ground to mark the river's edge and even before we turned in, it showed the level had dropped.

I wasn't convinced that the weather would stay clear all night as there were a few clouds hovering around. Steve and I pitched the larger of the tents and both decided to sleep in it. Dick chose to sleep under the stars and he described it as a very special night – the stars were incredibly clear. He'd seen quite a bit of them during his solitary walk in the crisp early hours of the morning, as he alleviated another bout of cramp. An early check of his stick showed the river was much lower than when it had defeated us. A family of early birds came along in a cart drawn by a donkey. After a fair bit of dithering, they made their way across the watery challenge. This gave us more confidence, but we needed to get away before the snow-melt got going, causing the river to rise again.

Once we had a spark at the magneto it didn't take long for Penelope to speak to us in her usual way. We'd pulled away all the river weed and now she looked her normal self. We happily crossed the river and headed away mid-morning, re-crossing later without drama. The rest of the morning was spent climbing towards the border. Dick was again my passenger. I always felt that he was brave to sit placidly in place whilst I charged at the many

THE LAST HURRAH

KKH TRIUMPH

obstacles that presented themselves. It could be that he was immobilised by fear and he'd suctioned himself to the seat with the reverse-thrust of the sphincter. Either way he was a good pillion.

The road was variable, some of it not much wider than a farm track and the terrain was as extreme. Yet from time to time there were signs of hardy souls living in the hills. At one stage I watched two young men racing away on yaks. Although yaks look bovine, they gallop like equines. In other words, they look like cows but run like horses. When they are small (relatively speaking) they gambol and could easily be mistaken for St Bernard dogs, lolloping away into the distance. We also saw numerous large marmots scurrying away to their holes. Buzzards were wheeling above. It was quite surreal. How much higher could we get? The snow-clad peaks were getting closer and closer and our excitement rose accordingly. After more than 20 years of waiting, I was riding my dream. It was exciting and ethereal, yet the physical side remained hard and demanding. The air had thinned even more and we were struggling to find it pleasant to be there. Even Steve, younger and fitter than us two old buffers, was struggling. More than once he proclaimed that he was stuffed.

At lunchtime we reached the Chinese checkpoint for the final stamping of our passports. The top was within sight. We cooked up some noodles and some more of our back-country de-hy delights. We needed feeding even though eating and breathing is harder at altitude than just breathing. It was only a kilometre or so to the top and, despite the physical drain, we were soon euphoric. We were standing at the top of the world, at over 16,000 feet, on the road I'd so long dreamed of riding one day. Well bloody hell, here I was.

We were puffing away like Thomas the Tank Engine, yet happy to endure this minor debilitation just to be there. A lone Pakistani soldier greeted us in a most friendly and informal way. A Pakistani family was also at the top. They'd driven up for a holiday outing. Their border checkpoint was a couple of hundred metres down, and as they weren't intending to go through to China, they had to leave their car and walk the last bit. They were out of breath too. If anything, they were in a worse state than we were. I reckon we were pretty fit from our two months of riding. Soon they departed, leaving us to our extended photo shoot.

With interest and amusement we read the testimonial to the road builders. It was written in English and had the most flowery and emotive language.

... It was here that the stony wilderness of Khunjerab heard the mellifluous rasp of spades ... suffering the vagaries of freakish weather with a stoic determination. The oxygen-less thin air and blood-curdling winds made even a small exertion a fatiguing experience ...

The two-metre-high signboard told an amazing tale of endeavour. Standing there you could fully imagine the hardships experienced during the construction period from 1966 to 1978.

In some ways it was sad to leave the top of the Karakorum Highway. We'd detoured thousands of kilometres to get there. If we'd just been going to Europe we would have carried on past Samarkand, across Turkmenistan and into Iran and Turkey, etc. We'd always made the semicircle from Beijing to Islamabad our big adventure goal. The race to Europe was an add-on. This meant our adventure was nearly over. It was only 800 kilometres or so down the Karakorum Highway to Pakistan's capital – three or four days' ride. However, we were looking forward to Islamabad as we'd been corresponding with a friend's friend named Haroon. He'd indicated that he could help us with anything we needed. We'd already had Rollo send some suspension bolts to him, although Penelope's hadn't worsened since the initial bending was noticed. Crossing over at the top of the Khunjerab Pass also marked the spot where we had to start riding on the left side of the road again.

Riding down the 72 kilometres to the border-processing town of Sust

THE LAST HURRAH

KKH TRIUMPH

was absolutely amazing. You're probably sick of that expression, but that's what it was. Here we were, cruising downhill on a winding tarsealed road overlooked by some of the world's highest peaks. The river we first followed still had a 300 mm thickness of ice covering a lot of it. Unlike the Chinese side of the pass where we had made our way up an enormous, wide valley, we now had to make our way down a narrow valley with a substantial river below us. We sidled along awe-inspiring mountain faces. The river was boiling with menacing greeny-black water. The hillsides were close and rocky, and snow was never far away. The rivers we'd crossed in China had all been brown and the wide valleys were part of a plateau. We were now coming down off that plateau and it was spectacular. The road twisted and turned, often with switchback loops. We could often see Steve back up the road a bit, filming us as we wound our way down. Unlike most downhills, this one seemed to go on forever. We craned our heads around and around, as we were to do for a few more days yet. We needed 360-degree swivelling necks to do this section of the journey justice. Knowing that in these mountains were snow leopards, ibis and Marco Polo sheep, as well as Al Queda and the Taliban, made it even more thrilling.

The string of mountains appeared impenetrable but there is a gap between the Pamir and Karakorum mountains. Almost constantly I was pointing out scenery that amazed me and almost constantly Dick was tapping me on the shoulder and pointing at something else. We were almost hyperventilating with excitement. This was it, this was our orgasm. It had been sudden and glorious in its oncoming. The grind up through China had offered no inkling of what awaited us as we made our way down the other side. The exhilaration lasted all afternoon. When we stopped at the foot of the steepest part of the pass, we were still fizzing. We were now only 20 or so kilometres from Sust, at a small checkpoint. We rested and were treated to tea by one of the guards. He had a lovely little cottage

KKH TRIUMPH

on site and we sat in the sun there and enjoyed a comfortable interaction with him. His was also a park warden. We were crossing part of a national park which he helped patrol. He told us a little of his life and the wild animals in the hills that he was there to try and protect. Mostly, his role was observing and counting.

A couple more checkpoints were passed before we made it to Sust and the customs building. At the last checkpoint, they wanted to see something in Dick's under-armpit money belt. Dick's way of getting to it was to take off all his upper clothing. This amused everyone. We just hoped it wasn't offensive to the Muslem world we were now entering. The 'stans' had been followers of Allah too but not to the level that Pakistan demands.

Sust looked like a typical small dusty border town. A chilling sight on the way in was a container truck in the river below. A clear warning to keep

focused. The ribbon-like strip of tarseal through the town was bordered by dusty alleys leading down to cafés, and shops selling all sorts of trinkets. It took a while to locate a customs official and get our paperwork processed and we were pleased to settle into the first hotel we found. We were weary from our exciting day and in no mood to go off hunting and bargaining.

It always seemed eerie to change countries and find immediately that things were different. We were fascinated by the trucks. They had the most colourful decorations covering every inch of them, and hundreds of small dangling chains and metals clanged away as they moved. All through the ex-Soviet block the trucks had been blue with a white nose. These were also used in Mongolia.

The only exceptions were military vehicles. Even China seemed to prefer plain blue for her trucks. Maybe it was a communist thing. But in Pakistan the drivers spent considerable amounts of money making their trucks into

wonderful works of art. We quickly noticed that laughing came easily to these folk too.

We were too tired to explore far in Sust. We ventured down town for an evening meal and that was about it. The town only had limited electricity and a few places had generators humming away. What we noticed was the absence of women. We'd only seen one woman and that was at the hotel – a businesswoman had a quick breakfast, then left. There had been hundreds of men lounging around the town, but not one woman. No women were preparing or serving the meals. None were partaking of meals. None seemed to be selling any of the wares in the shops. None were apparent at the hotel we were staying in. We'd come from countries where women have very strong roles in society. This was a huge contrast, and gently amused us for the entire time we were in Pakistan. We mused that they were probably at home getting the men's long shirts immaculately clean, as they nearly always were.

Speaking of which, it has to be said that I'm not a natty dresser. There

doesn't seem to be any clothing in which I look elegant. My body shape means that I always look slovenly, but do I care? The power-egg shape means that if I hold my pants up with a belt, it keeps slipping down and my shirts always come out. For some years now I have used braces to stop this separation. The American film maker Michael Moore and New Zealand's Peter Jackson are my idols, when it comes to being at home with your shape and clothing. I realised in Pakistan that the loose 'poo-catcher' pants and the long overshirt would suit me completely. They're practical and comfortable. This sort of clothing would give me an elegant look with a smooth, even profile, quite different from the current sack of chaff outline (although I'm not sure of the pale colours – I can't see Steph being an invisible-at-home-washing type of wife). I did see mechanics in darker coloured, grease-stained garb, which would be more 'me'. My only worry is what my employers would think if I went native in this way.

On our first day heading for Islamabad down the Karakorum Highway, we passed another few hundred mountains. Pakistan has something like 121 peaks over 22,000 feet and quite a few of the highest in the top 20, K2 being second to Everest. Although the road was mostly good, there were a few sections where it had been recently washed out and the reinstatement wasn't yet complete. One of these was like riding down a small river; challenging, but OK in the end. It was becoming hot and Dick was back where he belonged, on Dutch Courage. We had a small delay when the recent puncture repair failed and had to be re-done.

It was hard not to suffer from 'breathtaking vista overload'. The peaks above were so often close, and the drops below so often spectacular in their dimensions. We didn't make a big distance although we were fairly keen to get to the supposed sophistication of Islamabad. We passed the turn-off to Gilgit, but decided not to venture there in favour of getting a few more kilometres under our belts. Soon after the turn-off, I spied a nice-looking tourist lodge on a bend overlooking the river and the small town of Hunza. I pulled up and consulted the others. The response was overwhelming. We owed it to ourselves to be treated occasionally. It wasn't expensive for one room and it had a wonderful balcony that Steve chose to sleep on. We always try and have a room that accommodates all three of us so we can share the off-field fun and banter. Only occasionally have we had to be separated. The Cabin Boy, as befits his role in life, usually sleeps on the floor at our feet while Dick and I have the beds, an arrangement that Dick and I have no complaints with.

Our stay in Hunza was sublime and Dick was moved to say that he could live there. The night was warm, the food was good, the town was interesting, and watching the day fade away while we sat on a high balcony was a simple experience to be treasured. It was funny for all of us to be exuding such strong feelings of contentment at the same time. We didn't have all our loved ones there but we had each other, and we were sharing something special. Across the river a muezzin started his prayer calling. It could have been annoying, but it wasn't. We would have loved to stay on a few days, but instead chose a slow start. We breakfasted well in the large attached restaurant. The Pakistani breakfasts for tourists are quite English, offering omelettes, toast and the like. We spent a little time with the proprietor's extended family, workers and friends. One was sent up a tree and he threw down cherries to another who held his overshirt out as a catch-all basket. Soon we were feasting on fresh cherries which were delicious.

The next day was a mixed bag. The Karakorum Highway provided some great riding despite the 40+ degree temperatures. We stopped to get apricots off two young lads who were sheltering under the only tree for miles and had another longer stop at a tiny settlement where we ate small meat pie treats and drank cartons of juice. It was the most beautiful spot, but marred by litter. The shopkeepers threw all their rubbish over the bank on the other side of the road. I hate littering with a passion.

KKH TRIUMPH

My obsession sometimes irked Dick, as I would insist on us not adding to local rubbish when the pile was already a mile high and one more bit wouldn't be noticed. He's a strong believer in the adage, 'when in Rome do as the Romans do'. One thing that fascinated us was the tiny tracks across the almost sheer mountain faces. They would be scary to walk across and often you could see where they'd dropped away into the river. We joined the holy Indus River some time during the morning (actually it joined us). We could have followed this river all the way to the sea if we'd wanted to. We lunched in a touristy place set high above the road, up hundreds of steps. From there we could see for miles in several directions, including up to an impressive glacier. A few backpackers and cyclists were about, Lonely Planet guides giving them away. I remember having a dose of the screaming shits shortly after dining and being surprised to find a clean toilet out the back. It also had running water, and even toilet paper! I couldn't resist. Bugger the medics, I'd take my chances.

In the mid-afternoon as we came off the end of a bridge and turned ninety degrees left, Penelope hit a big bump. So what, we'd hit big bumps a thousand times before, but this time something broke. We slewed wildly onto the wrong side of the road, then back, before coming to rest quite gently against a bank. Dick thought I'd dozed off, as from behind he could see no reason for the upset. This was one of the rare places where the road cut through a small gully and there was a bank on the river side. Otherwise we could have plummeted down many hundreds of feet into the river below. Yet again my good luck prevailed. Initially I thought a rear suspension bolt had broken, but it became evident that something was awry at the front end. The front wheel pointed one way and the handlebars the other. A fork leg had to be damaged. This wasn't a good thought. Until we stripped it, we couldn't ascertain what to do. We could see the small town of Jaglog only a few kilometres away. With the bars at a crazy angle and me leaning the other way, we crawled to the outskirts of town.

Dick and I set to work stripping the front end while Steve set off looking for refreshments.

The left fork leg had fractured where it left the lower triple clamp. The fork leg is a steel tube and it had corroded badly on the inside during the period it had been off the road. We should have picked up on it during the final trip preparations, but the forks had been assembled quite a few years earlier and weren't revisited. This was now a major problem. It even took Dick a few minutes to think of a way to repair it. Dick has seen first-hand every type of breakdown known to the motorcycling world, and fixed most of them. If he decides on a plan of attack you know it's well considered.

In my head I'd been running through the triumphant words I was going to send from Islamabad to our adoring public. Now, one day short of success, we seemed to have tripped at the last hurdle. I was also concerned about the time available if we were to get to Holland for Cinderella's party. But something that has been built once, can be built again. We'd be back on the road, even if it meant waiting while we sourced parts. Jaglog isn't a large metropolis and my thoughts immediately turned to getting us to Islamabad. We could stay here and find somewhere to do the repair or we could try and arrange a lift to Islamabad where maybe Haroon could help us. Deciding on the latter option, Steve and I went into town, leaving Dick with Penelope.

Say it quickly and it always seems like it was easy, but after a few false starts we managed to arrange for a van to come and get the bikes and take us overnight to Islamabad. We would catch up a day, vital now that time would have to be spent on the repair. When we got back to the bikes, Dick had made friends with an English-speaking military officer who could arrange for the repair to be done in their local workshop under Dick's guidance. Dick reasoned that the best repair would be to shorten the broken leg by taking out about 35 millimetres and weld it back together. The welded repair would be in the middle of the sturdy triple clamp and the stress-point where the leg leaves the clamp would have new metal present. Although this would make one fork leg longer, they would be stretched to the same length once the wheel went back in. One leg would be compressed a little more than the other, no big deal. Having the bike ride slightly lower wouldn't be a problem either.

Decisions, decisions! Should we cancel the van or decline the opportunity to repair the bike right here and now? History (pompous bugger, history doesn't care!) will show I probably made the wrong decision by plumping for getting to Islamabad as soon as possible. My rationale was that we gained a day by being transported at night. The repair would take the same length of time wherever we were and gaining time was vital. Already, I couldn't quite see how we were going to get to Holland on time.

Loading both bikes aboard the van meant we had to take out the second row of back seats and strap them on the roof. Finally we had both bikes, our mountains of luggage, the two drivers and the three of us all squeezed in. We were off. Well, not quite. They then decided to change the engine and gearbox oils before we departed. This was done on a vacant

bit of sloping land with the van driven up on a rock while a grimy youth carried out the work.

The early evening was still incredibly hot and gave rise to another trip legend. Dick decided to take off his boots for the all-night drive. Although the releasing of his feet from the constraining boots gave him some relief, he was almost overcome by the foul stench from his socks. In a magnanimous gesture he threw the socks out the window, only to find that the floor of the van was too hot to rest his feet on and he had to put his boots back on. It was equally hot whether you had the windows open or shut. It was like alternating between being in a hot typhoon and being stifled in a pressure cooker.

Driving in the Third World can be a scary experience. We aren't the fatalists that these drivers often appear to be. We aren't overwhelmingly confident that our maker will protect us if we drive around a blind bend on the wrong side of the road, and we drive accordingly. At times we raced with other vehicles and once, after a small bus had struggled past, our man pulled out alongside (as a matter of honour) to re-pass. The road had no barrier on the thousand-foot drop into the Indus. We drove mirror to mirror, with the other vehicle almost scraping along the rocky cliff side while ours seemed to be overhanging the drop to our death. After this manoeuvre, we told our driver in no uncertain terms that he was not to pass like that again. The bus got by again and our man relentlessly trailed it for an hour or so. Every time he looked like forgetting our instructions we had to hiss a warning at him. What bloody party-poopers we turned out to be.

In the mid-evening we stopped at a small town and had a meal and a rest, spying a leviathan-like BMW outside the cafe/hotel. Its owner, Antonio, was an Italian who had blasted across from Europe and was making for India. This was a pleasant meeting of similar adventurers, although he was a little distracted by being unable to find his passport. After a shared meal we swapped email addresses and squashed back into the van for the main night-time stint. Dick and I shared the front seat while Steve and the young second driver had the back row with the luggage.

The night continued to be hot and the road winding. The numbers of cars on the road gradually diminished and I relaxed a little. At least at night you can see the headlights of approaching vehicles. There were quite a few army checkpoints along the way, as this area was known to be rather unsafe. After one checkpoint, I felt sure the instruction from the soldiers had been to follow one of them on a motorcycle. He roared off ahead and we followed for a while. Then it started to rain and the bike shot off at a higher speed. Possibly he just wanted to get home before he got too wet. The rain didn't amount to much but we did experience an amazing electrical storm. Lightning gave us intermittent views of the countryside and sleeping villages.

In the last couple of hours before dawn the road began to straighten out and the going got faster and easier. This made it easier to sleep. Unfortunately that meant all of us, including the driver! Just on dawn we struck a truck going the other way. Luck was again on our side as the truck only took out the driver's mirror and peeled open

the side of the van like a large can opener. Steve was showered in glass from the broken window but the only casualty was a chicken from the truck's load. This was given to a passing taxi driver and everyone seemed OK about it all. It had been the younger driver who had dozed off, and we wondered about the consequences when he got back with the van in such a state. We presumed insurance wasn't in place. That largely seems to be a First World burden. An inch further over and we would have been hooked around and spun whilst going at 100 kph or so. The resulting roll, with a load of two motorbikes aboard, wasn't a pleasant thought. We all kept wide awake for the remaining drive into Islamabad.

We struggled to find our designated hotel so, in our tired state, we agreed to stay at a guesthouse belonging to a very persistent and very large, well-fed pair of brothers. We unloaded and found somewhere to lay our weary heads. The Karakorum Highway was behind us. We'd completed our big adventure. It was Saturday 2nd of July, two months and one day since we left Wellington. Now we needed to find Haroon, repair the bikes and plan how we could get to Europe in 22 days. Maybe we could take a short cut across Afghanistan or maybe we could get on a train to the bottom of Pakistan.

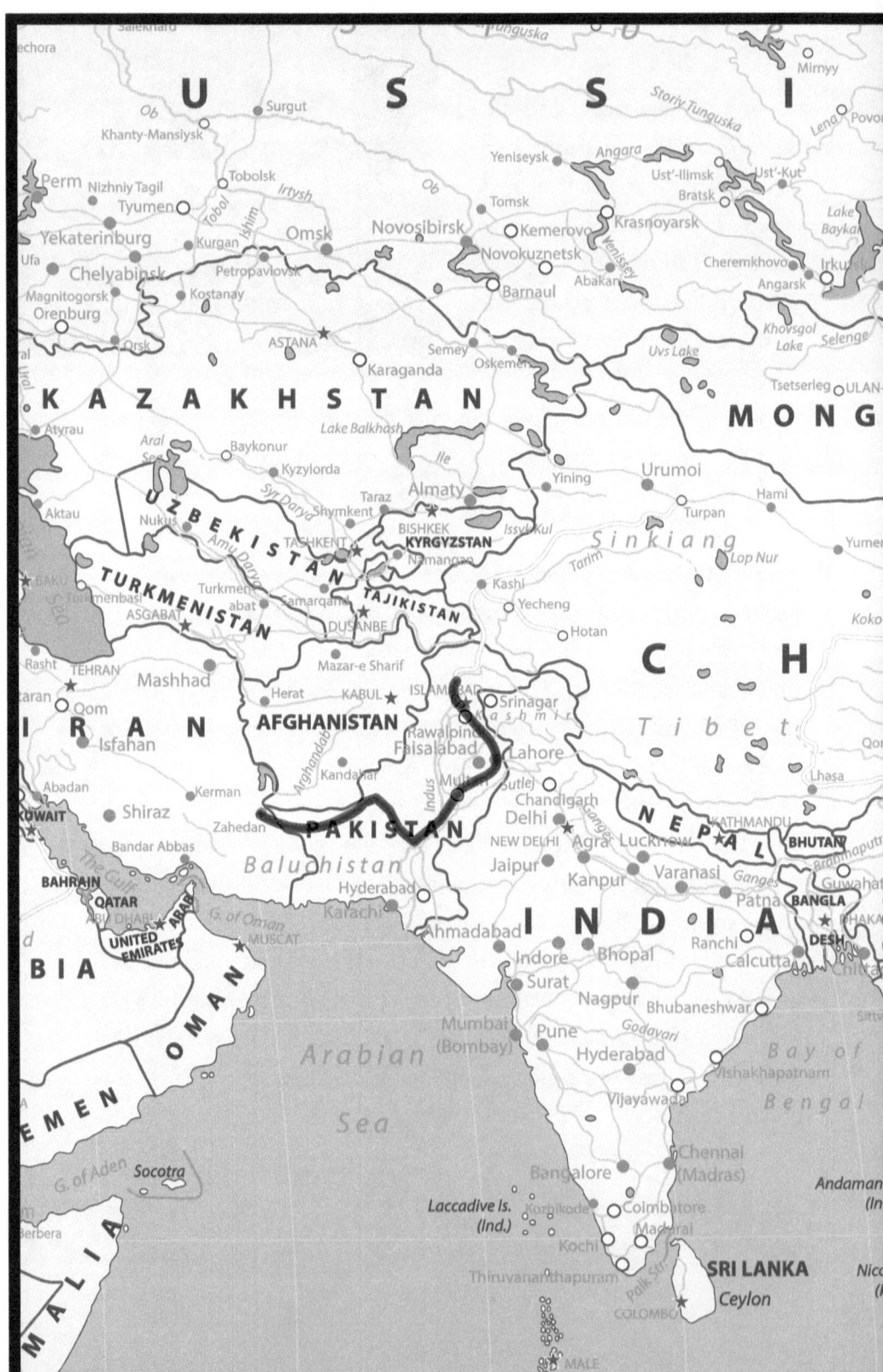

CHAPTER 8

PAKISTAN & PERSIAN DISAPPOINTMENTS

Islamabad is a modern, sprawling city. In the 1960s the Pakistan government saw the need for a specialised capital city and held a design competition. The winner was a Greek consultancy. They started with a green field and laid out the city in comfortable, regular grids. The old city of Rawalpindi is only a handful of kilometres away and the contrast is marked. One city has the high-intensity, the squalor, the light industry, and the exotic features of a Third World country. The other is an international capital, a trading centre with every feature and facility that goes with it.

It had been hot the week before we arrived, with temperatures reaching 46 degrees Celsius. Fortunately it was slightly more bearable while we were there. We contacted Haroon, who soon tracked us down. Short, sturdy and bearded, he was genuinely pleased to see us. He'd been following our adventures via our web site. On our first night, he arrived at about nine to take us out for a meal. With him were his father Mustapha and his son Mustapha. His father was a tallish ex-military man in his early eighties, a man clearly held in high esteem. Young Mustapha was a bubbly, confident youth who was home on holiday from California State University, also Haroon's alma mater. Like Haroon before him, he was studying to become an electronics engineer. These delightful people were to treat us to a wonderful time in Islamabad. Haroon has an electronics company employing about 50 people and it was probable that Mustapha would follow him into the business. These well-educated modern folk explained Islam to us and how it was an honour and their duty to look after us. Haroon told us all about the excitement of doing the haj to Saudi Arabia the year before and we enjoyed learning about Pakistan through their eyes. It was surprising to be told that the safest food here was chicken, as it has the shortest route from life to the plate, in both physical distance and time. Beef might come from 100 kilometres away and might take days to get to your plate, whereas a chicken would have been happily living around the back a few hours earlier. Coming from the relative sophistication of New Zealand, we considered chicken to be a slightly more at-risk food than other meats.

With Haroon's help (and a little Suzuki truck) we transported Penelope across to a tiny motorcycle workshop that had been recommended in Rawalpindi. The proprietors were two young brothers and their shop was no bigger than a shipping container. Most bikes were pushed out onto the roadside while the one to be worked on was taken into the bowels of this cramped work area. They were the local specialists in the bigger road bikes. We laughed at their card. It proclaimed them to be 'Heavy bike specialists' and their address as 'Tipu Road, near Petrol Pump'. They quickly caught on to what Dick had suggested as a repair, but thought that making a complete new fork stanchion was a better option. Their father dropped by for a look, as did half the town. The boys' dad was a machinist with a lifetime of experience with British bikes, including knowledge of Panthers. He would do the fabrication. A reasonable price was agreed to for the complete works. This would take a couple of days; longer than we would have liked, but it was reassuring to know that we would have a new leg at the end of it. Haroon took us to his factory in the afternoon and we were blown away by the complex intricate work they were involved with — everything from speed cameras to missile-tracking

devices. Each French missile-tracking device was going to cost the Pakistan Army $16,000,000. Haroon's company contracted to make four for that price. We like technical things so it was fascinating and enjoyable. Dick was particularly appreciative of their ability to adapt things for their own needs.

Afterwards, Haroon took us out for KFC. I'm a strong opponent of the multinationals and haven't had KFC for more than 20 years, so I was put in a bit of a spot. I rationalised that my real enemy was McDonalds and that would be my line in the sand. I last had McDonalds in Panama City in 1977, and that was a milkshake. My lone campaign against their worldwide spread took until the first quarter of 2005 to show a result, when the Golden Arches were tarnished a little by their first loss. We noticed that Haroon slipped some beggars a little money on the way back. Asked about it, he said it was his honour to be able to give the beggars something. Pakistan has homeless beggars, but it also has large numbers of big rotund people. Many don't match the stereotype of being thin with matchstick legs. Although the British haven't been here as a ruling power for over 50 years, there is still quite a good spread of English-speakers among both young and old.

Each day we would explore. We were only about a kilometre from a big shopping area that easily sustained our interest. One day Dick and I even managed to find strawberry cheesecake. As a city it had everything that you could desire. On the Monday afternoon I could feel a touch of diarrhoea approaching as I made my way back to the guesthouse. Such moments are always awkward. You know you want to run as fast as you can, but feel that the best control is with your sphincter squeezed tightly closed. This requires a smooth shuffle, not a bouncy run. Using a compromise, I managed to gain sanctuary successfully. There was no way I wanted to go out again until this little problem had passed. We'd been pleased with our healthy bowels to date and I saw this as a minor setback. I declined the teatime sortie and when the other two returned, Dick said he might be getting a little of what I had. Within a minute or so he had taken up residence in the loo, where he was to stay all night with only intermittent visits to the bed. When he wasn't in there I would oblige by keeping the seat warm and the air foetid. This was not our best night. Dick blamed the breakfast at the guesthouse. He and I had one sort of omelette and Steve didn't. I wasn't totally convinced, seeing it took all day to react, but the scenario did fit.

We weren't in great shape on Tuesday morning but we made our way across to Rawalpindi to finish off Penelope. We put new chains on both bikes and I swapped Penelope's wheels front to back for the big push for Europe. The boys had reassembled the front end and even tuned her a bit. I felt she might have been running a little better but it was hard to tell. We had leaned off the mixture while we were running at altitude, so everything was a compromise. Both brothers took Penelope for a spin before we made our way back to Islamabad. With Haroon, we'd been planning how to get across to Tehran as fast as we could. We'd briefly considered a short cut across Afghanistan but Haroon didn't think it wise. He had the local knowledge and was realistic about what was achievable and what wasn't. It seemed that our best option was to ride across to Lahore, then catch a train down to Quetta before riding through to Iran. This wasn't the shortest route to Iran, but the shortest route through Loralai was closed to westerners because of the lawless nature of the area. The train timetables matched our needs and we could even pick up a couple of days. I was already planning a train trip from Tehran to Istanbul to gain even more days. It left every Friday and would have us in Istanbul on Sunday, rested and refreshed. It required damn good progress all the way to make it, but with a bit of luck it could be done. We would be setting off on Wednesday morning and we had a week-and-a-half to get to Tehran, about 4,000 kilometres away. The local advice about not going around the southern tip of Pakistan because it was too hot at this time of year was a bit disturbing. When asked how hot, we were told 55–58 degrees – not something to look forward to.

In the evening Dick lapsed into an incredibly deep slumber. The night before had been virtually sleepless and now he was making up for it. Disappointingly for him, Haroon and his two sons came around quite late, to take us out one last time. We tried to wake Dick but he was almost comatose and, short of getting really brutal, it didn't seem he would awaken until his body was sated. We decided to leave him where he was. The second Qaresh son, Ahmed, was the youngest of the family (with a daughter in between the two boys). Haroon's wife had been going to join us too, but wasn't well. With much merriment and the two boys bullying their dad in the good-natured way that sharp young adults do, we went looking for suitable action. It was great to observe the family dynamics. I felt that there were parallels with our own family. We never met the daughter as she was away with cousins, but she sounded just like our Hannah, thinking that maybe she would be a fighter pilot, or a journalist or ... Nothing was settled, but nothing was impossible. Ambitious youth should be encouraged and listened to. It was a fun night. Steve had already bonded with Mustapha and now he did so with Ahmed. The trio of young ones chatted away about their interests and Haroon and I were able to be more like spectators. They took us to a pizza place where the well heeled of Islamabad society congregated, especially the young. Traffic management was required outside and entry was only allowed when there was there was room. We had to wait while we were booked in with a ticket system. Here, we finally saw Pakistani women in numbers similar to that of the men present. Many stunning-looking young women in local dress were out having fun with their male counterparts.

It was nice to be part of, even if it seemed a little too westernised and possibly a little contrived.

Islamabad had been a good end to our adventure and we'd had a lot of assistance from Haroon in planning our race for Europe. What worried me a bit was that it would be July 6th when we'd leave to ride down the Grand Trunk road to Lahore. The party in Arnhem was taking place on July 24, in only 18 days time. With more than 9,000 kilometres to travel we would have to cover more than 500 kilometres every day, including borders. Possible, but bloody tough on old chuggers like ours. We'd geared our bikes down for the deserts and mountains. The run to Europe on tarseal roads was going to be a drone of momentous proportions. We needed everything to go our way.

The Grand Trunk road was originally constructed in the 16th century. The brainchild of Sher Shah Suri, then ruler of the Indian subcontinent, it linked Sonagaon in Bengal to Lahore in an effort to ensure good governance and efficient administration. During the British colonial era it was extended in both directions and stretched from the Khyber Pass in Afghanistan, across Pakistan and India all the way to Calcutta. It was completed in 1848 under Lord Dalhousie's tenure as Governor General of India. It's still a major artery, even though a few expressways have sprung up in various places along the way. We chose it as a direct route to Lahore with the bonus of being a good day's ride, and so it proved. It demonstrated how treacherous the Third World's roads could be. After noticing that I'd passed several recent truck and bus crashes, I started counting them. We passed at least eleven. On the side of the road would be the yet-to-be-removed result of a recent crash. Sometimes it appeared that a wheel had fallen off and a bus had careered off the road. Other times it was obviously a head-on collision. It was sobering.

After a roadside stop for refreshments Steve told us that another customer, an old bearded man with bare feet, had paid our account. We were touched by his generosity. We'd only had tea and biscuits but there were three of us and his appearance suggested he had nothing to spare. But that was typical of Pakistan. The old guy felt it was an honour to be helping us.

Entering the turmoil of Lahore, and I don't use that word lightly, Penelope again suddenly veered off course. Unbelievably, our new fork leg had broken, or that was the immediate prognosis. The failure happened near a taxi station and within seconds there were dozens of people pressing in close around us. In the throng was a persistent beggar. It was hot, and everything was going wrong. There was the stress of trying to determine what could have happened and how we could extricate ourselves from this latest predicament. The pressing inquisitiveness was something Dick couldn't stand. He almost did the beggar some physical violence. Instead, he gave him a strong verbal outburst.

To get away from this unsatisfactory location we decided to shift the bikes down the road to the railway station and organise getting to Quetta. We'd worry about the repair when we got there. Another treacherous, but thankfully short, ride ensued. Haroon had arranged that his manager in Lahore would assist us, so we contacted him. He turned up with some underlings and Steve went off with them to arrange to get the bikes on a train. This was a long and involved process, and Dick and I were left to our own devices outside the railway station. We were tired and a little despondent. Again, typical of the nation, a couple of young brothers brought us some bottled water. One was waiting for a train and they were just filling in time. They were personable and generous.

One thing about Lahore that was beginning to drive us crazy was noise pollution. Every vehicle uses its horn. These are loud air horns playing either strident tunes or a shrill warbling sort of noise. Dick was about ready to take an axe to any driver that he could catch. As a rational man, Dick felt there was no reason for the incessant cacophony, but it seemed to be a local trait. It wasn't quite so bad in Islamabad, but was also prevalent in Quetta.

Finally, with the bikes off our hands we could search for our reserved hotel. An impish-faced driver in his thirties wanted to take us in his Vespa rickshaw. He was persistent, and wasn't going to be put off by the mountain of luggage. We agreed a price. It then became evident that he wasn't licensed to come into our part of the station. No problem – he ignored all officialdom. Our luggage was piled everywhere, including the roof. Dick and I squeezed into the seating area in the back while Steve perched up front alongside our determined driver. That the driver had little idea of where he was taking us only heightened our sense of adventure. Nor was he licensed to take us the distance he did. This created a minor drama as we approached a policeman on traffic duty. But we didn't stop and there was no way he could pursue us. We zigzagged all over the city. We tried one hotel, but it wasn't ours. We attempted to get instructions on how to reach ours, but to no avail. Finally, we found a local who knew where to go. This huge man also squeezed aboard our tiny conveyance and we putt-putted to the correct address.

This had been a monumental adventure with many dramatic traffic

skirmishes. If we hadn't been travelling these wild places for two months already, we would have been scared shitless. Dick was annoyed though, as he felt every taxi driver should have a map. I partly agreed, but also realised that in a city as huge as Lahore, with nearly seven million people, it would require a huge book of maps and these Vespas are tiny. I always reflect that you can't expect first world service at Third World prices. You'd pay a significant amount at a western fun fair for the adrenalin rush we had for just a few dollars.

The hotel had been booked by Haroon's man and seemed more up-market than we would have chosen. On closer inspection, as usual, not everything worked. We weren't sure which was worse, having no water or having water that wouldn't drain away. The heat, noise and dustiness of Lahore had exhausted us. We didn't venture out that night but had some food sent in, which was quite good. Our train wasn't departing until 2.55 p.m. so we changed some money and bought food for our big train trip which would take about 26 hours. The bikes had gone on a different train in a different direction, and would probably reach Quetta after us. Lahore hadn't endeared itself to us but we'd been appreciative of the assistance given by Haroon's men. The manager was a lean, bespectacled man nearing 60 who, whilst friendly and helpful, was a little imperious in his manner. His underlings jumped to his instructions with alacrity. He was a man of obvious standing. One of the two young lads working for him was a Christian. That must be difficult in a Muslem country but judging by the laughter, they seemed to get on well enough. We'd been impressed by the respect people had for Haroon. This seemed to be based on genuine affection. Back in Islamabad we'd gone out-of-hours to visit his factory. The on-site security guards seemed happy to see him and there was a relaxed relationship between them. Having his people in Lahore drop everything and see to our needs was just another of his services towards us that led to our refrain, "the man's a legend".

Pakistan is criss-crossed with train routes and thousands of people use them every day. There are a few terrible accidents, but we were impressed by the infrastructure and the trains looked neat and shiny. We were travelling first class. We'd got a taste for it in Kyrgyzstan. For a little extra, we were to have a sleeping compartment. We needed the space, as our mountain of gear was substantial. The coolie really struggled with it. It was interesting watching this regime of workers. Often they show off their strength and ability to carry heavy loads, even when quite elderly.

We were leaving the magnificent mountains and travelling south towards the flatlands. We saw what you see from a train, the unfolding countryside and people's back yards, which are always fascinating. The big difference from our normal mode of transport was that we didn't smell anything, or feel the heat, or hear the flies, or taste the dust. There was no difficulty to the journey. In a little over a day we travelled what would have taken us three on the bikes. We could become soft if this became the norm. I briefly spoke with a sophisticated young student returning to Quetta for the holidays. She asked me what I thought of Pakistan and we discussed the invisible nature of her gender. She felt this was changing in the big cities and not as dramatic as I portrayed it.

The next day we changed direction and headed back north westish again. We'd kept well away from the hills that separate Pakistan from Iran but we were now heading back towards them. This was Baluchistan, so there was an ethnic change as well. In the north, there'd been Pathans and Kashmiris; Punjabis dominate the middle areas and we'd not gone down to the Sikh area of Karachi. The Baluchis are present right through this area and across into Iran. Pashtuns from Afghanistan are also quite dominant.

We reached Quetta in the late afternoon and found a backpacker/guesthouse. There were two Dutch couples there, one travelling on a Indian-made Royal Enfield motorcycle and the other in a good Toyota landcruiser 4 x 4, done out for adventure. The guesthouse had an enclosed lawn courtyard that was a haven for us in the evening after the heat. It was nice catching up with travellers occasionally and learning and laughing with them. Listening to how hot it had been for the Enfielders coming across India was illuminating. I commented about their full-face helmets and how they must be unbearable in the heat they had described. "No, it was too hot for an open-face helmet", they said. This surprised us.

Although we went back to the railway station at 9 o'clock in the evening, the bikes weren't there. There was no alternative but to come back in the morning with fingers crossed. Our good luck held and on Saturday morning we reclaimed the bikes and got them to the guesthouse where we stripped Penelope's front end. We'd been duped by the young guys in Islamabad. There was no new fork leg. The old leg had been welded with a sleeve inside but this just put the repaired bit back where the most stresses were. Once the shrouds were in place covering it all over, it couldn't be seen and there was always the possibility it would work. Dick was justifiably pretty dark on the Islamabad 'repairers'. We now had to find facilities that could weld and machine as we instructed.

After a couple of false starts we located a suitable place and, with Dick strongly keeping the interested parties back, a repair was started. The happy machinist quickly grasped Dick's plan. The leg was cut in two at the old repair and another section cut out and re-welded. All this was done well and with a minimum of fuss. The machinist had a good workshop and when there was something he didn't have, he went next door to a similar workshop and used their equipment. While this was happening I watched an artisan hand-beating a sheet metal replica of a fibreglass handlebar fairing. In the workshop across the road was a small team who did the finishing of petrol tanks. They repaired and repainted tanks to a high standard, even using a small oven to bake the paint hard. Occupational Safety and Health inspectors wouldn't have been too impressed with the lack of personal safety equipment. Bare feet in sandals were the norm and there was no eye, ear or mouth protection. The tank painters got me some tea and we shared a few moments before the news came back from the machine shop that the work was complete.

The machinist was also a first class cricketer and had some trophies proudly displayed in the workshop. Like most Pakistanis he had a better knowledge of the New Zealand cricket team than we did, knowing who was out with injury and who had scored well in recent times. Although it was still several months away, the forthcoming tour by the English cricket team was big news and the entire nation seemed to be in a fever of anticipation. It was fun to be able to recall a magnificent Pakistani victory over New Zealand in a bygone One Day World Cup semi-final when their present captain, Inzaman-ul-Haq, took them from an impossible situation to victory. It was one of the game's most impressive single-handed displays of power batting. We all revelled in the shared memory. Dick and the repairer had clicked on a personal and technical level. On completion of the works, photos were taken of the pair of them with the freshly repaired fork stanchion. The vagaries and magic of Pakistan showed up again when

THE LAST HURRAH

all payment was refused for the work done. "It was an honour!"

We'd been ripped off on one hand and treated beyond all expectations on the other. No wonder people are fascinated by the country and love it so intensely.

We made our way back to the guesthouse and started our preparations to get back on the road. I felt that to have a show of making Willy's party we needed to gain on our itinerary. We had to get through into Iran as soon as possible and this meant crossing the scorching desert roads of Baluchistan, where there weren't many natural stopping places. There was a train every two days or so which took 30 hours, but the timing wasn't right and there was no surety that it would even run. Bearing these factors in mind, I hatched a plan where we would get a night ride across the desert using local transport and pass into Iran on Sunday 10 July. That would give us two weeks to get from the bottom of Iran through to Arnhem.

We'd always said that the race for Europe would be tough. Steve and I had even discussed the probability of failure and wondered if we could get Dick to leave us at a suitable spot and fly ahead to the party. I felt that this would probably be Istanbul, but we filed the prospect away, deep in the 'absolute last-ditch scenario' category. We were a team and had come the distance so far together, so we'd do the utmost to come in together as a team. Steve went off to arrange for a pickup truck to collect us in the late afternoon. It would take us the 800 or so kilometres to the border town of Taftan overnight. The Dutch couple on the Enfield would have loved to ride with us for a while, as they were also heading to Iran. We would have been increased security for them but sadly, with us having to rush this wouldn't be possible. Once more we cursed the time constraints we had put on ourselves. This type of travel does not suit a rigid itinerary. The flexibility of being able to decide on different agendas as the situation arises should be a foundation to the planning. I'd thought my youthful meanderings were so successful because I was young. In reality, the freedom to meander was just as important.

The pickup truck trip was a nightmare, starting with the loading of the bikes. For 50 years Dick has loaded bikes onto every type of conveyance. This has given him considerable skill at such tasks. The Pakistanis who brought the wagon around have probably loaded a few loads in their time also, but there was no coordination or leadership. Quite a few people swarmed over the back of the double-cab ute, with ropes flying everywhere. Someone would try to tie down a rope, and Dick would stop them because it was in the wrong place for pull-direction or it was impacting on a delicate part of the bike. Dick would try to put the rope somewhere else. He got a bit tetchy during the process. I've learnt that it's best to let Dick do things his way, as it will almost certainly work. He knows what he's doing. He may not always be the best person to assist as he can yell at you to, "get out of my f...ing light", when you're doing something on the same side as him and nowhere near getting in his light.

The situation didn't improve when we were just getting under way and the driver wanted money. Steve had paid the agent earlier on, so had to take the second driver back with him and find the person he'd paid. A protracted argument broke out because the agent had kept some of the drivers' money. All this took time, and Dick and I were marooned with the other driver. Dick was giving vent to some pretty dark mutterings about the Pakistanis ripping him off. These were hassles we could do without. Dick is at his best facing natural or mechanical challenges. Give him the stupid bureaucratic or organisation problems that the Third World throws at you, add some heat, some space-invasive, sometimes smelly local populace, and Dick starts to go into meltdown. We weren't off to a good start, but finally the financial flare up was resolved and we headed off across the desert. We hadn't expected two drivers, and the spare guy seemed more of a passenger. Having five of us jammed in meant the journey wasn't pleasant. It was one of the worst nights we were to endure. It was hot, we were squashed tight with some of our luggage and we probably didn't sleep at all. The only redeeming feature of the ride was that we didn't have an accident.

Ultimately we were delivered to the border early next morning so, rough as we felt, we were at least a couple of days ahead of schedule. We had to do the paperwork processing at a settlement a few kilometres back, so Steve and I did that and left Dick with the luggage. The paperwork was a huge hassle as there was no one to do it. The only people we could find told us that the customs officials would start at 9 a.m. Of course this meant 10 a.m. Then they discovered that the guy back in Sust hadn't known how to process the carnet de passage. The bikes hadn't been booked into the country so couldn't be booked out. This was a big problem to them. We could see it wasn't a problem; we were there with the bikes ready to leave, so we must have come in. It took quite a few phone calls and some time for them to agree with our point of view.

We were away from Dick and his pile of luggage for a long time. He'd handled this OK but there were now a million people all trying to get across the border. He'd made a few friends and had managed to keep out of the sun to a large degree. Once we were back the real fun began. The scrummage to get everything processed was probably worse than at any other border and it was afternoon before we were finally through. It had been hard and hot. We were naturally irritated (although not with each other). Finally getting the bikes fired up after the last permit had been gained was a relief but we knew there was no refuge from the sun until we reached Zahedan. Steve wanted to stop at the border and have a meal. He hadn't eaten much since breakfast as he'd been leading the paperwork battle on our behalf. Dick wanted to press on to Zahedan as he had all his gear on and the bike started. Much as I felt that Steve, as usual, was suggesting the rational and sensible course, I also felt that Dick had done a damn good job during a very trying morning. Agreeing to his request wasn't a big deal. It was only 80 kilometres to Zahedan, so we could rest and eat in around an hour.

The road was just as promised ... bloody beautiful. Iran's roads are all smooth and well-maintained blacktop tarseal. Our problem was that this corner of the world was way too hot for us. It was so much hotter than the 42 degrees of Samarkand. It had to be in the 50s and was more than we could handle. We were riding along with the hills of Afghanistan only 15 kilometres away on our right. This is the area that the Taleban are still in control of. The ride was probably most notable for our arrival. Dick recounted later that for the last few kilometres he was only just hanging on to reality. His concentration was beginning to wander and he felt he was beginning to lose it. We stopped at a big roundabout on the outskirts of the city centre and found a small roadside stall selling drinks and icecreams. We fell on these like men possessed. We were all at the end of our tethers. It was scary to have so quickly and so completely deteriorated physically. I could see a tourist hotel across the other side of the roundabout. I left the others in the shade and ventured across to find if we could stay the night. Our will to go on and look elsewhere was gone. We were all buggered. The walk across and back seemed like a major trek to me. I was pleased to report we were booked in to a hotel that had a restaurant. We got the bikes across to the hotel, parking them by the front door. We were too knackered to remove any more luggage than was necessary. Our room didn't have air conditioning but it did have a fan that at least pushed the air around. We always had water in our hydra-packs, but we all needed a lot of fluids once we'd stopped so we probably weren't drinking enough. After a rest we went down to the large and deserted restaurant area. It was about 6 o'clock and we weren't impressed to be told the meals wouldn't be available until 8 o'clock. We threw a bit of a wobbly and played the "This man is a diabetic and needs food NOW" card. Surprisingly Dick said he could hang on for another two hours. I remember saying, "well, we bloody can't, we all have to have food now!" Fortunately someone was in the kitchen and they agreed to rustle up some chicken kebabs and rice.

While we waited Dick took ill and said he needed a doctor. Steve, who had missed out on eating earlier, said almost snappily, "Can't it wait until after we've eaten?" Dick's response to that was negative. I questioned him again and his clear answer was that he needed help right now. Even I was a little grumpy that this should be happening when we were about to be fed, but I went to reception to make enquiries. Amazingly, there was a hospital straight opposite the hotel. I couldn't get a doctor to come to us, I would need to bring the patient over. Most of this was communicated in sign language. I returned to find Dick in our room. He'd tried some of the food and said that it tasted like shit. He couldn't even swallow the salad. We helped him across to the Persian equivalent of the Accident and Emergency Department. The paperwork was cursory as trying to get Theodorus Huurdeman written down in the Arabic script, Farsi, was beyond us. He was put on a drip immediately, and I think we all felt a little better.

Although a bit chaotic, the care was reasonably confidence-inspiring. A be- stubbled doctor seemed to be going from patient to patient non-stop. The nurses were all covered in the black veils that the Ayatollah decreed that all Iranian women must wear. There were a couple of women doctors similarly clad. After a few tests, it was ascertained that Dick wasn't bottoming off his diabetic scale at all. His blood-sugar readings were good, as they had been for most of the trip. If his readings were a bit high on a given morning Dick could almost always tell you why – maybe that extra beer the night before. He knows his diabetes and had managed it well to date, getting new insulin in Almaty. Once they knew his blood-sugar level was OK, they changed the drip and did other tests. The facility was crude and the hygiene was a bit on the basic side but we felt confident that he was in good hands.

It was interesting to observe that the doctors and nurses all interacted the same way ours do. You could see the flirting going on, even with the veils obscuring a fair bit of the women's faces. The human race is the same the world over.

When the doctor asked if Dick had diarrhoea, his answer was "Not really, no more than usual". We didn't think to mention the bout we'd had a week or so earlier. Whether they knew something that we didn't, we'll never know, but in about an hour Dick was barely able to walk to the toilet. Steve and I half carried him and his drip to the hole-in-the-floor and held him up. By now we had him in paper pyjamas and we threw away his undies, as we didn't reckon on reclaiming them. We'd have needed a whole sack-load of hungry enzymes and we just didn't have the stomach for it. Steve was again a champion, cleaning Dick up while I held him as well as I could. We got him back to his bed and faced up to the reality that this was looking like the end of the trip for him. The only real option was to look at how he could be repatriated to Holland when he was well enough.

We were pinned in this scorched corner of southern Iran with its searing temperatures and there would be no relief until we gained a little altitude, a couple of days ride further on. The problem seemed insurmountable. We were terribly forlorn and the heat was draining all the will out of us. Dick was quite clear that he didn't want to compromise the rest of his life. There would be lots more to enjoy and he wanted the comforts of the family in Europe. Initially he was lucid and able to contribute to the decision-making but once his gastroenteritis kicked in fully he was borderline, not being with it most of the time. Even while he was fading though, he remembered I still hadn't eaten and it was late at night. Towards midnight Steve and I left the hospital and retired across the road, for me to scoff the chicken kebab and rice meal that had been kept for me. I was a proud father when, as we made to leave, Steve bent over and kissed Dick on the cheek.

Later Dick recalled that when we left, he thought he might not see us again. He feared that it might be his last night. His body functions were now involuntary and uncontrolled. It wasn't a great environment to be in as he remained on the grotty bed that he was first put on. Accident and Emergency departments are never pleasant places. There isn't much in the way of recovery happening. The facility in Zahedan was a testament to this, with dramas unfolding throughout the night, people dying, relatives mourning and patients groaning in pain.

I was experiencing some unusual side effects of the heat and the beginnings of my own bout of diarrhoea. I suddenly and determinedly craved bubbles in my drinks. I'm not a consumer of Coca Cola. I'm not even keen on sparkling wine, but now I needed cola and fizzy orange drinks. This overwhelming desire was to last for a week or so. I didn't want water; I wanted a sweet drink with bubbles. I now needed to stay near my bed and my trusty toilet. It was a luxury being in a hotel where you had your own big, tiled bathroom. I was also appreciating the hand-held shower-like device that you can clean your nether regions with as I was still on the 'no paper' diet.

While I was recumbent and Dick was still on a drip in hospital, Steve was arranging flights. He contacted our agent in Tehran and put her in the picture. Our itinerary went out the window as we could only guess at Dick's recovery and our rescue needs. Scenario after scenario was run through. These difficult situations highlighted Steve's ability as a cool-headed, extremely competent organiser. Phone calls were made all over the place and everything had to be arranged on a 'maybe' basis. There was a flight out of Zahedan to Tehran on Tuesday and on early Wednesday morning there was a KLM flight to Amsterdam. Our agent had checked and there was no room on the Friday train to Istanbul, but we felt we'd cross that bridge if we ever got to it.

Mid-way though Monday evening, I heard the door to our room open behind me. When there was no greeting, I rolled over to see the haggard but happy face of the old fella. Steve was behind him, grinning away as he filmed my reactions. I wish I'd been a little more lively but I was feeling fairly drained. Dick was so relieved to be back with us and able to have a bed that wasn't vinyl-covered. He wasn't perky but he'd been signed out as OK. Steve had got a standby ticket for the flight to Tehran and our agent arranged an English-speaking person to meet Dick and transfer him to the International Airport. We weren't sure whether to be happy or sad. We were happy that Dick had turned the corner and whatever had ailed him was being beaten, but we were overwhelmingly sad to know that he'd not be with us for the rest of the trip. We kept reassuring ourselves with the thought that the big adventure was over and we'd done that together. The race for Europe was just an add-on. Dick wasn't yet firing on all cylinders and there were so many arrangements being made on his behalf that he wasn't taking it all in. Back in New Zealand, Silk Road Adventures picked up the tabs for the flight to Holland; we'd settle up later. We hadn't been able to contact Dick's nephew to collect him from the airport, but had left messages.

Mid-morning on July 12 we took a taxi and a far-from-well Dick out to the airport. Steve put on a tenacious display of youthful determination to win a spot on the plane. There must have been fifteen or so men, all wanting one of the standby spots. This group would run from one end of the booking area to the other when some action looked likely. There was no gentle queue-forming, this was full body-contact, every-man-for-himself stuff. Steve had persuaded a local to make calls to higher places within the airline, trying to ensure Dick was the first on. Dick and I were both still unwell. We were virtual spectators, nervous and edgy.

Shortly before the scheduled departure, a ticket was secured and we had an emotional parting. Dick wasn't well enough to be embarking on this journey, but it was the only solution. We wrote down some instructions about ringing his nephew from Tehran but I knew his nods and agreement to do so were just spontaneous reactions. I didn't believe there was real comprehension. His usual vitality was missing. This was a confused, doddery old man getting on the plane and starting a gruelling day that wouldn't end until tomorrow. He would reach Tehran about 2 p.m. but the flight to Amsterdam wouldn't leave until 2 a.m. and that flight would take many hours. Would he connect with the agent, would he manage to get food and drink, would he be met in Amsterdam, would his renowned stamina hold out? His departure left us with more questions than answers. Steve and I were concerned and relieved at the same time.

I'm a naturally buoyant person, always optimistic that the goal will be achieved, sometimes unreasonably so. Now I was in, and I love the phrase, a slough of despond. I felt we were pinned in the furnace, far from success. I realised that currently I was a burden. Steve was my rock, but I needed to make sure that the rock didn't get crushed by my relentless demands. I just didn't know how.

*We learnt later that Dick didn't contact his nephew from Tehran. Neither could he reach him once in Amsterdam, so he had to catch a train to his brother's place. This involved a long walk carrying all his gear. It would have been an extremely arduous journey for a fit person but was almost beyond comprehension given the state that Dick was in when he left us.

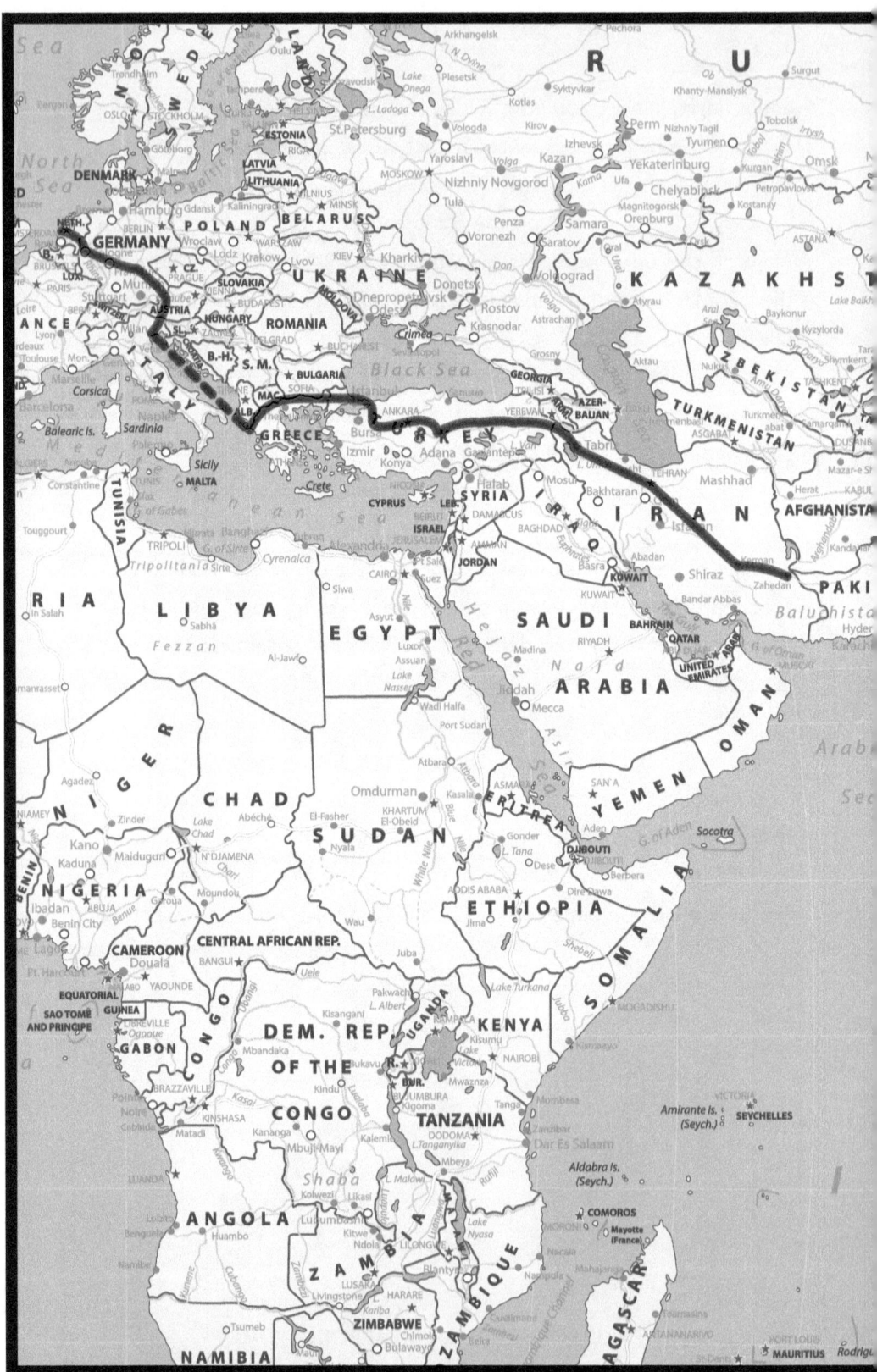

CHAPTER 9

RACING FOR HOME

After Dick left, our plan was to rest for the remainder of the day. We'd head off well before dawn and ride two days to a rail end where we would take a train to Tehran. My health problem was in no way as severe as Dick's, but I was low and unable to be far from the toilet for any length of time. Just before tea, Steve surprised me with the delivery of two beers. I was pleased that one was a Russian brand that we'd enjoyed often. The other was only just palatable, but I believe that beer starts at delicious and gets better. I had always felt that a beer from my youth encountered in Nelson called Harleys (known universally as Harleys' Horse Piss) was probably my bottom benchmark. This one, which I think came from Pakistan, came in well beneath it. (I was to learn more about these beers in a couple of days' time.) I was still craving fizzy drinks with every meal. Luckily, these were usually offered. The local copies of both Coke and Fanta were adequate for my needs. The meals, chicken or lamb kebabs and rice, were always quite pleasant. Even when ravaged by diarrhoea, my appetite normally remains intact.

Steve and I awoke at 3 a.m. with the intention of being on the road at 4 a.m. I was so lethargic and moribund I was not easily stirred into action. Steve slowly went through the motions of packing up all our gear and transferring it down to our bikes. I got up, abluted and lay down again several times. I remember the deep panting, the heavy sighing and the feeling of being so bloody useless. I was totally lacking in motivation. My willpower had been drained away with my watery discharges. It was 5.30 before we were down at reception paying the sleepy clerk the wads of money owed. It was a huge bill in local notes, although not when converted back to our currency. Changing $500 gives you over 4,500,000 rials. Even when the money is in 10,000 rial notes you have 450 notes - a whole lot of bundles. We had to spread the money around our luggage as it wouldn't all fit in our wallets or pockets. Not surprisingly we missed one bundle when we later left the country. C'est la vie!

It was still before dawn when we headed out of Zahedan and the temperature was just pleasant. Once seated on Penelope, I felt better and much more secure of bowel. On good roads, the kilometres slipped

quickly behind us. The day ripened into the blazing scorcher for which the area is renowned. Petrol was hard to come by, even though it's the Iranian's big wealth. It was amazingly cheap but gas stations were far apart. This had us worried at times as our range was limited to 300 kilometres. About 10 o'clock in the morning, when the intensity of the heat was almost as much as we could bear, we were flagged down at a checkpoint. The police told us to go no further than the next oasis and to wait there until evening when it would be cooler again. They gave me the name of the place. I thought it was about 30 kilometres ahead. Accordingly, when we came to a small group of palm trees and a few dwellings after about another 10 kilometres, we rode on. In error we'd ridden through the oasis and out into the desert looking for the oasis to shelter in. It's hard to describe the intensity of the heat. We couldn't ride with our visors up. It was just as the Royal Enfielders had described. It was too hot for open-face helmets. When we lifted our visors, the air felt like something from a hot-air paint stripper. You could feel your eyeballs drying out before melting. The region is known for temperatures of 55-58 degrees in the shade and the temperature in the sun above the tarsealed road would be considerably more. We'd already experienced temperatures in the early 40s but this was meltdown material. We couldn't handle the midday temperatures.

We found a small muddy river and I lay in it, fully clothed. I'd often regaled Steve with tales of the scorching heat in Central America; places like Honduras, Nicaragua and Costa Rica, and of my fully-clothed plunges into the rivers. It had a wonderfully cooling effect on the riding afterwards. The drying of the sodden clothing in the moving air is the same process as refrigeration. This river was the first we'd encountered that we could get to. It was shallow and muddy with a sticky bottom (a bit like me). Still, I couldn't resist. The ride was delightful for quite a while afterwards. We didn't reach a settlement and some shade until about 2 o'clock, by which time we were holding on for grim death.

Possibly I exaggerate, but it had taxed us to the end of our reserves. Steve's first words were, "Well, Dick would have said that was desolate". After a shared chuckle, we took refuge in the shade. We lay about on bed-like platforms, eating and drinking ... and drinking ... and drinking some more.

In the late afternoon we headed out into the baking countryside for our last session. It would get us to Bam, our intended overnight stay. Bam is known internationally for its dates and the earthquake that more or less levelled it on Boxing Day 2003. This shocking event killed more than 40,000 people and made many more tens of thousands homeless. Riding into town 18 months later was a humbling experience. People were still living in tents or shipping containers. There were piles of rubble surrounding cleared areas. Some rebuilding had been done but often it was by unskilled people just making do. The dire conditions dictated that the preferred processes of design and following an established building code were ignored. They had no relevance when put alongside the immediate housing needs of the people. This has led to the production of many substandard buildings. I talked with a couple of builders who were fabricating the reinforcing steel cage for a structural beam to go into their workshop. I asked if an engineer had given them the design. They looked at me the way people do when they are clearly thinking, "Why would we do that?"

The cage had only the most basic stirrups binding the longitudinal bars together and they were evenly spaced along the length, not closed up at the more heavily loaded ends. Even my untrained eyes could tell there was not enough steel going into the beam - a recipe for a future disaster. It's a sad fact that when this type of disaster happens, there isn't the time to plan the aid and reconstruction to minimise the likelihood of similar results next time. New Zealand is often called the Shaky Isles because of the large number earthquakes it experiences each year. These usually cause insignificant damage because our building code has been formulated around the need to have construction that won't fall apart and harm our population. If only the Iranian authorities thought the same.

Young kids on motorbikes were abundant in the town and some escorted us to the backpackers recommended by the Lonely Planet Guide. It was run by an ex-school principal who had tough standards when it came to shutting doors, taking off shoes and rubbish control. We put newspaper under the bikes as they were dripping oil, a worry to our house-proud host. Staying at the same place were Ivo and Jaquelin, a Swiss couple who were taking a couple of years to ride around the world on an early 90s BMW twin. They were personable and fun to be with. They both had well-paid jobs at home and no intention or pressing need to work while they were away. If they wanted more money, they could just go home and quickly earn more. Ivo raced an MZ back at home and in the German MZ Championship, a round of which had been held at the same meeting as one of the Moto GPs. He was chuffed to have raced on the same track on the same day as the stars. We were united in our awe for the skill of those stars, especially Valentino Rossi, the Doctor. They mentioned that they were missing being able to get alcohol. I chipped in that Steve had managed to get us a couple of beers in Zahedan. Steve laughingly informed us they had been NO ALCOHOL beers. I was gobsmacked. The Russian one had been delicious and just as I recalled the normal beer of the same brand.

Later we walked into the town centre for an evening meal and I remember it as just another pleasant father-son outing, notable more for the sight of a motorbike with a blue tail light than for the culinary experience. During the night I heard what I was sure was Dick's voice just outside our room, but in my sleep-befuddled state I couldn't rouse myself to investigate. I must've been dreaming.

It seemed a shame to be rushing away from Bam without exploring the remains of the heritage areas that abound, but I still harboured a forlorn hope that somehow we might be able to get to Arnhem on time, if we just kept going. The next day we made our way up to Kerman, a provincial capital. Finding the railway station was a big mission. At one stage we were turned back by a policeman who seemed to indicate that the way ahead was blocked by the results of a terrorist car bomb. Well, that was the inference I took from his persistent urging of us to go another way. Steve wasn't convinced that was what was being indicated and thought that maybe it was a car crash ahead. Who knows, but we did see smoke and we did go another way - only to get lost. Eventually we found the station and arranged for the bikes to be transported in the same train as us, the overnighter direct to Tehran. Information booths at places like railway stations were manned by women (if that's not an oxymoron). Despite being ruled by a very authoritarian regime, which the public seems to tolerate rather than like, more women than men go to university. I was told the ratio is approaching 65:35.

We'd got the bikes squared away by the early afternoon so we had quite a bit of time looking round the central city and the bazaar. Steve slept in the park while I chatted with a troop of five local kids who told me they were all brothers. The town was pleasant. We found all of Iran pleasant,

just as I had in the 70s. The Persian people are hospitable and friendly. They go out of their way to help strangers and are gracious with it. Some even apologised for their government. They felt that they were getting bad press around the world. We had to agree. Usually, after some kindness by locals, I would reflect on how they had been pretty damn nice considering they were from 'The Axis of Evil'. What a shame our world leaders couldn't do some real travelling and learn a little humility and forbearance.

Iran gets by despite the United States and other nations not allowing their businesses to trade with it. Iran's oil wealth helps its survival a lot, but the resolute nature of the Persian people is probably also a contributing factor. They make their own range of motorcycles and assemble several European cars. They even export their Citroens and Peugeots to countries like South Africa. In the past they assembled Land Rovers. Quite a few still trundle around in their inimitable way. Every time we saw a Landie I thought of Dick who has an orange Mk 1 he's had since before I met him in 1978. We spotted a few of the old Citroen 2CVs, but for travellers to Iran in the last 30 years, one of their most lasting memories is always of the main locally-assembled vehicle, the Paykan. I wrote the following piece on our web site heralding it.

The Paykan is dead. Long live the Paykan. Not the big bird with an orange beak (that's a toucan). A Paykan is an Iranian car that has been made since the late 1960s. It's the English Hillman Hunter. It has served the country well but finally after a few reprieves, production has recently stopped. You may think that this car is insignificant ... otherwise you would have heard of it. Perhaps, but there are over TWO MILLION of them on Iran's roads, almost all of them white, and they've been a huge part of the country's recent history. Iranians have always felt they owned this car. It had their Persian name on it. They also assembled Land Rovers and Citroen 2CVs but these were still branded as in the parent country. The Paykan was and is theirs. This became even stronger when the UK finished production in the early 70s and ultimately the parent died the normal death of England's car industry stalwarts. The climate of Iran is such that cars don't rust and as the car has been in continuous production for over 30 years, there's no problem with parts. All the bits that break or fail are available from one end of the country to the other ... no one-off light lens that cost hundreds of dollars. These are simple, robust cars, suited to a harsh land. A car from the 60s is not the fuel efficient, air-bagged, ABS equipped paragon of today's roads, so it should go. With fuel now only reaching 10c per litre, the efficiency wasn't a problem, but with Kias, Peugeots and Citroens being built locally (and exported) competition and progress has finally defeated the old Paykan.

It's hard to date the cars as it always depends on how well they've been looked after. We rode in one that was 33 years old. We also rode in one with the plastic covers still on the seats. There wasn't a lot of difference. The new one had central locking but externally they were identical. There could be problems with identifying your own car though. Often there are lines of white Paykans. I can imagine this being a nightmare for my wife, Steph. She has always had unusual cars that were easily identifiable including a Fiat 600

and Citroen Safari wagon. With her work Toyota she has problems. She just isn't interested in cars that look alike, and is always trying her key in Mazdas, Hondas and Nissans. If they're the same colour as the Toyota, they could be the Toyota. In Tehran with a street full of white Paykans, she could be all day getting home with the groceries.

One hour shopping, three hours trying to find the right car. Perhaps it was really women power that caused their demise, not poor performance or efficiency.

Whatever the reason, Persians have much to be proud of with the production of the Paykan. They made the sturdy Hillman Hunter a multimillion seller, something the English couldn't do.

The Paykan is dead. Long live the Paykan.

The train trip through the night to Tehran was uneventful although we were intrigued that there were prayer stops along the way. Folk would get off and pray at a mosque on the railway platform. This train ride was sad in that it finally spelt the death of my dream to find Ernie, my old ES2 Norton. I'd left Ernie in Esfahan in 1974. That adventure was like several in my youth; embarked upon without much planning. As the weather got colder we had ridden further and further east, with no way of getting back across Europe and without the funds to winter over in India as many did. After being snowed in, in eastern Turkey, Ernie had been put on a train to Tehran. The customs officials hadn't stamped our passports to show we had a motor vehicle, as it was in the back of the train and we were in the front. So we'd got into Iran without the bike being logged against us. This enabled us to later sell Ernie to Shaking Minarets in Esfahan for three Persian carpets. I still think of Ernie and that trip when I walk on those rugs. Maybe there could be another sortie looking for Ernie in the future.

You have to make compromises when you're travelling. I was still trying for Willy's party, even though it seemed highly unlikely we could make it. I was scheduled to fly out of Amsterdam on the Sunday after so there wasn't much time to spare even for that. All going well we would probably make it to Arnhem in the week after the party, maybe about Wednesday. There was no point in waiting around for a week to get the next train through to Istanbul, so we decided to take a train to Tabriz in the west of Iran and ride through to Turkey. We might even find another linking train service. I was sorry we were hurrying in such a special part of the world and felt I was cheating Steve a bit. I had so enjoyed my time riding slowly across Turkey and Iran in the 1970s, but this wasn't the time to be meandering about revelling in the exotic locations and antiquities. We were on a mission and we'd give it the best shot we could. Besides, Steve is young and can come back and wander about with the companions of his choice any time he likes. It won't be the Last Hurrah for him.

From my youth I recalled Tehran as being the most tumultuous city I had ever been to. The traffic was the craziest and most incessant. Tehran on a Friday meant that lots of places were closed, being the Sabbath, and it was a little less dynamic than I remembered. With a population of more than fourteen million people it was a huge bustling city. We'd booked the bikes on to Tabriz so spent the day tracking down an email facility and visiting the museum. The museum has lots of interesting old stuff from the ancient city of Persepolis and also a 2,000-year-old preserved head, which had recently been found in a salt mining area. With his wispy long hair and big beard he looked like an antecedent who had perished on an earlier Molloy adventure.

In Tehran we also ate pizza. Pizza is now a staple of the Iranian diet. Don't ask me how this came about, but there are now towns that vie for the title of The Pizza Capital of Iran. On my previous visit, standard fare was always spicy minced lamb as a kebab on a pile of steamed rice, served with flat bread similar to naan from Pakistan and India.

The temperature now ranged between 30 and 40 degrees which was just hot, not screamingly, debilitatingly hot. This slight drop in temperature and an easing of my problems meant that a little of my vitality was returning. I was feeling more resilient and stronger with each day; fortunate given what was ahead of us. It was now July 15. We only had nine days to get across to Europe and up to Arnhem. It still didn't look likely, but I thought we might only miss by a couple of days. We could rest on the overnight train to Tabriz before riding from Tabriz to the Turkish border. We hoped this border wasn't like the Mongolia to China and Kyrgyzstan to China borders - closed on the weekends. The train ride was filled with memorable travelling companions. We shared with a salesman who traded in onyx and other semi-precious stones, and an expat dentist. Nik introduced himself in good English. As well as a dentist he was a magician. Although as a student he had protested against the Shah, he had fled Iran when the Ayatollah Khomeini came to power. He'd spent five years doing further training in Sweden, went to the United States for 15 years then to Australia, where he'd been for the last 10 years. He had just attended a dentists' conference in Tehran and was now visiting his family in Tabriz. He was informative about Iran. He told us he could come back and earn a good living but his teenage daughters, having been brought up in Australia, wouldn't countenance living under such a restrictive regime, although they quite liked visiting.

Nik got great service for us by doing a magic trick for the steward. He then offered to do a couple of tricks for us. Before he began he drew the curtains tight as one of the tricks involved cards, illegal in Iran. There were only two rules. We weren't to ask how the trick was done and he would only do each trick once. We agreed. His tricks defied belief. We watched closely for the sleight of hand but none of us saw anything other than magic, pure magic. We saw things happen that we know can't have happened. This made us laugh. We knew we'd been hoodwinked, but who knew how? Nik and the stone salesman gave an insight into Iran's recent past. They were both middle-aged but one had lived 30 years in the west looking in. The other had endured the restrictive regimes that had followed the fall of the Shah. They were both Muslims, but moderate in their beliefs.

Occasionally we saw religious leaders on our train travels. They all looked fierce and staunch. They never seemed to crack a smile or pass the time of day with any of the teeming masses that passed through the railway stations each day. This was such a contrast to the almost universally jovial demeanour of the Iranian people.

At 6 a.m. we were folding up our beds and preparing to say goodbye to our companions. We made our way into the city for breakfast. The bikes were arriving on a later train, due around 9 o'clock. Regaining our bikes was to prove quite a challenge. Even after the train arrived and the goods carriages were shunted off onto a siding, it looked like a classic case of 'first on, last off'. Steve did a lot of negotiating and urging while I wrote a dispatch on my pocket computer. In the end we completed the unloading when the stevedores went off for lunch. It was quite an effort shifting things around in the wagon and finally getting the old girls down to ground level. It was two in the afternoon before we rode out of the railway station.

It was hot but not unpleasant and the ride across to the border was

an excellent afternoon's achievement. The surroundings were greener and hills were shadowing us a bit. There was always something to look at and ponder on. The countryside was lush and whilst not affluent looking, it was very different to the harsh desert environment we'd encountered in the south east. Perhaps it was my improving health, but all seemed well in the world of The Last Hurrah. We almost ran out of petrol but reached a gas station in the nick of time. Getting to the border while there was still daylight was a great reward. Up ahead was Mt Ararat where Noah's Ark is reputed to rest. The colours in the late afternoon, early evening were a purple and blue treat. The border crossing took three hours or so and was the usual test of patience. You always think your paperwork is valid, the officials make you think that it isn't, and several hours are spent proving you are right. We passed into Turkey after dark and made to the nearest town and a welcome bed. At the border I'd seen a sign which was like a revelation to me. Istanbul was listed as being a bit over 1,600 kilometres away. I'd thought it was quite a bit further.

Suddenly, being encouraged and feeling strong, it came over me that if we rode and rode and rode, we could do this in two days, couldn't we? Before bed I asked Steve if he was up for the huge challenge of averaging 800 kilometres for a couple of days. "Of course", he replied. It was like a light going on. If we could ride to Istanbul in two days, ride to Igumentia in two days, take a boat to Venice for a day and a night, we'd have two-and-a-half days to get to Arnhem. It was bloody possible, just.

The hotel we stayed in overnight had no lock-up and advised us to put the bikes in the back bar area. So in through the front door we rode on our thunderous great steeds, past the surprised patrons quietly drinking in the front bar. We again put newspaper under the old girls and retired, having told the staff we'd be off early in the morning.

Dawn wasn't a welcome arrival as she found us still in bed and feeling drowsy. However the excitement of the day's challenge soon had us up

and preparing for departure. Today we were going to show how tough and dedicated we really were. The routine of riding all day in chunks had already been established, but today we would do it with more fervour. We rode until morning tea, had a break, rode until lunch, had a break, rode until afternoon tea ... just like a work day. I remembered eastern Turkey as being strongly Muslem and quite unlike the west of the country which is more like Europe (well, the land west of Istanbul is in Europe). This was still so, but as we didn't ever pause for long it was hard to know how much it had changed.

This first day's ride introduced us to European petrol prices. In Iran, 10 or 12 litres of fuel in each bike would cost between $2.20 and $2.40, in total. We were astonished to find that our first Turkish fill-up set us back $55.00. This was the sort of price we were to pay for the rest of the trip. Even though the price was so high, there were gas stations everywhere. They all had enormous signs urging you to buy. They would sometimes be alongside each other and in the spirit of free enterprise, there were many different brands. We could recall about twenty. They were mostly ultra-modern facilities with food outlets included. There was no excuse for running out of petrol now.

The roads were good and the undulating countryside interesting without being stunning. The bikes were humming along well although I could sense a flatness in Penelope's performance. The exhaust note sounded a little different. I just hoped it wasn't a valve beginning to burn. We didn't have time to stop and give her a valve grind. I wasn't sure either if we had a valve spring compressor with us so I tried not to waste energy worrying about something that might not happen.

Quite a while after dark and 15 hours after we hit the road, we decided to call it a day. We'd reached a town called Savas and on the ring road was a petrol station with an attached motor hotel. We'd covered a bit over 700 kilometres, a good achievement even though it meant there were still 900 kilometres to go to reach Istanbul. We were knackered but quite buoyant. Even if we didn't get all the way next day we'd set a daunting benchmark. Seven-hundred kilometres in a day, on an old classic bike, is something you tell your mates about. We were getting a bit pissed off at Dawn, but again she dug us out early and we hit the road with grim determination. We decided to keep going that day until we reached our goal.

Our longest day ended at 1.30 a.m. in a grotty hotel in Istanbul, yet there isn't a hell of a lot to tell about it. We relentlessly ground our way across the Anatolian land mass. There were some great fun hilly bits and generally everything went according to plan. Some time after dark we finally saw the sea. Aptly, it was The Black Sea. It had been 15,000 kilometres or so since we'd seen the sea and that had been from an aeroplane (Beijing is a little way inland). It had been a long trip to the beach.

At our last stop for petrol and sustenance, about 100 kilometres short of Istanbul, a couple of young bikers came across to see us. They had what are known as Motard bikes. To the lay person, these look like trail bikes with smaller front wheels and road tyres, which is more or less what they are. One of them had a pretty fast one (200+ kph). He was reputedly the Turkish road racing champion in the road bike class and next year he was moving up to Superbikes. His brother in Germany was currently second in the Superstock 600 class and quite famous, with a web site and fan club. As is often the case when you meet friendly folk who don't speak your language, we weren't sure whether these guys had been drinking or whether they were always that way. When we were getting ready to leave, the champion biker said he would wheelie with us all the way to Istanbul. Hardly had we got out onto the motorway when they came by showing off. They both had great skills, but the champ had astonishing control. He would come by wheelieing quite happily in the fast lane, juggernauts up his bum with horns blaring. It was 10.30 at night and he was riding at the even speed of the traffic in whichever lane he chose.

To pop a wheelie needs a bit of power to get the front wheel up. To keep it there you can either keep accelerating or go to the point of overbalancing, then keep it there with skill. If you seem to be going to go over backwards, a touch of the back brake will bring the bike forward again. If the bike starts to drop frontwards to the ground, you give it more throttle. To go around corners you just lean a little. Well that's what I presume you do because physics says that would work. This guy could do it at all sorts of speeds and he could maintain it, go around corners, change lanes, nothing was a problem. It was bloody scary for us. I had to keep telling myself that it was going to be his skin not mine that was going to be lost. They did all sorts of tricks as we made our way along the motorway. The piece de resistance was mono-wheeling while standing on the seat. This means you can't use the back brake to keep yourself up, you have to do it all by balance and throttle control. Watching this loony doing this at night with the headlight pointing up into the sky, on a crowded three-lane motorway, going at probably 120+ kph was a surreal and scary experience. They also rode with their hands crossed over on the wrong sides of the bars. I tried this and it isn't easy. Steve filmed some of their antics but unfortunately the camera had been knocked off autofocus and the result was crap. We were relieved when they got bored with playing and left us to get on with finding Istanbul.

This day had taxed us to the limit, but 900 kilometres had been cracked. We were now only 1,000 kilometres from the ferry at Igumentia; two good days' ride. At my peak, I'm pretty good with sleep deprivation, but these two massive days had been really tiring and Dawn didn't get a look in next morning. We were sluggish and idled away a few hours sorting out emails and gaining strength. We had a cheery email from Dick and were relieved to learn he was on the mend. It was a shame Steve wouldn't get a good look at this jewel of a city either. It was nearly lunchtime before we were saddled up and away. We crossed the huge bridge over the Bosphorus and were now in Europe, with Asia behind us. The ride out to the Greek border took us past a few resorts. People were basking in the sun and playing on the beaches. This was alien to us, having spent so long away from the coast and travelling through Muslem countries. We'd noticed the mosques giving away to Christian churches as we got across into the west of Turkey, and they became more common as we headed towards Greece. The overt commercialisation of the area was a little too overpowering for me. I don't like huge roadside signs at the best of times. It was late afternoon before we reached the Greek border but it was our easiest crossing to date. The carnets made all the difference when it came to convincing officials that we own the bikes. They show they're registered somewhere. We aren't going to sell them in their country because if we don't take them out the other side, we won't get our money back.

As usual, the day was quite hot. The riding became more varied as we skirted some hills and passed through or around small Greek towns.

We rode until just after dark; another 400 kilometres were behind us. We would possibly have carried on but Penelope's light switch decided to call it a day and refused to allow current to flow to the lights. I'd ridden with my lights on throughout the trip. I'd noticed in the previous couple of days that the switch had become a little notchy, and I thought that it was fair enough as we'd been through some dusty times. Electrical fittings on British motorbikes of Penelope's era were usually made by Joseph Lucas, known by all as 'The Prince of Darkness', a title that was well deserved. To provide reliable generation of the white stuff that comes out the front of the headlight, I had resorted to a modern French invention called an Alton, an alternator that fits in the same space as the old Lucas generator. This had powered my lights reliably since Beijing, even after being submerged during our dunking in the Chinese river. It was a shame it was being let down by the switch gear. I reasoned that there were enough daylight hours to avoid riding at night any more. If we had to then I was sure I could direct-wire something to make it work.

Kavala was a small bustling holiday town. The young were all out, parading up and down the streets as only the Europeans do. Lots of scantily clad young women were racing up and down the streets on motor scooters. Sometimes they were pursued tenaciously by their male equivalents, who were usually popping wheelies to show how cool they were. We stayed the night in an old family hotel, and the proprietoress wanted us to bring the bikes into her marble-lined lobby. That night however, we took the risk of leaving them out on the road. The old girls aren't really valuable enough to steal and are too distinctive to just go joyriding on. Neither bike needs a key to start them, but the rituals to be followed to fire up a big long-stroke single cylinder British motorcycle are like the Masons' secret handshake - you need to be trained and inducted.

We were a lot friskier next day and were on the road reasonably early. It was over 600 kilometres to the port town of Igumentia. Most of the day was interesting, but hardly memorable in the context of where we'd been and what we'd seen. The last 200 kilometres were the exception. The road went through the mountains and a tanker driver told us it was the worst road you could imagine, being twisty and hilly. We salivated at the thought. Corners, yum. Ups and downs, yum, yum. This ride was delicious - a veritable feast with no resulting indigestion (or other unmentionables). I'll remember it for ever. The scenery was breathtaking, with deep valleys often lying far below the road and rugged hills towering above. The road itself twisted and turned and dipped and rose and snaked; it was challenging and rewarding. All the aggressive drivers would pass us on the straight bits, then every time they encountered a slow vehicle or a tight twisty section, we'd be by in a flash. This was invigorating. Even after nearly three months of riding, it was great to have an afternoon of such good fun. It wasn't an easy day because of the heat and the distance, but the stops were good and the mountain section outstanding.

It was dusk when we finally reached Igumentia. We stopped outside a ferry booking office on the hill leading down to the town centre. A lot of friendly banter went on as we provisionally booked a ferry for the morning. Steve went off with the manager to get the tickets and then find a hotel. I stayed chatting to the 16-year-old nephew in the warm evening and reflected on our achievements. Seeing a thermometer still reading in the 30s, I asked the young lad how hot the day had been. "40 degrees", he replied. I probably smirked a little, knowing that we'd faced a lot hotter than that. No wonder it had only seemed moderately hot.

Once tickets and a room were sorted, we set off down town to find the email facility. The bar was way out past the docks where all the ferries were moored. This is the jumping off point for Corfu and ferries abound. Most of them were drawn up to the land front-on with their mouths open, ready to take cars and people. Our emails included another posting from Dick that further encouraged us. I responded to the group and included a few words about the temporary inhabitants of the town.

The summer season is well under way here and the town is full of sun-loving folk. And doesn't that look good on the young! Not quite so good on the slightly older though. Ladies, please keep the bits you want to preserve, out of the sun. Personally, I've always liked ladies' white bits, soft and smooth. Hell, you can't tell that I've been away for three months can you?

It's a weird feeling knowing you're racing hard for a goal yet tonight you will rest, tomorrow you will rest and the next night you will rest, before all hell breaks out again. The bikes were finally starting to ail a bit with the Norton now leaking oil. Penelope was definitely burning a valve and becoming harder to start and there was a squeakiness to her exhaust note. We were tired, but happy. I was only a little disappointed that we would not be going up the old Yugoslavian coast. I would have liked to ride it again to see if it lived up to my memories. We had hoped to travel through Albania, something I couldn't do 30 years ago. The ferry would get us right to Venice in a day and night, whereas we'd take three or four days by road. It was an easy choice and we would luxuriate in the idleness of a sea cruise.

In the morning we had to push start Penelope for the first time. Compression was down, so this was the only way to bring life to her. It wasn't far to our ferry and soon we were on board asking for tie-downs to secure the bikes. The crew looked at us as though we were from another planet. They indicated we should put the bikes on their stands and just go upstairs. We're used to the temperamental Cook Strait separating the North and South Islands of New Zealand. On a bad day it also separates ferry passengers from their last meal. If you didn't tie down the bike if would fall over during the voyage. The Mediterranean wasn't like that, we were told. Begrudgingly, the crew found us a couple of rubber wedges to put somewhere. They weren't really suitable, but we shoved them under the bikes and figured that if it did get rough then probably the crew would run around tying things down. As it happened, they were right and we were wrong. The sea stayed as flat as a pond for the 24 hours that we were on board. If you didn't look out the window, you wouldn't know you were on the ocean. Shortly after the voyage I penned a few words.

Igumentia and the ferry to Venice were a huge contrast to where we've come from. Sun worshippers flock to the Greek Islands and this is their route home. Not a Chador or Burqa in sight. These folk have worked so hard on their all-over tans that they must show them off, otherwise it has all been wasted. Some of these men and women are stunning examples of what can be achieved in the way of improvement over what our maker created. There are also many, many examples of what the rest of us achieve. There are elephantine folk wearing less than is required to wrap an iceblock. I can't say that I found it appealing in the slightest. Also, no one has told the middle-aged, overweight European male that the wearing of skimpy Speedos is not a good look.

I don't want to labour the point but most of us should remain fully clad, in public, for most of our lives. Yes, there is probably a short time in our youth when we look pretty good but other than that, I don't think so. A couple of nice-looking girls, whom I took to be twins, loitered around the area we had established ourselves in. They were still in that youthful short time. There was also a slightly older, tall, statuesque beauty who, if there is a creator, had been made in her image. We had travelled huge distances without seeing overweight or obese people and now suddenly, not only were we surrounded by them, but most of them were semi-naked.

We didn't have a cabin so our time was spent on the back deck. We read and had a few beers and icecreams - quite boring really as there wasn't anything to look at overboard, just open sea. On board there were the people frolicking by the pool and mostly that wasn't pretty. It was funny being so anonymous. There wasn't a soul there who knew we had just ridden from China. They probably just dismissed us as scruffy down-and-outers and maybe wondered about the pairing of one middle-aged, balding chubby guy and one fit, virile young guy. But all the time we rested, our batteries were being recharged, so sleep deprivation shouldn't be a problem up ahead. I figured on only about 1,200 kilometres to go once we hit Venice, with two-and-a-half days to do it in. Our only concern was the bikes.

Day became night, things got a bit rowdy (led by some Kiwis, of course), things quietened down, we found some floor-space indoors, then night became day again. It was quite a bit cooler than we'd been used to and the mood on board seemed to change a little. The holiday was behind, getting home was now the focus. The crowd at the rail was sombre, yet also interested in Venice unfolding before us. It was fascinating to watch the Venetians going off to work in water transport, barges moving cranes around, police boats bustling along and all the while we were gently moving through the main waterway into the docks. We could see up the main canals as we passed by. The beautiful old buildings and stunning architecture in general held us spellbound. This was a wonderful introduction to Venice for those who hadn't seen it before. For Steve and I, who had visited previously, it was a fresh insight into an old acquaintance.

It wasn't long before we were gassed up and on the highways of northern Italy. We were heading across towards Slovenia. We would turn north before we reached Trieste and then pass through Austria and Bavaria. After Munich we would head for Stuttgart, then Frankfurt, to Cologne and on to Arnhem. It looked like a reasonably straightforward route and had the benefit of taking us past Dick's friend Erik's place in Ludwigshafen. Erik had been an officer on a freighter. He was introduced to Dick as a person who could take him hunting in New Zealand. That had been 40 years ago. For many years they hunted together whenever Erik was in town. He had retired from the sea and was now running a successful trucking company in Germany. He'd been in touch earlier telling Dick if help was needed, he could have a truck to us in no time, wherever we were. I also knew that

RACING FOR HOME

some of their workshop guys were motorcyclists who had been following our adventure, and they were keen to ride along with us for a bit if it fitted in. Sadly it didn't look like it would. Ludwigshafen was too far for us to get to in one day but we wanted to be past there on the second day, so as to only leave a couple of hundred kilometress for the Sunday morning. The ride across Italy was dull until we turned into the hills and crossed into Austria. This was again spectacular alpine countryside. Sadly, we had decided that the only way to make good time in Europe was to stick to the motorways. We could see the most wonderful minor roads following our route, often hundreds of feet below as we scooted along a straight, smooth autostrada which ducked in and out of tunnels and over many bridges. Now that we were in the European Union the borders were just lines on a map and we swept by two of them in one day. Six-hundred kilometres later we reached Gunzburg, and stayed at a motor hotel which cost as much as we'd spent in a week in Central Asia. We felt it was way too good for us but beds seemed to be at a premium and it was getting dark. Earlier, near Munich, we'd been flagged down by an expat Kiwi who'd offered us hospitality. But because of the need to get miles under our belts we'd declined. Our 'NZ' stickers and odd-looking registration plates were creating a lot of interest. People passing by would often give us a cheery wave and a thumb's up sign. At gas stations people would look at the old, very soiled bikes and the stickers, put two and two together and realise we'd just ridden from the other side of the world. We did a lot of smiling as the enormity of it finally began to sink in. We'd done just that - ridden half way around the world.

Our second to last day was just another day behind bars, a day at the office, but like one just before the Christmas break. You tough it out without enthusiasm knowing that there's a welcome break to follow shortly. The Norton was still making like the Torrey Canyon and putting out quite a bit of oil from the cylinder head region. We couldn't trace its origin as the speed smeared the oil everywhere. A battery wire broke off causing us a short delay while we located the fault and rectified it. Meanwhile Penelope was only just holding her own. She could usually give me 80-90 kph but she was dying away, with no acceleration available. She needed a rest but she wasn't going to get one. There wasn't time.

We found the autobahns of Germany quite scary. We were too slow for the traffic. Even the trucks were much faster, so we were constantly being passed by everything. It was dangerous. Some of our closest shaves came on these roads. Certainly, they were the most stressful because of the big speed differentials. They are amazing arteries though and I remembered Dick telling us that Hitler had them built with a 50 kilometre radius curve to them. Although they appear straight, they aren't. They curve and you get to see the countryside. A tender side to the tyrant? We'd missed Dick immensely, often posing questions we felt he would know the answer to. Often it was just trivia that you'd normally discuss at the end of the day. "Where are Scanias made? Have you worked on 2CVs?"

Our last night was spent in a small village about 75 kilometres south of Cologne. We'd done 400 kilometres in colder conditions than we were used to and with only the 200 left we felt we deserved an early finish. We chanced upon a small family hotel and it suited us just fine. There were plenty of hours of daylight left to have a bit of a look around. The hosts were friendly and hospitable but asked us to move the incontinent bikes away from the pristine front of the hotel. That was OK. The girls looked lovely resting over by the trees. Our final start needed to be early and we'd arranged for the breakfast to be left outside the door. We had a date with destiny at noon.

I'd emailed our supporters that we would be reaching Arnhem at that time. Dick had told us of a suitable spot just out of town where we could meet anyone that wanted to be there. Dick couldn't come as he didn't have easy access to transport, so we'd be seeing him at the party. We knew

Rollo was coming over from England, and he'd be bringing something with bubbles in it. We were looking forward to meeting him as all our contact, bar one telephone call, had been by email.

We got away early and Penelope kept chugging along. It looked like we would make it OK. Of course nothing was certain, as we'd found in Pakistan with the broken fork leg. Fortunately, there was no repeat. With half an hour to go we stopped, refuelled and took stock. This was the end. It was funny trying to imagine life after today. We wouldn't have to ride. Was that nice or wasn't it? We weren't sure. I knew that within a few days I would return to being a worker drone, a wage slave. Our novelty value was almost over, but not yet. There was one Last Hurrah to go.

We sat across from the gas station and tried to set up the helmet camera again. A photo shows us looking happy and relaxed. This was when we found the dry-soldered joint in a cable connection had broken, rendering that function of the camera useless. We watched as a convoy of brightly coloured Citroen 2CVs, some with matching trailers, pulled up. Just as we

were finishing our adventure, they were starting theirs - an international rally in Scotland.

We were justifiably euphoric as we rode those last few kilometres to our rendezvous. It wasn't hard to find, as it was where commuters left their cars before taking the train into Arnhem. There, waving crazily, was Rollo. With him was Hans, a Dutch Panther owner. We were a fashionable 10 minutes late, not bad after three months of riding and all the trials that had been put before us. It was a joyous moment. Within seconds we were slugging back the champagne. Rollo and Hans were both appreciative of our efforts to get there, just as we were of theirs. Hans' Panther wasn't running so he had come on a BMW twin. Rollo's Panther was as stunning in real life as in the photos. It was great having an audience each. Rollo and I yakked away while Steve and Hans did similarly.

It was funny in a way. I'd expected a few others to turn up, judging by the interest we'd received through the web site. I'd thought some from the Dutch Norton club might have turned up, along with other locals who

THE LAST HURRAH

RACING FOR HOME

knew Dick. Apparently my emails to the 800 or so supporters, saying where we were and giving them details of our arrival, hadn't been getting through to more than a few at the front of the alphabet. This had happened earlier in the trip and we thought the problem had been fixed.

As it happened, it was nice to have quality over quantity. Rollo and Hans both took piles of photos before we decided it was time to find the old fella and his sister. We farewelled Hans, and Rollo led us into the town centre. From there we found our way out to the party which was just across the road from Willy and Jan's house. The venue was part of a huge facility for returned soldiers, and was set in big park-like grounds with a long driveway winding up to the beautiful old buildings. Just as we parked our bikes we met Dick's older brother Rijj and his wife (another Willy) and also Sharon's daughter Megan and son-in- law John who had also come over from England. As we crossed the road Megan leant over and quietly asked, "How's your arse?" I gave a non-committal answer and we laughed. Then we saw the man himself.

Dick had left us 12 days earlier a scruffy, befuddled, sick old man. Here before us was a trimmed and scrubbed up, 20-year-younger version of the man who left us in Iran. He looked a picture of health and vitality. This was a hugely emotional moment for us. The video camera catches us both blubbing. This was probably an unexpected outpouring of relief. Dick had worried over us, just as we'd worried about him. Arm in arm we made our way up the drive, pausing for photos at a cannon before making our entrance to Willy's party. We were conscious that this was Willy's big day. We were just a tiny sideshow, especially as Dick had been recuperating for nearly two weeks. Willy welcomed us effusively and with more warmth than we deserved. We were still road- soiled and very unkempt-looking (probably smelly as well). It had taken Dick more than a week to gain any strength but now he was positively chipper. He was in his new pants, teamed with a clean, white patterned shirt, belonging to Jan. This was the smartest I had ever seen him.

There was little time for collectively wallowing in glory. One minute we were all together and then we were all heading off in different directions. Megan and John went back to their hotel late on Sunday night after the party. Rollo headed back to the UK on Monday morning, after promising to come out to New Zealand soon. Tuesday morning Steve left us to go off to Belgium before returning to Grenoble where he'd worked earlier. He still had a month or so before he would return to New Zealand.

Also on Tuesday Dick and I hired a car and went back into Germany to see his friends Erik and Ilona. A few wonderful days followed before we returned on Friday to the accepting warmth of Willy and Jan. Saturday was spent reflecting, doing some preparation work on the bikes for the freighting home and having a couple of local walks. Dick and I had enjoyed many walks together in most of the countries we had travelled through. It was fitting that we finished with a few in his home town. Arnhem is a pleasant, verdant town. Dick's family were wonderful hosts and it was great hearing him talking in his native tongue. Often he wouldn't know which language he was speaking and frequently spoke to me in Dutch, then wondered why I was unresponsive. But my time was up and on Sunday 31 July 2005 I started my 40-something hour trip home. Dick was to stay for another couple of weeks. Some of it would be spent showing Geoff around, the friend who'd seen us off in Beijing. Geoff wasn't there for our arrival, but he was in Europe for business and would be going home on the same plane as Dick.

The Last Hurrah was now over. It had been a magnificent charge across the world. On Tuesday I was home in the arms of the family and on Wednesday I went to the barber for a number three hair and beard cut. By late morning I was back at work, leaner and …

THE LAST HURRAH

CHAPTER 10

AFTERMATH

When Rollo Turner, our publisher, read the first draft of the manuscript, he said he needed more of me. He felt that by the end of the book he knew little more about me than when he started. I reread and added a few words but still didn't know how to achieve the insight he was after. I had already, in Kiwi parlance, 'spewed my guts out'. What more was there to know? I hadn't had a roadside epiphany. I didn't have another persona giving rise to deep and meaningful wisdoms that I could share. Photos show me to be very ordinary, and that was the nub of this whole journey. It was an ordinary person's adventure. I know that lurking inside this soft exterior is a soft interior. I lack physical hardness. I'm not a very good 'details' person. I'm not a good mechanic, cook or hunter-gatherer. I know I don't have high energy levels or drive. To the contrary, I've elevated lethargy to a golden pedestal and pay homage daily. I have always, jokingly, given out advice that "if you aim low enough, you'll always be successful"! I am, however, happy with my space. I have a reputation of 'rolling with the punches' and being easy to get on with. What you see is what you get, although in the words of one of our Toyota ads, "I would say that". I'm also fairly resilient and unfathomably optimistic.

A pre-edit read of the manuscript was also done by an English teacher friend who said I didn't tell her enough of the landscape for her to envisage it. My overuse of the adjective 'amazing' had irritated her – it told her nothing. She wanted the 'crumpled blanket of brown' and 'rust-red cliffs' type of description. I was literally amazed on so many occasions. I can fob off my descriptive inadequacies as being a deliberate ploy to make you buy the DVD to see the sights. If there's a colour in nature, we saw it at some stage. We saw craggy, we saw lush, we saw 'river deep, mountain high', we saw shimmering deserts stretching further than the eye can see. We saw pollution, congestion, procreation, devastation, forestation and any other 'ation' you care to name. We experienced solitude, gratitude and every tactile, aural, nasal and visual sensation. At times we suffered sensory overload. When we were camping without the glare of a city to intrude, the night sky sometimes produced a fairyland of twinkling stars like a glow-worm grotto, the Milky Way so three-dimensional it was breathtaking. It was wonderful to experience and share those moments.

On our return, a five-minute feature was broadcast on national TV. Although he didn't say a lot, Dick produced a couple of pearls of wisdom. He advised the viewers, "not to wait too long, as before you know it, you're knackered." This was particularly poignant for many of us, as Dick was then recovering from a stroke. Fortunately, his recovery has been successful and he's back, able to ride his Nortons. During the interview he also made the telling statement, "Some people have said that it must have been wonderful. It wasn't wonderful, every day. It wasn't beautiful, every day".

A couple of my own groan-inducing quotes have gone down in family folklore. Even the kids' friends parrot, "we had the best of days and we had the worst of days". My other inanity has been trotted out by several friends, on returning from their travels, "We went as mates and we came back as mates". Often the two quotes are put together and everyone rolls about laughing at my expense. Luckily I'm not a sensitive soul.

I believe I chose my companions well. They were the extraordinary components of The Last Hurrah. I would never subjugate the legend to 'mere mortal' status and describe Dick as ordinary. Although we talk of sequels, this truly could be his last hurrah and he should be revered for what he achieved. As for the Cabin Boy, this trip showed me that Steve is exceptional in many ways (beyond just being tied to me by a blood connection).

These two wonderful companions made this venture the memorable event it became. One older and wiser, with a million tales; the other younger, with dynamic vitality and drive. After returning to his studies Steve received a grant to do a couple of months' research in East Timor, on the management of aid at the community level. He spent the early part of 2006 doing this in his usual self-effacing way.

The narration doesn't always address the mundane questions friends ask like, "Where did you get petrol?" or "Where did you sleep?". This chapter attempts to provide those snippets of information, and may even answer questions you never thought to ask.

Wherever there are people, there will be petrol. Our research had told us that we would struggle to find petrol in the Gobi region of Mongolia (remember, we only had a range of 300 kilometres in our tanks). As it happened, we never needed more. We carted a jerrycan for a while, and the guide carried extra for us. Often the petrol depot would consist of a single pump, locked in a small enclosure or shed. In both Mongolia and Pakistan, the pumping was done by hand on numerous occasions. Where there was a choice of 80 or 91 octane, we usually chose the 80. It was much cheaper and our bikes grew up in a time when that would have been the norm. At times we had petrol that was listed as low as 76 octane. The low compression of both bikes was ideally suited for this usage.

We slept where we could. Sometimes it was in guesthouses, often we camped and on one occasion we scored a four-star hotel. Similarly, we ate what was available. In China it was Chinese, in Mongolia it was nearly always boiled lamb with a few potatoes and noodles included, in the 'stans' people were big kebab eaters and so were we. In Pakistan we ate chicken every day and Iran gave us pizza. Many of the countries had three-minute noodles, always a good standby for breakfast. Eating wasn't a problem.

We had our dehydrated food as an emergency back-up and we also had some NZ Army rations which had been gifted to us. Although these come in quite a few flavours, the writing on the package is tiny and hard to read. Dick inadvertently packed only one flavour, and we soon became bored with that. These sachets can also, supposedly, be eaten cold as the food is for combat troops. It's a hideous thought. Wars should be decided by who can eat these rations cold and survive. Emptied out, they look a bit like a cross between dog food and the pulp that babies are given. Hot, they're passable, cold, they're like something participants might eat on the reality television show Fear Factor.

Bottled water was available everywhere we travelled, even though it was quite often evident that the manufacturers were using false labels. A surprising number of the fruit juices in Central Asia are owned by Coca Cola, whilst the biggest water company seems to be Nestlé. A dead give away in the forged version is the lack of the acute accent over the e in Nestlé.

Most countries had wonderful icecream. We didn't indulge much with sweets, but one of the big delights of the trip was Dick's sharing of his one kilo of jelly beans. (He had these as an emergency sugar boost.) After quite a few weeks of not using them, he rationed us a few and what a treat that was. Later still, he gave us what was left and we pigged out in manic fashion.

We rode with Nolan open-face helmets because of their comfort and lightness, being also airy in the hot conditions. They had the added advantage of having a visor that could be lifted when it was hot or kept down when it was cold, or kept down when it was bloody hot.

Each of us had different types of clothing that satisfied the needs of the trip. My eight-pocketed army surplus trousers enabled me to carry a couple of kilos of stuff in my pockets, albeit with the braces groaning under the strain. The merino wool Icebreaker™ tops proved to be good in both hot and cold conditions. They had the added bonus of not getting smelly too quickly. Ditto with the merino/possum socks.

One of the most difficult trivial things of the trip was keeping all the required documentation in good condition. We had paperwork inches thick. Add that to the guidebooks and maps and the total was impressive. Usually we had the relevant Lonely Planet Guide with us. As we left an area we would trade it if we could. Lonely Planet Guides have revolutionised backpack travel and are a wonderful resource. They're constantly being updated by travellers. One of ours provided a bit of humour early in the trip. We were walking down a Beijing street, consulting the Guide, when Steve's cellphone rang. A voice said, "This is the Wellington City Public Library. You have an overdue Lonely Planet Guide for Beijing." After falling about laughing, we shamed Steve into giving it to Dick's friend Geoff to take back.

Primarily we kept in touch with friends and family through the wonders of email. All the major towns had an email facility somewhere, even though they didn't always have USB ports to enable me to send the Word documents. Steve had his cellphone and we were able to use it in China and Russia. If we'd had time to stop and get the necessary card loaded we could have used it in Europe too.

One of the most successful inclusions in our gear was Dick's book of photos. This showed his family, motorbikes, old Studebaker, his hut, Land Rover and hunting trophies. There were also shots from some of our old adventures and lots of pictures of New Zealand. This book needed no words and it broke the ice with many families. Dick would show Sharon, mime his relationship and compare his situation with theirs. In many places the men were interested in the hunting shots and good-natured banter would result. The people we were with would then get their photos out and show us. These were experiences way beyond the scope of any packaged tour.

Having Steve along was another ice-breaker. Ordinary folk seemed to love the fact that a father and son were doing this big ride together. Often we joshed that Dick was my father as well. Probably, they were all pleased to know that the relationship was familial, and the Cabin Boy was not just a plaything for two old debauchees.

The bikes were successfully returned to New Zealand and Dutch Courage was quickly refurbished by Dick and the sidecar reattached. Penelope is resting in my shed awaiting time and motivation. For her, the challenge of Australia in mid-2007 might be the next big outing. Maybe, it'll be The Last Hurrah Meets Skippy!

We've kept in touch with Eggi, Wang, Marat and Haroon by email. Dick sent a gift to the machinist who repaired the fork leg correctly in Pakistan. He's also put the wheels in motion to try and have the machinist's brother come to New Zealand to play cricket. The military officer from Jaglog who we didn't use to repair to fork leg, rings Dick and Sharon at odd times. However he always gets the answering machine, so they have yet to actually talk to each other. (Disappointingly, in the fourteen years that have passed since Edition One of *The Last Hurrah*, contact has been lost with all these folk who helped us so much.)

Finally, here are some details for the anoraks or trainspotters among you!

- The team – fantastic. As travelling companions and friends they couldn't have been better.
- The bikes – ditto. We never took a spanner to either bike's engine or transmission. We didn't do the tappets or check the primary drives. We didn't need to. Apart from Penelope breaking a fork leg, any breakdowns were resolved at the roadside within a few minutes.
- We put new chains on the bikes halfway round. Regina rules OK!
- Penelope made the entire distance on the same tyres (Dunlop K70s). The wheels are identical so were swapped front to back in Pakistan. Dick

put a Russian tyre on the back in Bishkek and it had plenty of tread left at the end.
- Panthers use oil, so we added about a third of a litre every second day for most of the trip. The Norton used less oil and had periods of negligible consumption. By the end of the trip both bikes were a little incontinent. A couple of lay days would have sorted them out.
- How far did we go? – It's hard to be completely accurate, but more than 3,000 kilometres were on unmade roads or tracks, often with corrugated stretches lasting hours at a time. There was probably another 12,000+ kilometres of roads ranging from appalling to autobahn. There were also some train rides and a ferry from Greece to Venice so we did have trains and boats and planes as the song says. The journey's total distance was around 20,000 kilometres.
- For some of the journey Penelope was two-up.
- Our guides – we were so resistant to the requirement to have a guide in China and Mongolia but in both instances we would have struggled without them.
- There was no back-up vehicle as alluded to in Classic Bike except in China and Mongolia.
- We used medical facilities in Mongolia, Kyrgyzstan, China and Iran. All gave immediate, inexpensive, good care to the best of their abilities.
- We had two snowstorms but no significant rain in three months. Temperatures were well into the 40s, maybe higher, in Iran and Pakistan.
- Approx 15,000 kilometres were travelled before we reached the seaside – a long way to go for a paddle.
- The Norton had four punctures, including one front wheel one. Penelope had none.
- Scary moments – too many to mention or dwell upon and almost all relating to other road users. Many occurred in Europe, as vehicle numbers and speed increased.

- We crossed three passes of more than 10,000 feet. The highest was the Khunjerab Pass (between China and Pakistan) at more than 16,000 feet.
- Biggest downhill – 800 kilometres of the Karakorum Highway from the China border to Islamabad. Most impressive was the first 72 kilometres to the country's entry point at Sust. A steepish, winding descent all the way. Magic.
- More than 30 one-hour video tapes were recorded and about 750 photos taken.
- Countries passed through – China, Mongolia, Russia, Kazakhstan, Kyrgyzstan, Uzbekistan, Pakistan, Iran, Turkey, Greece, Italy, Austria, Germany and Holland. China, Kazakhstan and Kyrgyzstan were all visited twice.
- Longest time at a border – three days (Russia/Kazakhstan).
- Longest day – 915 kilometres (18 hours) in Turkey.
- Hardest day – possibly the first day in the sand of Mongolia. Would we ever get out of second gear or look away from the track ahead and see some scenery?
- Best looking women – Russians narrowly over all the others but not sure about the black-shrouded girls of Iran. They might be the best of all, but it was hard to tell.
- Cheapest petrol – US9c per litre in Iran. To fill both bikes cost about $2.50.
- Most expensive petrol – US$2.00 per litre in Turkey and Europe. To fill both bikes cost $55.00
- Biggest grins – finally leaving Beijing and starting the saga.
- Most dramatic moment – dropping Penelope in the river and pinning Dick's leg under the luggage. This mini adventure resulted in an unexpected night camped at 12,000 feet.
- Most baffling sign – see photo section. What the hell does that mean?
- Unexpected pleasure – rolling thunder fart (without a wet spot) when

'stoppers' kicked in after a bout of diarrhoea.
- Real happy moments – Seeing Dick running towards us in Holland looking a million dollars. Finding Rollo and his welcoming champagne at journey's end.
- Good gadgets – Palm computer and folding keyboard, digital max/min thermometer.
- Useful item – antiseptic gel hand cleaner.
- Item left behind deliberately – water purifier. It could suck water from a puddle and make it potable. I decided early in the planning that this wouldn't be the trip where we drank out of puddles and that we would buy our water where necessary.
- First aid kit – selected by a doctor friend, it included lots of bandages for road abrasions which we didn't use, and several antibiotics and strong painkillers which we did.
- Unnecessary gadget – voltage inverter. We could have hooked this up to a 12 volt motorbike battery to produce 240 volts for charging batteries for the cameras. We always found electricity of a more useful sort and never resorted to this heavy hunk of magic.
- Most disappointing gadget – helmet camera. It had faulty wiring to batteries causing an intermittent fault and much frustration.
- Best support – families. They let us go and, even more surprisingly, were there when we returned.

CHAPTER 11

POSTSCRIPT

The completion of The Last Hurrah finished one reality and returned us to our 'other' lives, for me the low-level drudgery of work, the joy of family life and the thrill of minor celebrity status. Of course an adventure like this doesn't just end. It is natural that there will be reflective times and the glow that is satisfaction. Satisfaction that we dreamed big and somehow we … just ordinary Little Joes … managed to successfully and safely complete a pretty damn good adventure. It had been sub-titled Odyssey or Idiocy … and now we knew which it was.

Often when finishing a travel book, I wonder about what happened next. This is usually strongest when I have felt a connection with the participants. Maybe I have enjoyed the ride and want a little more. Was their wonderful adventure just a once-in-a-life aberration? … or is there more? What happened to the protagonists? Travel and adventure is often life-changing. Sometimes you travel because you want your life to be changed, other times because … well it seemed a good idea at the time. It was different for all three of us, as we were all in different stages of our life's paths.

After experiencing a minor stroke shortly after our return, a few weeks later Dick had another more intrusive one which necessitated hospital time and subsequently an exercise regime was introduced to ensure he regained some of his legendary walking capability. Dick's house is on a very hilly part of Wellington above the zoo and there is only 20m of flat road by his garage. The steepness meant he couldn't practice his perambulation without a car ride. During this period, we were still living nearby and it was a delight on the weekends to be able to uplift Dick and give him his 'walking'. Initially he could only manage a couple of lamp posts of very slow shuffling. Gradually we did longer walks, all the while of course, there was the chat ... wonderful, trivial chat. Inanities were shared, experiences recalled, family-times remembered, the trip relived. We enjoyably discussed so many things on these slow contemplative walks, as Dick inched his way along the pavement. After getting pretty competent and almost speedy on the flat footpaths of Evans Bay Parade, we graduated with a long morning's circuit of Wellington's zoo. This is quite undulating, so a good test. Neither of us had been to the zoo for some years despite both living close by. As a local Berhampore boy I had been a regular visitor with my mates, especially during our teenage years, when some of the local girls worked there 'mucking-out' etc. Later when our kids were of an appropriate age it was a great place for an outing, and was the setting for the family folklore tale of a runaway-pram. All parents will have had that moment when you have taken your hands off for a seemingly important reason ... and next minute the latest product of your loins is off down the hill in a rudderless carriage. Although the wee one involved didn't end up tipped into a bear cage or even the meerkat's enclosure, the incident generated enough excitement and drama to ensure it has been remembered for posterity.

A pleasing coffee after our morning in the zoo, informally finalised our walking commitments. Dick's speed and agility were returning with repeated exercise, but for me one of the most amazing bonuses was realising how much better his recall had become for specifics on the trip. There was a period in Central Asia when Dick was a little confused and I can remember getting irritated because he couldn't name which country we were in and often needed reminding. Months later, after two strokes, he had superb clarity and accurate recall. He was very impressive, as was his immense pride in having been part of an epic outing. In pride of place above his mantle-piece was a framed copy of the front page of the Russian newspaper we featured on. Mongolian memorabilia were also to the fore and a photo album never far away. I was gently proud of Dick's enthusiasm because he was already someone of note and substance … a motorcycling legend. After a notable racing career of his own, he had engineered race bikes that had taken on the world. He had created the fabulous Fast 'n' Fragile Ducati that had demonstrated Dick's engineering was on a par with anything in the world. Races at Daytona and Assen had shown what he could do. I would have been happy for our adventure to have been a side-note to his achievements … but no, Dick always had it centre-stage. He really did see it as his Last Hurrah.

Dick's balance issues meant that whilst he could usually manage a solo bike, the road up to his house included a very tight uphill bend that was a very tricky one to get right. After having a mishap there one day, Dick abandoned solo riding and resorted to always riding Dutch Courage with a camping-box sidecar attached. This meant he became a three-wheeled hooligan instead of a two-wheeled one. He loved entertaining the young and staid, by cornering with the sidecar wheel waving around in the air 250mm above the tarmac, tyres screaming in protest.

It was always an intention to produce a film of The Last Hurrah and when we had consulted an award-winning film maker before we went, his main advice was "Take lots of footage!" Luckily it turned out that Steve had a good eye for what should be filmed and how, as this had not always been practical. The timing of the ride had been such that digital equipment was not yet of a technical standard to produce a TV-quality product. We had two cameras, both of semi-professional level … one being described to us as the sort of thing that war correspondents used, a balance of weight, size and quality. They both recorded to mini tapes which needed to be looked after or dispatched home when possible.

Unfortunately, we'd suffered technical issues with our helmet camera never working successfully. It would be set up and checked, yet when the tape was reviewed after the section of ride being recorded, it would be either not there or not viewable. Only on our last morning did we find the cause, a dry soldered joint in one of the cables from the battery pack. We did however take more than 30 hours of footage which needed to be made into a suitable entertainment. Dick's enthusiasm and focus on the trip was such that he insisted in getting a copy made of all of the footage so he could see it all again ... every recorded moment.

Of course, I thought I could make a movie. I even mocked-up a script, got the tapes back from Steve, only to realise that it was beyond me. I was writing the book and working full-time, as well as trying to be the family-man I should be. Steve was similarly stretched. He was completing his Masters in Environmental Planning and producing his thesis. As part of that process he was away in East Timor for a few months. It finally dawned on us that we needed a proper film-maker to help us. To this end Steve placed an advertisement with Student Job Search down at Otago University where he was based.

This brought Katrina Jones into our realm. Katrina was a recent graduate of the Natural History Film Unit and the backstory was that she had crashed her boyfriend's car, needed some cash and was willing to accept Steve's meagre offerings. She reviewed every minute of film and decided how she would tell the tale. Ultimately she produced a movie that we are all proud of. There is one anecdote from the time that I enjoy. About two thirds of the way through the production, she put her hand up and asked for more money, asserting she was better than what she was being paid. I admired her for that, didn't see it as blackmail and dug deeper without telling Steve.

I am sure it was largely Dick's star power that dragged in the big numbers for our 'premiere' … a combined big-screen movie showing, and book launch on Sunday night July 15th 2006. Wellington's Courtney Place was filled with motorbikes, mostly from the classic years. Old-stagers appeared from everywhere and it was astounding to find riders coming in from all over the North Island. *Penelope* and *Dutch Courage* greeted them in the foyer. For most it would be the first time they had seen a Panther in the flesh. Suddenly the 500-seat Paramount didn't look quite big enough. The theatre inadvertently over-sold and on the night there was drama and confusion with me holding back family and friends so others could get in. I think in the end quite a few contravened the fire rules and sat on the steps in the aisles. I remember standing on stage with the spot-lights only half shielding the eager throng in the steeply-sloped auditorium. Not really being big on expletives, I couldn't help myself, opening my arms in a gesture I hoped was inclusive, I said "Holy Shit!"

Seeing ourselves on the big screen was a bit overwhelming, especially when set in the most wonderful scenery from the roof of the world. I think we were all pretty emotional and I know I teared up at the end when Dick and I are re-united in Holland. I was blubbing on the screen and blubbing in the darkness of the Paramount. Subsequently, the wine flowed, the books sold … what a night! Some of Dick's mates whisked him off for meal nearby and it was quite late when Steve, Dick and I were together again. The ride home through the crisp winter-air was a great one. Strung out behind friend Michael's Ural outfit, our bikes' baritone single-cylinder exhausts boomed through the deserted streets. Steve was on *Bessie*, our 1937 BSA which like *Penelope* had been a participant in our youthful folly, riding from New Orleans to Buenos Aires … but that is another story. It was an euphoric experience, especially as here we were, the three of us, carving through the night. We had conquered beyond our wildest dreams.

Whatever I was on during this period, it sure worked. Even while writing *The Last Hurrah* I was planning another adventure that would help promote the book and DVD, which of course didn't exist. During a 600 km night-ride on Bessie back from the classic races at Pukekohe in the Feb preceding the 'premiere' I hatched a plan ... I would storm the US promoting and selling the book, giving movie-screenings, maybe even doing TV appearances. Possibly Jay Leno would be taken by our adventure and feature us? The night-dream had started with me wanting a more comfortable, faster bike ... and slowly evolved into procuring a 1965 BMW R69S in Michigan, persuading friend Myles to get a similar age Honda 305cc Superhawk. We'd re-create the *Zen and the Art of Motorcycle Maintenance* ride of Robert Pirsig on the correct period motorcycles, all the while promoting and selling *The Last Hurrah*. We'd also film the ride and I'd write another book marrying Pirsig's ride with ours. Phew ... fantasies don't always come to fruition but once you've spoken aloud and involved others, you have to carry through. Of course it was too much. The fact that it even got off the ground was due to Myles's help and commitment from daughter Kitty to come along and film. We didn't have the skill and knowledge to arrange an itinerary of movie screenings whilst still fully-engaged in our NZ lives. The tyranny of distance defeated us but we did manage to book a site at the Mid-Ohio Vintage days, we did arrange a production run of the US specification DVDs (one frame per second different), we managed to get a batch of the books to be sent to the US, we even booked (and later cancelled) a site at Sturgis (the biggest motorcycle gathering in the world). All of this was being done in tandem with getting ready for the premiere in Wellington. Still hyped-up from the 'night of the stars' Myles and Kitty flew out to Michigan the very next day. I had work commitments which meant I didn't follow for a week.

Our USA adventure was a mixed bag. Mid-Ohio went pretty well, but we could see it was going to be impossible to both promote *The Last Hurrah* and re-create the Zen ride. We had no local promotional skills or ways of getting suitable publicity. Reluctantly, the decision was made to abandon the promotion ... we would just focus on ZAAM. We cancelled our stall at Sturgis which was for a week and just ducked in for the experience, as it was almost on our route. It turned out to be good ride across the top of the US on backroads to California, and maybe one day my manuscript will see the light of day. I have even bettered Robert Pirsig's 131 letters of rejection. Luckily I have broad shoulders and perhaps success would have spoiled me anyway.

Life went on, Steve returned to complete his thesis and then went off to Bougainville for a year with VSA (Volunteer Service Abroad). He was based on the Island of Buka and liaised with the 'Big Men' (politicians) as well as helping and hosting the local seven-a-side rugby club. This brought him into contact with UN Peace-keepers and one older American in particular became a mentor and inspiration for Steve to aspire to be an 'Aid Professional'. Howard had made a career of assisting war-torn nations get back on their feet after civil wars etc. Around this time Steve had met Maud, a French girl doing her Law Masters (and how it applied to refugees) in Dunedin. Steve had some French language from his period working in Grenoble prior to his spell as a volunteer at the Athens Olympics in 2004.

My work role as a presenter and technical writer for BRANZ (Building Research Association of New Zealand) involved me in delivering educational seminars from one end of the country to the other. In November 2006 following my return from America I had the opportunity to take my books and DVDs on the road. During the day I was 'The Old Geezer' for BRANZ and at night I was an adventurer from *The Last Hurrah*. I had an enthusiastic co-presenter who knew about film things and was happy to help. Not all theatres had moved across to digital projectors so I had to purchase my own data viewer which another friend helped me get a good discount on ... still not much short of $5,000. Speakers were also needed, so an enormous old 'Ghetto-blaster' was found. This set-up made me self-sufficient and I could pop a DVD into my Macbook Pro and do a screening anywhere. A great five, three-day weeks followed. Where possible I went 50:50 with the theatres on costs and profits, which meant they had 'flesh in the game' and would put in a good promotional effort. We only had one dud, where at a provincial Multiplex only five people turned up to a theatre I had paid $500 for. Subsequent to this failure, I would send a couple of DVDs to the local radio stations as give-aways and always got good audiences thereafter. One of the most enjoyable was the last of the tour. The BRANZ work had finished in Christchurch and we had booked a screening in tiny Kaikoura on the way home. Steph had managed a few days off and had done the last circuit of shows with me. We arrived in seaside Kaikoura mid-afternoon and soon spotted the community-run, old-fashioned movie theatre. It always gave me a thrill to see our posters up and this time was no different, except the poster had been amended ... it had a bold addition ... SUPPER PROVIDED. Being just a small settlement there were no staff on duty that we could confirm our commitments with. Luckily, our afternoon's planning of a supermarket raid was not needed, as when we turned up nice and early in the evening we found the theatre committee already there with mountains of home-baking. What a night, people came from all over the area to attend, taking up the opportunity of having a 'live' guest.

Overall the experience had been a very positive one, with 18 movie screenings generating good book and DVD sales, which when added to my share of the gate-takings, meant a good return. We would never recover the costs of the adventure, but we certainly got back the outlay I had invested in camera gear and the subsequent projecting equipment. The Last Hurrah was getting good reviews for both book and DVD.

After 12 years living in Wellington's Lyall Bay, in early 2007, Steph and I decided to move on to the next part of our lives' path. This involved shifting to Golden Bay at the top of the South Island and buying The Nook, a backpacker guesthouse property of a couple of acres. I also decided to leave my role writing about construction and giving educational presentations. It was time to have a stint back nearer the coal-face. To this end I agreed to be part of a construction project on Wellington's waterfront with the civil engineering company I had previously worked for. The Kumutoto Plaza Civil Works would only take a year and I would work with familiar faces in a contract management role I enjoy. This did mean that I would weekly commute for 2007 which when I was taking motorbikes up and down meant an eight and a half hour journey each way with Friday night's ride being in the dark. We both saw it as worthwhile and a new exciting venture. There was a period when we were childless for the first time in our lives, but first Hannah came down and got a job with the local bus company, then Kitty came back from her time in Canada, Mexico and India ... and got a role as night-care for a paraplegic. Finally, Steve re-appeared and got a job on the mussel boats. Only Joe was absent, making his life in Melbourne. With Steph getting a position as a social worker, it needed all of us to muck-in to run the 11 bed backpacker facility, straw-bale cottage, Bohemian house truck and camping paddock that we rented out. Somehow we managed to do this.

Rollo from Panther Publishing decided that a promotional visit to the UK might be a goer if done in conjunction with the Manx Grand Prix races held in September 2007. I'd been to the Isle of Man in the 1970s and loved it, so of course agreed to be part of it. A wonderful six weeks of getting around meeting Panther Owners followed. We had some great successes but a couple of failures meant that overall we just covered our costs. One highlight was getting to the Panther Rally in Yorkshire that includes a visit back to the factory site and meeting with old employees. Local club member and historian Doug Stockley introduced me to the actual man who had breathed life into *Penelope* all those years ago. Not many people can say that about their bike. After a good screening at Whitworth Hall in Darley Dale I'd answered Jennie Strawford's enquiry about a Panther ride in NZ with the response "You bring a group, and I will take you on the ride of your life around our South Island." A deal made over a beer is not one to be broken and two years later a whole container-load of Panthers landed in nearby Nelson.

Of course time ticks by and slowly the kids all left home again, Hannah to Australia, Kitty to start nursing training and Steve back to Dunedin and a planning job. Sadly, Dick's life with Sharon had come to an end, which disappointed many of us, his friends. Each of them had envisaged growing old together but there were other matters outside of their immediate relationship which could not be overcome and they parted. Never one to shy away from solo travel Dick visited once on the way to mutual friends about two hours away. When he hadn't turned up there after four hours we knew he would have been happily lost, not a care in the world … maybe another adventure had intervened.

So in early April 2009 I hosted a group of the Panther Owners' Club members and showed them around the South Island for two weeks. This was a joyous adventure. Motorcyclists have mostly not seen a Panther and yet here we had nearly 20 of them thudding along through the autumn countryside. Dick was with us for the early part of the ride and entertained all with his tales and obvious joie de vivre. This would almost be the last time we would ride together. Steve and Maud joined us for a night in the tiny Central Otago settlement of Naseby and struck up an easy rapport with several of the group. They were talking of going to Europe and riding down to Albania to see if there was any 'aid' work going. This hatched another plan. I knew there was space in the club's shipping container to squeeze one more bike in. I would swap Steve's Aprilia Moto 6.5 Starck for my BMW R65 and that could be the 'Europe' bike. Accordingly, I paid a share of the return trip and everyone won. There was the small issue of the bike going to Liverpool but Nick and Karo from the south coast of England offered to uplift and store it for them.

And so it was that later in the year, we had both Steve and Maud back in Golden Bay with us, desperately sending off CVs and job applications. I recall one occasion when Steve was in one room trying to do an application in French while Maud was struggling in another room with one in English. Ultimately Maud scored an internship in Paris (Fieldwork in Kabul) with Médecins du Monde just before they set off. Steve went to the UK and did a logistician's course and in time got the bike from Nick and Karo. It now sported panniers courtesy of Nick and was an ideal bike for touring and getting them down to the South of France where Maud's father lived. Steve hadn't managed a work visa for France as the Embassy in Auckland had failed him on his French fluency. This meant any jobs he got in Paris were poorly paid and under the table. Ultimately Steve did get a job with an Italian aid agency in the Republic of Congo and in time Maud followed. Although they were not quite in the same region, they were able to have furlough together in some of the nicer parts of East Africa. I think their time in the Congo was both rewarding and scary. Maud's village up near the Sudan border had no electricity or running water and on one occasion she was only a minute ahead of a LRA (Lord's Resistance Army) attack, getting her crew to a UN base, and having to camp outside for a few days while Steve arranged for them to be evacuated.

By mid 2011 they were ready for a spell and got married in St Nazaire, near Perpignon in the South of France. It was a fairy-tale wedding in the grounds of an old abbey with friends (including Panther Owners from Germany and the UK) and family from all over the world present. After using the BMW R65 to honeymoon in Corsica and Sicily, they took more aid work. Steve went off to Dadaab (World's largest refugee camp) in Kenya, up on the Somali border, for Handicap International, whilst Maud went out to Pakistan to run a women's refuge there. Their lives certainly weren't dull and it was nice to follow along vicariously without the heat, flies and general deprivations.

For me, life stuttered along, I did some contract work for BRANZ, I had a short stint in Christchurch helping set up a ground improvement company after their earthquake, and all the while did my bit with the accommodation business which was trickling along, giving us a life-style rather than an income. There was a small cry for attention when early on New Year's morning 2011 I had a heart attack necessitating a helicopter ride off to Nelson Hospital. Ultimately I had a stent put in and remain breathing to this day. Mid-2012 I had the opportunity to go to Australia's North West to make my fortune. This spawned many a dream ... of which toys I was going to refurb and which new ones I was going to buy. It was going to be hard, hot and I knew I would be miserable at times, being away from Steph and the family but it would be worthwhile, enabling the mortgage to be kicked into touch. After an enjoyable six weeks or so in Newcastle, an hour or so up the coast from Sydney, out of the blue, the client BHP pulled the pin on the project. That began the big mining collapse of 2012 and in three months 10,000 mining workers were laid off. We'd spent $1.2M mobilising people and gear to site and it was all over in an instant. There would be no new toys. The company who had recruited me also had another project in Port Hedland cancelled and now were desperately short of work ... so let me go, to slink back to NZ with my tail between my legs, fortune-less.

A pretty disastrous flood at The Nook in Dec 2012 further set us back, with the season being pretty much wiped out. This came at just the wrong time as we had done some significant improvements pre-season and when added to the outlay for getting to and from Steve's wedding in France earlier and the non-fortune from Aus, we were running on empty, hanging out for the summer influx. When there were very poor returns

THE LAST HURRAH

and more money to be spent recovering from the flood damage, we knew we needed to change the accommodation business over to full-time tenants so we could go from The Bay as required to work away. To this end I proposed another go at Australia to crack the lucrative big-project work ... what was remaining of it.

But in the meantime, there was fun to be had. Dick celebrated his 80th birthday at home in Wellington towards the end of January 2013. What a day! It was an all-day, drop-in of motorcycling or hunting folk from all over the country. Dick had mates of both worlds from way back in the 1950s when he arrived in New Zealand. I was a Johnny-come-lately, only meeting Dick when I returned from overseas in 1977. The sun shone, and the old fellow was in his element, reveling in the memories and the joy of the occasion. Photos of the day show legions of smiling faces ... and Dick wearing the black Icebreaker top from our 2005 ride. It had been so worthwhile making the nine-hour ride and ferry-trip to get there. Many of us had also been present for his 70th, which had been a camping weekend at his notorious hut in the hills and all of us wondered where the decade had gone. That previous celebration had seen 75 or so hardy souls camped-out in the wilds of the Orongorongas, with not all our tents surviving the vicious Wairarapa winds. It was a memorable weekend, suitable for a legend, and so was this one, more gentle ... but so was he. All day his garage was open and visitors could re-acquaint themselves with his three Nortons, and the mighty Studebaker Hawk in the corner. Several times during the day it was started, just so we could hear how slow it could idle. I felt a slight sadness when I left that day as I knew Dick's riding days were coming to an end. I knew he'd never ride Bucephalus, his racing Manx again and was unlikely to get out on his staggered-crank Dominator either.

In mid-2013 Steph and I crossed to Melbourne to not only see the kids in Melbourne (Joe and partner Jess, Kitty and partner Cam) but to uplift the little Citroen Berlingo van I had left there in 2012. We headed north trying to find meaningful work but ultimately were unsuccessful. The big projects were slowing up and Steph's social work qualification was not going to be recognised in Australia for another year or more. After a wonderful time meandering up an inland route to Cairns and re-connecting with friends … it was time to fall back on Plan B. I would seek work in the earthquake recovery phase of Christchurch's rebuild. We returned to NZ and I rang an old boss who had been heading Fletcher Engineering South Island's operations.

"Hi Alan, Des Molloy here, who do I talk to about work in Christchurch?"

"Gidday Des, nice to hear from you … why Christchurch?"

"That's where the work is isn't it?"

"How about the Kapiti Coast? I am heading a $650M expressway project. Do you want to come for lunch next Tuesday?"

That took care of the next four years. We had good tenants looking after The Nook and enjoyed a spell back earning proper money for a proper job in the Lower North Island near to Wellington. A bonus was having our youngest also living with us for the last couple of those years. We shared a cottage that we jointly bought in Otaki Beach. Having thought that with the kids all being more or less over 30-plus, Steph was lamenting that there were no grandkids presenting themselves. Wonderfully, three came in a year.

Steve's life in Dadaab had been interrupted when the aid agencies all pulled their staff out after two Spanish aid workers were kidnapped. This meant a very boring time marooned in Dadaab amongst the humanitarians and not out in the camp itself. Ultimately this became too much for Steve and he took a position as an operations manager for a Dutch dairy company in Pakistan. Steve and Maud were now together in Lahore, albeit neither loving their work too much. Working conditions were tough for both of them and ultimately when one contract ended, they bailed out and headed to France. Maud soon had a role co-ordinating Womens' Refuges around Lyon, her old home town. Needless to say we were thrilled with their return to more benign surroundings. Further good news followed in early 2014 when they announced their pregnancy. Simultaneously, Joe and Jess gave us similar news, although the joy was tempered with learning that the 20-week scan showed Jess to have ovarian cancer. Steph spent Oct and November being the new Granny in both France and Melbourne.

Dick's balance had deteriorated and he could no longer live at home. Initially be was in care at Porirua Hospital about 45 minutes south of where we were living at the time. I probably didn't visit as often as I should have, but treasured each one. Dick was still very much a 'character' who entertained staff, visitors and other patients. Quickly he struck up a bit of a relationship with a similar aged woman there … he always was a charmer, even though almost toothless in his later years. I remember going to see him on Bessie the old BSA. Dick heard me come into the parking area of course and identified the unique single-cylinder thump as being quite different from a more regular visitor who came on an early 1950s twin-cylinder Triumph. I actually parked where I hoped he could see me come and go. Unfortunately, as he couldn't use his walker unaided, he had to wait until I walked in to be certain it was me. A broad smile broke across his face exposing his almost gummy grin. "I thought it was you!" he beamed. Later he was arranged so he could see me go through the starting procedures necessary to get old Bessie on fire and snarling out of the carpark. I could imagine him up on the fourth floor chuckling away. It was becoming clear that long-term care in the community was needed.

He was shown a small number of places and settled upon the Vincentian Home in Berhampore, a suburb he had lived in for an extended period when his children were growing up, and co-incidentally the same home where my mother spent her last year … and the same street I had grown up in. We'd been very happy with the care given mum so confidently assured Dick that it would be a good place. He hid his sorrow well, of knowing he wasn't going home or back to his workshop. No more would he be spinning the hand-wheels on his mill or lathe. No more would he be tinkering or improving a mechanical component of the machines he loved. We often talked at length about how we were not really the owners of these gems, we were custodians. To that end Dick was very clear about the fate of his Nortons. They were not to be sold to random strangers. Nor did he think his family were the ones to be those next minders. The family would be looked after suitably from Dick's canniness with regards to property investments. Dick shared with me who he had selected to gift the bikes to and why. There were reasons for each, and the choices were good ones. I must admit my eyes filled with moisture when he told me he wanted The Cabin Boy to have *Dutch Courage*. Steve and Dick had bonded very deeply during *The Last Hurrah* and continued the relationship when it was possible. Each time Steve came home to New Zealand he would make time to go and see his old buddy. Dick didn't care that Steve was still primarily overseas … he knew he would come home sooner or later. Steve had also been very proud to introduce Maud to Dick … to show him the future.

During the next couple of years there were a few significant motorcycle events around the Wellington region and Dick was not forgotten. For *'A Bit of a Do',* which was a celebration of 50 years of a family-owned motorbike shop, he was collected by a mutual-friend in a sidecar and brought in, to much fanfare and enjoyment from the throng of milling, drinking bikies. He'd known all the family players for all of the years. Whilst there we were interviewed by Radio NZ for their National Programme, Spectrum. Dick was now a bit slow in speech but still fully cognitive and firing on all cylinders. Sometimes slow to get a sentence started, it never lacked relevance when delivered. He was also sidecar-ed to the *Distinguished Gentlemen's Ride*, so not forgotten or left to moulder. His friends were many and true.

The Vincentian Home was much further away and each visit was not on a 'whim' but a fully-planned outing. Once more he charmed everyone, always keen and quick to show his photos. Again he found a girl friend who he would hold hands with in the lounge in front of the TV. Even though his mobility was now quite compromised Dick always seemed very chipper and pleased to see visitors. He kept himself busy reading and it was always good to catch up on what had interested him. I took him a book called *Gasoline Gypsy*, a tale I knew he would enjoy, of a young English woman riding across Canada, down into Mexico to Veracruz and back up the East Coast of the US, ending in New York. This huge ride was done in the mid-1950s on a tiny two-stroke BSA 125cc Bantam. She had along as a companion an enormous terrier which would jump off the back and run up the hills beside her. Of course he loved it, he loved dogs and he loved the incongruity of using such a small and on the face of it, unsuited motorcycle for such a ride ... just like our old girls on *The Last Hurrah*

By November 2015 Dick was not in good health and I took a call from his good mate Geoff just before I headed off on a ride to the bottom of the South Island for the Burt Munro Challenge in Invercargill, saying he wasn't in good shape. In the words of Richard Thompson's cult song Vincent Black Lightning 1952 ... *'He was runnin' out of road. He was runnin' out of breath.'*

So it was no real surprise when I got another call from Geoff in Franz Joseph, where we had stopped for a brunch, telling me that the great man had passed the night before, 25 Nov 2015. A giant totara had fallen. It was the end of an era. This was sobering but not unexpected. Many memories and emotions flooded back and I cut short my weekend in Invercargill to head back to Wellington for his funeral. This was not a miserable time and in particular I almost enjoyed the Sunday's ride, because normally I would have shared the details of the ride with Dick, because it was suitably tough. I over-nighted in St Andrews, south of Timaru and from there it was close to 700kms before I reached Otaki Beach ... and the ride had included the three-and-a-half-hour ferry ride. I knew Dick would have been proud, as he loved 'an epic' ... a ride that is a struggle, one that is respected by others. I recalled one of his epics, being as a result of hearing the news that another of NZs legendary racers had passed. Dick had just got home from riding back from the annual Pukekohe Classic Races up near Auckland when he learned of Len Perry's death. With no hesitation, Dick turned the Norton around and dashed back the 600 kms to get to the funeral. The thoughts also brought back one of my own efforts, which included our last ride together.

In early February 2011, a mutual friend lost his battle with cancer. There was no doubt that I would be at the funeral and on a bike, Jim was part of the inner-sanctum ... our crew ... and I felt it would disrespect him if I flew in and hired a rental car. Co-ordinating ferry crossings meant that I left our home in Golden Bay at 4.00am on the Zen-ride BMW and caught an early morning boat. Dick met me at the other end and we rode together to the sorrowful, poignant event which incorporated a massed motorcycle ride behind Jim's race BSA. After the wake, Dick rode with me back into Wellington to the ferry terminal. Our last ride hadn't been filled with joy but I knew it was important. Deep down we knew there wouldn't be many opportunities left. We'd had a coffee together, we'd shared our updates, we'd shared our memories of our good riding buddy. It was time for me to head home. After an evening crossing I was faced with the four-hour ride home from Picton through the night. Riding a bike at night when there is no traffic is a special experience. You are following a pool of light but surrounded by inky darkness, there is a solitude that gives rise to reflection and satisfaction. I remember pausing at Pelorus Bridge to add a layer, I was cold and suffering from double-vision. A ruru, our native morepork, gave forth its haunting, melancholy call. It was nearby and I felt that somehow this was a spirit's presence. I wasn't disturbed by the call, but acknowledged it with a smile, hoping it was Jim saying goodbye. It was 5.00am when

I tumbled into bed. I knew Jim and Dick would both be pleased.

Of course, as befitted motorcycling royalty, Dick's own funeral was a celebration of his 60 years of actively being part of New Zealand's two-wheeled fraternity. As with his 80th celebration, they came from all over the country. His race bike Bucephalus took pride of place at the front of the chapel. Outside there was the most wonderful display of motorcycles representing many eras, genres and countries. A six-cylinder Benelli was feted no more than the tiny BSA Bantam that parked nearby. They were all there to pay their respects to the passing of a true legend. A few years earlier at a National Classic Motorcycle Rally I had presented Dick with a medal awarding him 'Living Legend' status. I see no need to amend that status. Along with others, I said a few words of tribute acknowledging the passing of a true friend and wonderful adventure companion.

I chuckle when I read in the Aftermath chapter that Penelope was resting and I was aiming for a mid-2007 Aussie adventure. My strike-rate has never been high, or accurate ... and it was Oct 2016 before *Penelope* made it across the Tasman Sea to the big red continent. After arriving in Melbourne we rode the 'Pretty Average Ocean Road' (trumpeted by the Aussies as The Great Ocean Road) to Mt Gambier where we had a pleasant overnight stay. I was heading to the Australian Panther Owners' rally on the Fleurieu Peninsula out of Adelaide. This proved to be a wonderful event and the area is one I wish to return to. I looped back to Melbourne via Swan Hill and Echuca on the Murray River, leaving *Penelope* with Kitty and

Cam in Melbourne. In 2017 I returned and embarked on the next leg of the adventure, initially with Victorian John Ferguson on a Panther Deluxe sidecar outfit from 1938. Ferg led me through the back-roads of Victoria and introduced me to their back-country pubs. A wonderful 1,100 kms were enjoyed getting to that year's rally up in the Southern Highlands of New South Wales. As to be expected, a good time followed, and then after the rally, I went solo up the inland roads, skirting the outback, to Cairns in Far North Queensland so *Penelope* could rest with friends there. In Mid-July 2018 I returned again, for a more ambitious bite of the cherry. From Cairns I headed across to The Gulf of Carpentaria at Karumba and then down to Mt Isa and straight down the Birdsville and Oodnadatta Tracks to South Australia. Once back on proper roads I went up the middle via Alice Springs (a detour to Uluru included) to Darwin where *Penelope* rested with other Panthers in the famed Qantas Hanger courtesy of club member and friend Dan Leather. In the winter of 2019, after some pretty serious 'fettling' we continued down the west coast, pausing for respite and assistance in Toodyay with Bruce and Linda Sharman before 'doing the bottom corner' and crossing the Nullabor Plain to complete the circle in South Australia. Still not quite finished, I went home for a few weeks before returning with Steph to ride up to NSW for the 2019 Panther Rally where I launched a book of our first big ride on Penelope. *No One Said It Would Be Easy* records our youthful ride from New Orleans to Buenos Aires. *Penelope* now rests in Melbourne after 24,000kms of mainland Australian roads. She'll get a freshen-up before Tasmania is visited in early 2021 – health and wealth willing.

Steve and Maud now have two children, Jude and Nelson Atawhai, live in a tiny village on the edge of the Beaujolais area of France and hope to commence cycling home to New Zealand as a family some time in near future. It is thought this will take a year. Steph and I respect their adventurous desire but question their sanity.

Steph and I are enjoying being grandparents, albeit from a distance. Joe and Arthur are a tight team in Melbourne, making a good fist of things on their own since Jess's sad passing in 2016. Kitty and Cam live across town with Isaac and baby Nina. Currently Hannah is our only resident Kiwi. We miss all of the kids and resulting mokopuna but are so proud that all have also travelled and explored both the planet and themselves.

Des Molloy
December 2019

Available Online Now
www.kahukupublishing.com

An outrageous sortie on a pre-war BSA and two obscure, obsolete Yorkshire-made, single-cylinder Panther motorbikes. Poorly funded, with little planning, the ride depends on good luck, blind loyalty and terminal optimism. The struggle is managed with a youthful naivety.

This is a recollection of a youth well-spent. Love and adventure are in the air with every chapter a precarious adventure.

In July 1968 a mentally insecure philosophy teacher began a motorcycle ride across the US with his not-yet 12-year-old son. Robert Pirsig's journey was immortalized in his best-selling book *Zen and the Art of Motorcycle Maintenance*.

Des Molloy and team, on the correct-period 1965 bikes follow the wheel-tracks of their antecedents, recording their thoughts and comparing with the best-selling philosopher.

Kahuku
Publishing Collective

Everyday People.
Amazing Adventures.

www.ingramcontent.com/pod-product-compliance
Lightning Source LLC
Chambersburg PA
CBHW021053080526
44587CB00010B/238